Feminist Approaches to the Body in Medieval Literature

University of Pennsylvania Press
NEW CULTURAL STUDIES
Joan DeJean, Carroll Smith-Rosenberg, and Peter Stallybrass, Editors

A complete list of the books in this series appears at the back of this volume.

Feminist Approaches to the Body in Medieval Literature

Linda Lomperis and
Sarah Stanbury, Editors

University of Pennsylvania Press
Philadelphia

Library of Congress Cataloging-in-Publication Data

Feminist approaches to the body in medieval literature / Linda
    Lomperis and Sarah Stanbury, editors.
        p.   cm. — (New cultural studies)
    Includes bibliographical references (p. 235–243) and index.
    ISBN 0-8122-3117-1. — ISBN 0-8122-1364-5 (pbk.)
        1. Literature, Medieval—History and criticism.   2. Women in literature.
    3. Body, Human, in literature.   4. Feminism and literature.   5. Sex in
    literature.   6. Symbolism in literature.
    I. Lomperis, Linda.   II. Stanbury, Sarah.   III. Series.
    PN682.W6F37   1993
    809'.93352042'0902—dc20   92-33033
                                                                               CIP

Contents

Introduction: Feminist Theory and Medieval "Body Politics"

In its distant beginnings, this essay collection dates back to a conference panel entitled "The Body as Spectacle in Medieval Literature," which took place at the 1987 convention of the Modern Language Association (MLA). Formally, the panel provided the occasion for investigating a number of questions surrounding the visual display of bodies in medieval texts; informally, the panel also functioned as the occasion for a number of collegial discussions between panel organizer Sarah Stanbury and panel member Linda Lomperis. Since both of us were avid readers of contemporary feminist theory, our conversations often turned into discussions about feminism, a topic that was having an increasingly visible impact on literary studies as a whole. Indeed, the program for that MLA meeting included numerous feminist papers. As an academic critical practice, feminism seemed to have reached what one might call a watershed.

Our sense of this was in fact confirmed the following spring at the International Congress of Medieval Studies held in Kalamazoo, Michigan. There in a roundtable discussion sponsored by the *Medieval Feminist Newsletter*, six panelists spoke to a large audience about feminist scholarship in the field of medieval studies. For us and for many others as well, no doubt, this session seemed to represent a genuinely new beginning: feminist-medievalists were mapping new critical terrain, and the intellectual enthusiasm generated by this enterprise was both abundant and infectious. Not surprisingly, therefore, given our own recent work, we began at this point to contemplate putting together a feminist essay collection about body questions in the Middle Ages. Clearly, we thought, the timing for such a project could never be more right, and the number of feminist presentations at this conference alone assured as that there would be no lack of material to work with.

In 1993, it is perhaps even more accurate than before to speak of the volume's timeliness, for just as medievalists have been engaging with the materials of contemporary feminist theory, so have feminist theorists been turning their attention increasingly to questions of history. This move toward history has come about largely in response to feminists of color in the United States who have criticized mainstream (i.e., white, Western, middle-class) feminist theory for unacknowledged models of racist and totalizing thought (e.g., the use of "woman" as a tacit code word for "white woman," and the employment of such concepts as "patriarchy," "family," "marriage," and "reproduction" in indiscriminate and universalizing ways). Acknowledging these pitfalls and at the same time working to avoid them, a number of contemporary feminist theorists have made explicit their resistance to the homogeneous and the monolithic. In her own way of de-essentializing feminism, Teresa de Lauretis insists on the complex and contradictory nature of subjectivity. The female subject, she writes, "is a site of differences; differences that are not only sexual or only racial, economic, or (sub)cultural, but all these together, and often enough at odds with one another."[1] A call for historical specificity pervades the work of feminist philosopher Denise Riley, who not only emphasizes the "temporality and malleability of gendered existences," but also reconceives the task of contemporary feminist inquiry as that of "tracing the (always anatomically gendered) body as it is differently established and interpreted as sexed within different periods." What Riley argues for, in short, is that feminist scholarship pay attention to "the historical crystallizations of sexed identities" rather than to some timeless understanding of either "Woman" or "women."[2]

Within recent feminist theoretical writings, however, this recognition of the centrality of history typically does not extend back further than the early twentieth century. This is indeed unfortunate, since one of the central issues fueling present-day feminist and cultural theory—namely, the sociopolitical significance of the body—was in fact a central concern of cultural inquiry—literary, philosophical, scientific, religious, and political—during the Middle Ages. As the writings of historians Jacques Le Goff, Peter Brown, and Caroline Bynum have demonstrated, the Middle Ages was anything but a purely metaphysical time period.[3] It was, on the contrary, a moment of history governed by what we might call an incarnational aesthetic: the Word having been made flesh, the spiritual and the somatic were necessarily intermingled, and the body itself in the Middle Ages became a significant grounding of religious experience. Medieval spiritual abstractions and ideas about morality, moreover, were typically given bodily form: the seven deadly sins were represented as people, that is, as fleshly bodies, just as Dante Alighieri's spiritual journey to God was cast in the form of an actual, physical journey. Saint Bernard's condemnation of religious ornamentation reminds us, in part, of the numerous physical decorations—images of the dying Christ, effigies of holy persons, saintly body parts—found in medieval cathedrals.[4] Cathedrals and local sanctuaries, of course, were also places where medieval women and men regularly received instruction, via sermons, in matters having to do with bodily restraint, even though, to be sure, education about bodily activity and bodily conduct was not at all confined to the Church. Indeed, everyday life in the Middle Ages was what we in the late twentieth century might see as supremely, if not unrelievedly, "bodily." The proliferation of outhouses and public baths, the overall lack of legislation and facilities to promote sanitation, the typically communal nature of familial sleeping arrangements, the public surveillance of marital sexual activity, and the homely setting of such eminently bodily events as birth and death all serve as concrete reminders of the fact that body in the Middle Ages was in no way simply an abstract concept.

Thus, one of the main purposes of this book is to introduce contemporary feminist inquiry to this orientation of medieval culture toward the body. More specifically, however, the collection as a whole focuses critical attention on representations of the body in medieval literary texts as a means of investigating the politics of gender-body relations in the Middle Ages. To conceive of these relations in political terms is to acknowledge the fact that the signifiers "gender" and "body" function within the space of this volume not simply as object designations, but rather as socially based categories that are eminently and inextricably connected with questions of power. For as the essays themselves make clear, the study of the body in the Middle Ages necessitates an understanding of its ideological structuring: the critical task of making the body intelligible—indeed, of establishing its literal existence—demands that one regard it as a politically charged discursive construct, a representational space traversed in various ways by socially based power relations.[5] Similarly, the essays' collective insistence on matters of gender promotes an understanding not simply of sexual difference—"man" versus "woman"—but rather of the various ways in which sexed identities take shape, in all their complexities and contradictions, according to historically specific configurations of power and power relations.[6] Engaging simultaneously, therefore, with questions of gender and body, the essays in this volume lead to an appreciation of what we might call medieval *body politics*, an appreciation, that is to say, of the ways in which representations of gender-body relations in medieval writings both stage and challenge the defining force of dominant ideologies.

Some of the essays situate their explorations of "body politics" historically in very specific terms. Margaret Brose, for example, assesses Petrarch's figuration of Italy as a wounded female body in relation to the political turmoil of Italy in the mid-1340s. Linda Lomperis reads bodily representations in Chaucer's *Physician's Tale* through the lens of the sexual practices of the English ruling class in the late fourteenth century. Peggy McCracken's discussion of the representation of adultery in Chrétien de Troyes's *Cligés* foregrounds the disparity between the politically significant reproductive power of queens in late twelfth-century France and the conventional display in medieval French romance of a barren or nonreproductive queen. Each of these essays, moreover, locates the political pressure of bodily representation differently. Whereas Brose features the part played by the Petrarchan wounded female body of Italy in guaranteeing the security and hegemony of a masculine Italic political community, Lomperis insists on a more subversive functioning of bodily representation in Chaucer. The concept of the body as a site of instability and gender confusion, as seen in the *Physician's Tale*, Lomperis maintains, exposes and indeed contributes to the demise of the late medieval British monarchy's hold on political power. According to McCracken, the power of the adulterous queen's body in *Cligés* operates doubly: threatening the security of dynastic succession through its own duplicitous power plays, the politically disruptive potential of Fenice's body in Chrétien's romance is ultimately usurped, her body's own reproductive agency consistently displaced through the simultaneous idealization and castigation of the theme of adulterous love.

Doubleness and duplicity in relation to body-power questions are particularly striking in representations of the body of the Virgin Mary. Theresa Coletti's reflections on the contradictory cultural constructions of Mary's body in medieval cycle plays lead her to analyze the potential of these plays to unsettle dominant ideologies of marriage and sexual relations in late medieval English urban life. Dramatizations of the "troubles" between Joseph and Mary over her apparently transgressive body, Coletti suggests, work to undermine not only the patriarchal ordering of society, but also the domestic regulation of the sex-gender system in the late Middle Ages. In Coletti's eyes, the dramatic representation of Mary is not to be separated from the lives and social realities of medieval women; on the contrary, the plays' insistence on Mary's physical existence, especially on the domestic problems posed by her pregnancy, functions for Coletti as a reminder of the ways in which female sexuality in the Middle Ages could upset the power structure of the patriarchal medieval household.

Indeed, both for medieval culture and for twentieth-century critics, powerful maternal bodies are capable of eliciting contradictory and anxiety-ridden responses. In a discussion of the Middle English *Pearl* that draws on feminist film theory as well as on late medieval domestic history, Sarah Stanbury argues that a preoedipal maternal body is implicated in the poem's shifting incarnations of female loss. Desired though constantly displaced, this maternal body, Stanbury proposes, functions as a source of resistance, impeding the narrative's achievement of any simple or salvific sense of closure. Similarly, Gayle Margherita points to the repression of a maternal body—the original textual "mat(t)er" of history and literary history—in Chaucer's *Book of the Duchess*. Drawing a parallel between anxieties surrounding maternal origins in the Chaucerian text and similar anxieties in recent historicist studies of Chaucer, Margherita emphasizes the ability of the maternal body to disrupt the smooth operations of relations between men. Each relying on psychoanalytic models of interpretation, the arguments of Margherita and Stanbury also stage the part played by the feminist critic in retrieving that which a particular culture represses or marginalizes.

The representation of the female body in the Middle Ages, however, does not always function as a source of anxiety. The essays by Elizabeth Robertson and Wendy Harding, in fact, explore the ways in which medieval women exploited the cultural codes of gender-body relations for the purposes of self-empowerment, especially as a means of authorizing their own spiritual lives. Reading the spiritual practices of female mystics in relation to the gender-specific descriptions of body functions in medieval medical literature, Robertson points to a new way of understanding the manifestly bodily preoccupations of medieval female mystical writings. The medieval medical construction of women as creatures of excess moisture provided late medieval female mystics, Robertson claims, with a specific vocabulary for creating their own distinctively somatic spiritual expressions. In a similar manner, Harding is concerned with the display of Margery Kempe's own embodied spirituality in *The Book of Margery Kempe*, though Harding's discussion focuses mainly on the complex ways this display functions. Embodied spirituality in Kempe's *Book* becomes, according to Harding, a means of subverting conventional, gendered hierarchies (e.g., body vs. text, passion vs. reflection, female vs. male) and, ultimately, of reestablishing them in a nonhierarchical, dialogic relationship.

The collapsing of binary oppositions having to do with the body is also crucial in both E. Jane Burns's discussion of Old French fabliaux and Helen Solterer's investigation of the *Roman de la rose* of Jean Renart. Focusing in particular on fabliau representations of talking vaginas, Burns discusses the ways in which this form of female, bodily speech both undermines the hierarchically gendered distinction between (masculine) mind and (feminine) body and makes the body itself into a mode of knowledge, a vehicle for thought. Solterer's discussion of female figural activity in Renart's *Rose* highlights the ways in which this text undoes the conventional binary representation of the female body: by ultimately refusing to cast the female body as either purely literal body or simply symbolic mirage, the *Rose*, Solterer argues, encourages readers to recognize the existence of a greater range of female representation in medieval narrative. Attending to the textual deployment of oppositional or counter-voicings, both Burns and Solterer read against the grain, holding on to those moments in texts when "something else happens."[7]

As the foregoing discussion suggests, no single or all-encompassing "feminist approach" is embraced in this volume. Nor is there an attempt here to represent in the space of one volume all the various forms of feminist critical practice at work today. As editors, we have tried to allow each essay in the collection to stage its own "feminist approach," thereby demolishing any monolithic understanding of "feminism" and "feminist approach," and cultivating at the same time a sense of feminist solidarity amidst differences. We take our cue in this regard from bell hooks's recent suggestion that feminists acknowledge their differences, difficulties, and struggles with each other, all the while that they remain in solidarity (though not in unity) as they work together for common goals of world transformation.[8]

The concept of transformation has indeed been an important aspect of this project right from the start, for one effect of this volume, we hope, will be to change the way in which the study of the Middle Ages in the academy today is often consigned to the unexamined margins of contemporary thought. For in their collective display of the complexities and contestations of gender-body relations in the Middle Ages, the essays in this volume also seek to undermine a certain mind-body split that is maintained on the level of much practical critical work. That is to say, insofar as literary studies in the academy tends to construct theoretical projects as a kind of professional "mind," contemporary feminist theory often comes to represent the "brains of it all" in relation to a medieval text, itself conceived as a dead body, a lifeless, unintelligent *corpus* from the past. Such a dualism, we might note, falls into categories nuanced by gendered hierarchies: "feminine" medieval textual matter is cast in a position of dependency to the "masculine" contemporary theoretical mind. The essays in this volume, however, eschew all such hierarchical relations between the materials of texts from the past and the materials of contemporary feminist theory. Instead, they seek to demonstrate the various ways in which medievalists do in fact "think through the body"—that is, engage in knowledge-making projects of "mind" that are also historically "embodied"—at the same time that they provide a set of new and historically specific dimensions to contemporary feminist theoretical thought.

In orchestrating this challenging dialogue between academic "mind" and academic "body," between texts of the present and texts of the past, we are aware of the way in which the project we have embarked upon will no doubt find itself displaced at some later time owing to the ongoing processes of academic culture work. This book, in other words, no less than any other project of knowledge-making, emerges out of a particular set of currently felt contingencies, and remains, therefore, inevitably limited and "situated."[9] For the moment, however, the volume represents a sincere attempt to disrupt the boundaries that have kept feminist theoretical scholarship on body questions and textual scholarship on the Middle Ages as twin preserves, comfortably inured one from the other, each holding up, as it were, with the untainted safety of their "own" analytical categories, their "own" self-definitions, their "own" political positions.[10]

Notes

1. Teresa de Lauretis, "Feminist Studies/Critical Studies: Issues, Terms, and Contexts," in *Feminist Studies/Critical Studies*, ed. Teresa de Lauretis (Bloomington: Indiana University Press, 1986), 14.

2. Denise Riley, *"Am I That Name?" Feminism and the Category of Women in History* (Minneapolis: University of Minnesota Press, 1988), 103, 111.

3. Jacques Le Goff, *The Medieval Imagination*, trans. Arthur Goldhammer (Chicago: University of Chicago Press, 1988), esp. "Part Three: The Body," 83–106; Peter Brown, *The Body and Society: Men, Women, and Sexual Renunciation in Early Christianity* (New York: Columbia University Press, 1988); Caroline Walker Bynum, *Holy Feast and Holy Fast: The Religious Significance of Food to Medieval Women* (Berkeley: University of California Press, 1987); idem, *Fragmentation and Redemption: Essays on Gender and the Human Body in Medieval Religion* (New York: Zone Books, 1991), 1:160–219.

4. The reference here is to Bernard's *Apologia, PL* 182, esp. cols. 914–16, in which Bernard attacks Clunaic monasticism, censuring at the same time the religious display of sculptures of the body, especially of the grostesque body.

5. See, in this regard, Judith Butler's discussion of the discursive construction of the literalized, physical body in her *Gender Trouble: Feminism and the Subversion of Identity* (New York: Routledge, 1990), 79–141.

6. Joan W. Scott's definition of gender as "a primary way of signifying relations of power" is relevant here. For this definition and also further discussion of the connections between gender analysis and political speculations, see her *Gender and the Politics of History* (New York: Columbia University Press, 1988), 42–50.

7. This expression comes from Jane Gallop's *Thinking Through the Body* (New York: Columbia University Press, 1988), 8.

8. bell hooks, "Feminism: A Transformational Politic," in *Theoretical Perspectives on Sexual Difference*, ed. Deborah H. Rhode (Stanford: Stanford University Press, 1991), 185–93.

9. For an excellent discussion of the provisional and historically situated nature of all knowledge-making projects, see Donna Haraway, "Situated Knowledges: The Science Question in Feminism and the Privilege of Partial Perspective," *Feminist Studies* 14 (1988): 575–99.

10. We wish to thank Carla Freccero, Nadia Medina, and Sheila Conboy for reading earlier versions of this introduction and for making useful suggestions for revision.

Margaret Brose

Petrarch's Beloved Body: "Italia mia"

Recent feminist criticism has directed our attention to the pervasive presence of images of the wounded or fragmented female body in our cultural
production. In a commodity culture such as ours, we are compelled to
interrogate both the exchange system that assigns value to this proliferation of a specific image and the ways in which this exchange system is itself
gendered. Our interrogation is thus twofold: What role in commodity
exchange does this figuration of a wounded female body play? And how
does this image function in our sex-gender system? The ultimate goal of
such questioning is to reanimate our understanding of the force of figural
language in all aspects of our sociocultural production.

  In the following pages I will focus on a specific literary use of this
image of the female body, tracking its function within an exchange system
internal to a specific medieval textual space. But I want to suggest at the
outset that this autotelic textual space is paradigmatic of other cultural and
psychosexual terrains as well. My specific topic is the rhetorical figure of
prosopopoeia or personification: the figure of Italy as a wounded female
body in Petrarch's justly famous political canzone "Italia mia." In this canzone, poem 128 of the *Rime sparse*, the figuration of Italy as a vilified female
body serves both to enable a specifically male poetic language and to justify the call for a rebirth of Italic political consciousness. Of course, Petrarch's "Italia mia" is not the first text in the Italian literary tradition to
figure Italy as a vilified female body. His most immediate models can be
found in Dante's Epistle VII (which represents Florence as an unnatural
Myrrha) and the famous invective in *Purgatorio* VI, which opens with the
image of the enslaved and prostituted Italy, "Ahi serva Italia, di dolore
ostello, / nave senza nocchiere in gran tempesta, / non donna di provincie,
ma bordello" ("Ah, servile Italy, hostel of grief, ship without pilot in great
tempest, no mistress of provinces, but brothel!") (vv. 76–78).[1] "Italia
mia" is, however, the founding text of a complex Italian poetico-political
history of female *sparagmos*, in which figurations of a wounded and scat-

tered female body sanction the construction of both poetic and political subjectivity.[2]

Petrarch's "Italia mia" is more than a canonical literary text; it has been invoked over the centuries as a powerful instrument of political propaganda and persuasion. It was appropriated as a banner by the Italian Risorgimento in its efforts to unify Italy in the middle of the nineteenth century, and by Mussolini and the Fascist party in their totalitarian efforts to conquer Europe and Africa in the early twentieth century. As we shall see later, it was appropriated and craftily retroped by Machiavelli in *The Prince*. How is it that such different political projects can claim sanction under the same figural aegis? Posing this question provides an inroad into the political unconscious of our forms of representation, or more modestly, it can serve to open an inquiry into the processes by which rhetorical figures are formulated and assigned commodity/exchange value within a poetic text/cultural context. The metaphors of our cultural production must be de-aestheticized—or rematerialized—if they are to be held accountable for what they in fact do. In this case, they contribute to the reification of the "femaleness" of the body of Italy so that its fetishized parts can be exchanged for the production of song and speech, which are in turn utilized to fortify male power.

In describing the metaphorical system in Petrarch's poem, I will have occasional recourse to terms such as *binary gender system*, or *male* versus *female*. Despite the convenience of this usage, I want to acknowledge the importance of the work of Teresa de Lauretis and to subscribe to her insights that simplistic binary notions of sexual difference "have now become a limitation, something of a liability to feminist thought."[3] For Petrarch and his epoch this binary mode of conceptualization was deeply entrenched, and the female body was generally represented as the site of visual and sexual pleasure. And yet, in Petrarch's (and Dante's and Saint Augustine's) intuitions, representations of female figures always evidence anxieties about absence and representation, language and desire, signification and the Logos. As late readers of these texts, we can appreciate the ways in which such representations of the "female" are grounded in culture rather than in nature. But we might also entertain the possibility that for writers such as Petrarch, anxiety about the "constructed" nature of femaleness, and hence—and more terrifingly—that of maleness also, may be at the heart of the appropriative dynamics of this rhetorical scenario.

In this essay, then, I will try to defamiliarize Petrarch's "Italia mia" and its central representation of the female body of Italy, and to suggest that the famous Petrarchan fragmentary poetic techniques, which have been masterfully analyzed by several readers in reference to the body of Laura in Petrarch's love lyrics, are also at play in this political canzone.[4] The best critics of Petrarch tend to ignore the rhetorical and metaphorical similarities between "Italia mia" and the poems addressed to Laura, however.[5] This critical tendency indicates how our reading practices have so naturalized the gendered commodity system that violent images used to fortify patriarchalism can be sublimated into the value of "patriotism."

Critics of Petrarch frequently divide his poetic corpus into love poems and political poems. Not surprisingly, there is a tendency to sentimentalize the political poems, especially "Italia mia." Let me offer a representative example:

> The most celebrated of Petrarch's non-amorous poems is the beautiful "Italia mia," 128, written at Parma in 1344–45. This and Dante's lament over divided Italy in *Purgatorio* VI, 76–151 are the loftiest expressions of Italian patriotism . . . yet how they differ in tone and feeling. The difference is apparent in the opening words of each, in the contrast between Petrarch's tender "My Italy" and Dante's harshly admonitory "Ah, servile Italy" . . . Petrarch's canzone is subjective and lyrical throughout.[6]

Although Kenelm Foster describes well the tonal difference between these two canonical figurations of Italy, he fails to recognize that both are predicated upon the imaging of Italy as a vilified female body and the metamorphosis of female degradation into male power and speech. So, too, Foster fails to note that Petrarch's tenderness does not preclude images of sexual violation of the maternal body. As with Petrarch's love lyrics, the central project of "Italia mia" is the construction of male subjectivity at the expense of female creativity.

i.

A brief description of "Italia mia" and its historical moment is in order here. The poem was written in 1344–45. The date is significant in its proximity to several important events in Petrarch's life: the popular uprising in Rome of 1343, which marked the political emergence of Cola di Rienzo, whose efforts to revive the Roman Republic were briefly supported by Petrarch; and the fall in 1344 of the Correggio family, Petrarch's patrons in Parma, at the hands of mercenaries fighting on behalf of the Visconti and the lords of Mantova. The divisive situation in Parma reflected the general condition of the Italian polity as a whole. Moreover, in 1343 Petrarch wrote his *Secretum,* a dialogue with Saint Augustine on the subject of the divided will of the poet. Finally, in 1345, Petrarch made his most extraordinary philological discovery, a manuscript containing large portions of Cicero's familiar letters. Taken together, these events point to the two dominant themes of "Italia mia": on the one hand, the topos of internecine strife, divided will, and political division; on the other, that of the possibility of an actual material revival of the Roman past.

The canzone "Italia mia" contains seven stanzas of sixteen verses each, followed by a *congedo* of ten verses. Stanza 1 opens with an invocation to "My Italy" and a rhetorical disclaimer that "although speech does not aid those mortal wounds of which in your lovely body I see so many, I wish at least my sighs to be such as Tiber and Arno hope for" ("a le piaghe mortali / che nel bel corpo tuo sì spesso veggio") (vv. 2–3).[7] The poet then switches interlocutor, from "Italy" to God ("Rettor del cielo," v. 7; "Segnor cortese," v. 10; "Padre," v. 14), to whom he laments the civil war being fought on Italian soil by foreign armies and mercenaries. He asks for divine inspiration ("ivi fa' che 'l tuo vero / qual io mi sia, per la mia lingua s'oda") (vv. 15–16) and prays that the hearts of his ultimate interlocutors, the lords of Italy, may be softened and made receptive to his poetic word.

This first stanza, then, initiates figural connections between the wounded body of Italy, a political crisis, and poetic inspiration. The wounded body is grammatically marked as female and rhetorically described as "bel corpo," a recurrent syntagm in the poems to Laura. It is the injury to this female body that is supposed to inspire the effort to resolve a political crisis and to enliven male speech.[8] Let us also note the specular or scopophilic nature of this opening scene: Petrarch stresses it is the sight ("veggio") of wounds that inspires him to song. As is well known, and we shall return to this point later, Petrarch's love lyrics to Laura rely heavily on various Ovidian myths of metamorphosis involving voyeurism, rending and scattering of bodies, and the production of narrative.

Stanza 2 swerves toward the third interlocutor, from the upper-case "Segnore," God, to the lower-case and plural "signori," the ruling lords of Italy. The intimate "tu," first addressed to the beloved body of Italy and then used in supplication to God, is now transformed to the plural "voi" and directed to the lords of Italy whose "hard and closed" hearts have allowed the country to be violated. In so addressing his lords, Petrarch defines himself as more than a political "subject": he constitutes himself a subject of the God of Love, of the Christian God, and of his secular lords; and from these multiple positions of subjection he constructs his literary subjectivity.[9] Historically, we should remember that Petrarch was completely dependent upon the patronage of these secular lords. Although a cleric by profession, Petrarch had no long-term affiliation with any one benefice, and his various moves between France and Italy, and between cities within Italy, were necessarily influenced by his relationships to his lords.

Stanzas 3 and 4 portray Italy in geographical and historical terms. In stanza 3, Petrarch describes Italy's body as providentially formed by Nature with "the Alps as shield between us and the Teutonic rage" ("Ben provide Natura al nostro stato / quando de l' Alpi schermo / pose tra noi et la tedesca rabbia") (vv. 33–34). But this shield has failed to protect Italy from the Italian lords' "blind desire," which has made her healthy body "scabbious" ("ch'al corpo sano à procurato scabbia") (v. 38). Stanza 4 then recounts past Italic glories, contrasting the heroic deeds of the noble Roman generals Marius and Caesar with the pettiness of contemporary Italian warlords. As in the love poems, the dominant image is of *sparagmos*, but this time it is the "divided wills" of the rulers of Italy that "are spoiling the loveliest part of the world" ("Vostre voglie divise / guastan del mondo la più bella parte") (vv. 55–56).[10] All these instances of division and dispersion suggest a recurrent scenario of male desire dismembering the female body.[11]

Stanza 5 grows more rhetorically agitated as the poet reproaches the Italian lords for their anger, which is causing a rain of blood: "Ma 'l vostro sangue piove / più largamente, ch' altr' ira vi sferza" ("But your blood is shed more copiously, for another anger whips you on") (vv. 69–70). Blood begets blood, even rhetorically: Petrarch's opening image of a rain of blood is condensed synecdochically into the more powerful figuration of "Latin sangue gentile" (v. 74). Description becomes desperate exhortation as Petrarch implores "Noble Latin blood" to "throw off these harmful burdens" (v. 75): again the plural "voi" becomes the singular, intimate "tu."

The sixth and penultimate stanza opens unexpectedly with an anaphoric series of rhetorical questions in which Petrarch explicitly invokes Italy as the body of the mother:

> Non è questo 'l terren ch'i'toccai pria?
> non è questo il mio nido
> ove nudrito fui sì dolcemente?
> non è questa la patria in ch'io mi fido,
> madre benigna et pia,
> che copre l'un et l'altro mio parente?
>
> (vv. 81–86)

("Is this not the ground that I touched first? Is this not my nest where I was so sweetly nourished? Is this not my [homeland][12] in which I trust, and my kind and merciful mother which covers both of my parents?")

Italy's body is nest and womb, the "homeland" of a prelapsarian, preoedipal symbiosis between mother and child: the poet receives his first sustenance from the mother-body. Italy's soil is mother as well as sepulchre of both parents. The wounding of this body is the precondition for the production of speech, the occasion for the poet's invective. Images of female blood (the wounds of stanza 1) are to be transmuted into exhortations to destructive bloodletting and male self-begetting.

Again, blood begets blood; Latin blood is destined to overcome barbaric blood. As dramatic climax to stanza 6, the poet calls Italians to arms and battle: "manhood shall take up arms against rage, and the fighting shall be short: for ancient valor is not yet dead in Italic hearts" ("vertú contra furore / prenderà l'arme, et fia 'l combatter corto; / che l'antico valore / ne l'italici cor non è ancor morto") (vv. 95–96). The myth of Roman male destiny pervading the entire canzone is especially prominent in this apostrophe: contemporary Italians have betrayed their Roman heritage. Envisioning the remedy for the contemporary political crisis in terms of a revival of a lost virtue, Petrarch exhorts the Italian lords to assume the moral and political burden of their Roman ancestors: "ancient valor is not yet dead in Italic hearts." But the force of this backward glance is profoundly elegiac. It is cast in the mode of loss. Hence the dominant tone of mourning and regret.

Stanza 7, the last stanza before the *congedo*, provides a final unexpected swerve as the poet suggests to the princes of Italy that they turn their affection to God rather than to the pursuit of secular power. Instead of a call to arms, it is a call to death and a reminder of the Last Judgment. Petrarch's ambivalent attitude toward secular power manifests itself most clearly in this Christian epilogue. The *congedo*, which as usual is addressed to the canzone itself, sends the poem out to seek the protection of "the magnanimous few who love the good," crying "Pace, pace, pace" ("Peace, peace, peace") (v. 122). Petrarch here identifies with that patriarchal authority which has femininized the body of Italy. The poem considered as a synecdoche of the poet now seeks the protection of that regal male power.

Machiavelli was aware of Petrarch's ambivalent political stance. Readers of Machiavelli would have recognized the irony of his truncated quotation of "Italia mia" at the closing of *The Prince*:

> vertù contra furore
> prenderà l'arme, et fia 'l combatter corto:
> che l'antiquo valore
> ne l'italici cor' non è ancor morto.
>
> (93–96)

("manhood shall take up arms against rage, and the fighting shall be short: for ancient valor is not yet dead in Italic hearts.") [13]

Machiavelli stopped quoting here, just before Petrarch launches into his Christian sermon on the transience of all life, which would have undermined the powerful call to action of the verses quoted above. The last chapter of *The Prince* does invoke the coming of a redeemer, but a secular one. Machiavelli exhorts his lord, Lorenzo de' Medici, to those "just enterprises" ("le imprese iuste") that will liberate Italy from foreign domination, and his rhetoric is crudely unequivocal: "A ognuno puzza questo barbaro dominio" ("This barbarian domination stinks to everyone"). [14] Petrarch's classical *sentenza* quoted out of context—or, rather, embedded within the context of Machiavelli's own rhetoric and logic—takes on the exhortatory tone of *The Prince*. Yet this reference to Italy's "ancient valor" would have been rendered powerless had Machiavelli included Petrarch's closing appeal to a transcendent form of Christian peace.

ii.

Having outlined the progression of topoi and images of "Italia mia," I want to speculate briefly on the genealogy of this imaging of Italy and on the way in which the poem utilizes the notion of *figura*, that is to say, the

Christian exegetical concept of the figure and its fulfillment. Then, in the last section of this essay, I want to emphasize the need to bring recent feminist theories to bear on Petrarch's "Italia mia," so as to highlight the violence inherent in the nexus of images (the semantic field) of the wounded female body, blood, voyeurism, and the production of discourse.

What are the interconnections between literary figures and possible political futures? Surely we owe to Dante the first self-conscious definition of Italy as a linguistic, hence national, entity. In the *De vulgari eloquentia*, Dante separates Italy from the other geographical areas speaking Romance by virtue of the affirmative particle "sì," thus distinguishing Italy from those other national configurations that speak "languedoc" and "langue-doil." As is well known, subsequent literary historians follow this typology when they distinguish the different genres and styles produced by medieval French writers: northern France, in "languedoil," created the anonymous war epic, the *Chanson de Roland*, while southern France, in "languedoc," spawned the subjective Provençal love lyric. The literary historians remind us, however, that Italian literature failed to produce its own indigenous epic hero—adducing this as an explanation for the fact that Italy failed to produce itself as a true nation state until very late in the nineteenth century. We are reminded of the fact that even Ariosto's Orlando was French in origin, and thus inauthentic as a hero.

In the *De vulgari eloquentia*, Dante defined Italy as the "lingua di sì." Was Italy, then, in its first incarnation as a linguistic entity, already a yea-sayer? Did this characterization by means of the affirmative particle presage a nation riddled by prolonged periods of foreign invasion? A nation whose battles were fought by foreign mercenaries? The pragmatic rejoinder would be simply that since the negative particles in these Romance idioms are unmarked, the affirmative particles would necessarily be used to render difference. We should recall, however, that even in this linguistic practice of differentiation, marked versus unmarked functions as a genderizing inscription, in which the unmarked as male subsumes female. Female as difference is that which is not male and which therefore must be rhetorically figured.

The issue here is not the *De vulgari eloquentia* as such, but rather the question of a figural determinism. Following Christian exegetical practice, we have been trained to look for the rebirth of the spirit beyond the letter.[15] And yet, perversely, we may want to reverse the familiar adage and ask whether the birth of the letter out of the spirit is possible. We need to re-dress our habitual gendered forms of metaphorization, to rematerialize our representations of national and linguistic identity, which are grounded in the politicization of gendered images.

Stephanie Jed's recent book *Chaste Thinking: The Rape of Lucretia and the Birth of Humanism* examines what she terms the founding scenario of Western humanistic thought. As Jed comments, in "historiographic literature, the legend of the rape of Lucretia is always contiguously related to questions of law."[16] In Lacanian terms, this law is the "nom du père," the symbolic phallus, the instrument that penetrates, wounds, dismembers the female body, and that allows for the very possibility of speech. Furthermore, since the story of the rape of Lucretia functions narratologically to confer legitimacy on the foundation of Republican Rome, Jed asks "if there is some kind of reciprocal relationship: do republican laws and institutions also legitimize the conditions of sexual violence?"[17] Indeed, relationships that are adduced to legitimize sexual and legal practices are more than contiguous or metonymic. They are causal and sanctioning as well.

This question becomes all the more pressing when we recognize, as recent feminist critics have, that figurations of the female body are not innocent metaphors. The more deeply entrenched these figures are, the more they appear "spiritualized"—that is to say, only "a figure of speech" or merely "a dead metaphor." And yet metaphors never die; they are recycled into new semantic packages, usually smaller and offered at discount prices. At work here is the Althusserian concept of interpellation—the process whereby a sociocultural representation becomes domesticated, so to speak, and absorbed to the point of appearing natural or real, rather than fictional and thus an arbitrary construct. When images of sexual violence become so interpellated, we dull our understanding of how they in turn generate real acts of sexual violence, and how narration itself is the act that dispossesses the female of speech.

It is precisely these Roman virile laws and virtues—originally purchased with the blood and body of Lucretia, suggests Jed—that Petrarch seeks to resuscitate in the historical moment of 1345. His impassioned plea for peace re-tropes the same scenario of sexual violence recounted by Jed by personifying Italy as a wounded female body. It is the mutilation and debility of the female body that requires the speech of the male poet and his summoning of male virtue as the presence that completes the opening figure of loss and absence. In "Italia mia" readers must understand the meaning of the figure of Italy to be incomplete and absent until the metaleptic return of Roman virtue. And yet, suppressed in Petrarch's figuration is the apprehension of the impossibility of return. In Petrarch's canzone, the figure can be fulfilled only by making the female body a commodity. Within the economy of the poem, the bleeding body of woman is exchanged for the liquidity of male song. Fulfillment as thus conceived is the transumption of the male Law or Nomos.

As is well known, in the Western metaphysical tradition, male is privileged over female, aggression over peace, war over poetry. Gendered binaries give rise to class and race hierarchies. That the scene of male creation is played out on and at the cost of the desacralized female body is a view now amply explicated by such diverse works as *The Lay of the Land* and *The Land Before Her* by Annette Kolodny, and *Sowing the Body* by Page duBois.[18] Despite the extreme divergence in time and place of subject matter (Kolodny works on North American frontier myths of the eighteenth and nineteenth centuries, duBois on such metaphors of the female as field, furrow, stone, oven, and tablet in pre-Socratic Greece), these two critics share a concern for how the putatively innocent metaphors of our sociocultural production encode an ineluctable psychosexual dynamic by means of which Woman as Virgin/Mother/Procreator is inevitably dispossessed of her fecund, paradisiacal attributes. The fertile self-sufficiency of woman, as duBois might characterize it, is then transmuted into male virtue so that he may conquer that very "virginal/maternal" land that gave him birth. This process of acculturation, as it were, involves what Julia Kristeva has called the transition of the semiotic to the symbolic.[19] Page duBois terms this move "the Platonic appropriation of reproduction," which she locates in a precise historical moment in ancient Greece, and which we may view as recapitulated in the psychosexual development of each individual (Western, modern) human psyche.

Petrarch's "Italia mia" occupies the same semantic field as Kolodny's frontier tales and duBois's telluric metaphors. Petrarch posits the figure of Italy as a once-generative female body now mutilated, from whose wounds blood flows and from which he derives his own inspiration to speak. The blood of Italy is transfigured into the effluent voice of the male poet. The forceful fiction of prosopopoeia (personification) endows that symbolic space, which by convention we now call Italy, with name, body, and voice. The seemingly innocent tactic of endowing the ruins and stones of Italy with body and voice and emplotting Italy's story as a Fall thus implicates this poetry in the figural logic of the katabasis and its corollary of the return. The return envisioned is of the lost Law of the Father. How can this poetry, then, speak the language of the future, let alone of a multigendered polis?

iii.

Petrarch's "Italia mia" is of especial interest because it allows us to consider the conjoining of the manifestly political and the latently erotic into the figure of the female body. As we shall see later, this is often the body of the mother, in which case the poet seeks a return to a preoedipalized union before individuation, before genitalization.[20]

In Petrarch, the metaphor of the body politic is extended beyond its primarily political connotations; it is also conjoined to the iconography of the courtly love lyric, which, with its dramatis personae of antagonists and assassins, comes to enact its psychomachia on the body politic. The dominant image is that of *sparagmos* or dispersion, In Canzone 128 this lacerated, dismembered body is that of Italy only secondarily. Indeed, I would like to suggest that Laura and Italy are, fundamentally, always specular projections of Petrarch himself, the poet as synecdoche of the divisive desires of love and peace within the human psyche. Love and politics are merely the two most obvious stages for the ritual reenactment of that drama. It is in this light that we can begin to see how well Petrarch's "Italia mia" fits into the larger fabric of the *Rime sparse*. The Latin title of the *Rime, Rerum vulgarium fragmenta*, characterizes not only the nature of the individual poems comprising the *Canzoniere*, but also the ontology of the whole work. Those famous poetic strategies of fragmentation and scattering, which have come to be viewed as the hallmark of Petrarch's poetic and amorous stance vis-à-vis Laura, are the distinctive features also of the canzone "Italia mia."

Petrarch's model of the anatomical and geographical coordinates of Italy derives from Christian interpretations of Virgil's *Aeneid*, which traditionally view Rome as *caput mundi*.[21] Two traditions merge within his figuration of Italy as a female body: first, the universalist, Virgilian myth of Italian destiny, which underlies Petrarch's lament for a lost Italian hegemony; and second, the rhetoric of the courtly love tradition, which is transferred from the psychomachia of the poet-lover to the female body of the motherland. The battles for peace, control, and integration of the passions and reason are played out on the flesh of the mother. Consequently, Petrarch's myth of Italy as fatal geographic body merges political and erotic allegories and establishes a connection between female wounding and the male poetic creativity.

Although Petrarch addresses himself, in the body of the lyric, to the warring petty lords of Italy, the poem's *incipit* immediately establishes the connection between words and wounds. In an aporia somewhat like a *praeteritio*, in which the speaker emphasizes a point by appearing to pass over it, Petrarch states that although speech does not aid the many "mortal wounds" that he sees in the lovely body of his Italy, at least his "sighs" may be such as hoped for by Arno and Po (this metonymic representation of ruling powers by the rivers contiguous with their cities is another instance of reification). Petrarch would like to heal the wounds in the body of his beloved Italy by means of his speech, but his speech is itself a product of wounds, that is to say, of both the originary separation from the mother-body and the specific figuration of Italy's wounded body in the canzone.[22]

Most of the rhetorical devices in Petrarch's poetry serve as strategies to contain and forestall the dispersion of speech (blood) that always signals the dissolution of the self and loss of control. It is in this sense that blood imagery in Petrarch's poetry (and in the Ovidian myths that inspire him) subsists as a figure for the disruptive potential of speech itself. The rhetorical moves of Petrarch's "Italia mia" are stylistically consonant with his love poems to Laura in their strategies of containment and ingathering. We see the same chiastically balanced lines, geminated adjectives, and reduplicative syntax. As examples of chiastically balanced lines, let us recall the syntagms "di che lievi cagion' che crudel guerra" ("from what trivial causes comes such cruel war") (v. 11); "Or dentro ad una gabbia / fiere selvagge et mansuete gregge" ("Within the same cage savage beasts and gentle flocks lie down") (vv. 39–40); and finally, "perchè 'l verde terreno / del barbarico sangue si depinga?" ("Why is the green earth covered with barbarian blood?") (vv. 21–22). Geminated adjectival syntagms such as "Marte superbo et fero" ("proud fierce Mars") (v. 13) and "le fortune afflitte et sparte" ("afflicted and scattered fortunes") (v. 59) abound.

By means of these stylistic devices, along with tightly binding end rhymes and logically coordinated stanzaic display, the thematics of dispersion in "Italia mia" is mitigated by a syntax of integration, balance, and conciliation. The centrifugal dispersion of body parts, city states, and poetic psyche, if you will, is countered by a centripetal ingathering. The dialectic of dispersion of the female body and containment by means of the male poet's techne is a hallmark of Petrarchan poetics. It is also the representational pattern underlying the rape of Lucretia and the constitution of the Roman law. Indeed, the models imitated by these classically balanced syntactical periods are those of Roman control.

My remarks above accord well with the observation of Umberto

Bosco that Petrarch's political attitude is best characterized by "sogno e rimpianto piuttosto che di decisione" ("dream and regret rather than by decision").[23] Bosco goes on to note that Petrarch's seemingly contradictory political opinions are united by a single theme, his love of Italy. "E questo amor d'Italia era tutt'uno . . . con l'amor di pace." Love of Italy is identified with love of peace, that same haven or "porto" so often invoked by Petrarch as a refuge from the conflictual nature of love in his lyrics both to Laura "in vita" and later to the Virgin Mary "in morte di madonna Laura." Bosco defines Petrarch's patriotism as the "rimpianto" and "auspicio" of the return of an Italy without war, an Italy synecdochically identified with Rome—the dream of the restoration of the Roman Empire. The dual crises of the polis and Eros, both arenas of the body or the material, if you will, are sublated into the myth of the return of the spirit of an Italic halcyon unity.

We should recall at this point that the archetypal mythos of *sparagmos* implies the ritual dismemberment of a sacrificial victim, which serves, through scapegoating, later to reunite the members of the community. In *sparagmos*, according to Northrop Frye, the theme of the disappearance of the hero often takes the form of the tearing to pieces of his body. "Sometimes the hero's body is divided among his followers, as in Eucharist symbolism: sometimes it is distributed around the natural world, as in the stories of Orpheus and more especially Osiris."[24] This mythos is pervaded by "the sense that heroism and effective action are absent, disorganized or foredoomed to defeat, and that confusion and anarchy reign over the world." Rather than ingesting the dismembered body, we have in "Italia mia" a displacement from ingestion to gestation: the image of incorporation as return to an amniotic identification with the mother-body.

Francesco de Sanctis, who was perhaps the first critic to characterize Petrarchan poetics as a strategy of dispersion, had commented that Petrarch's *Canzoniere* lacks all story or plot ("ci manca li romanzo o la storia").[25] We might say that for Petrarch, the primal myth is that of the Roman Empire. It is in this story that he finds precisely those characteristics missing in his own personal story: integration, plot, progress, permanence. In both the erotic and the political aspects of Petrarch's own life, the notions of integration, hierarchy, and domination are especially valorized because these are the most problematic. Petrarch's rhetoric of an embodied Italy is profoundly contradictory, balanced between a yearning for return to a maternal home and a need to rend and disembody that very form. Through *sparagmos*, therefore, the negation of woman's reality results, on the thematic level, in the glorification of the patriarchal Roman period and, on the formal level, in poetic creation itself.

iv.

Above all, images and metaphors of blood bind into one matrix the tropes of the female body, the body politic, and the voice of the poet. The shedding of blood, mentioned four times in "Italia mia," inspires the poet's words and yet reduces them to sighs. Petrarch's attempt to heal wounds with words reveals the incommensurability between these two terms. As we have seen, even his appeal to a return of a past virtue is displaced once more, now to the plane of ultimate spirituality, that of heavenly peace. Life is the perilous path ("dubbioso calle")(v. 102); peace can only be obtained by turning on to the "road to heaven" ("strada del ciel")(v. 112).

The chain of associations with blood in the central sections of "Italia mia" recalls a specifically female scene of creativity, inasmuch as in parturition the flow of blood signifies not death and destruction but life and production. In the Petrarchan version, poetizing is a surrogate form of female creativity, a virtual theft of a distinctively female mode of creation. We have come, then, to images of parturition and menstruation and, by the logic of psychoanalysis, to another famous scene in which female creativity is expropriated and transformed into an instrument of male power: Perseus's decapitation of Medusa. For like Perseus's power in battle, Petrarch's poetic powers depend upon the dismemberment of a female body—either Laura's or Italy's.

It will be recalled that Freud saw Medusa's head as symbolizing the terror of castration, but it is not often noted that he saw it also as serving to isolate "the horrifying effects" of representations of female sexuality "from the pleasure-giving ones."[26] Freud's argument is that the hair on Medusa's head, conventionally represented by snakes, derives from the castration scenario; they represent the penis. Freud then swiftly substitutes the "horrifying" with the "pleasure-giving." "It is a remarkable fact that, however frightening [the snakes] may be in themselves, they nevertheless serve as a mitigation of the horror, for they replace the penis, the absence of which is the cause of the horror." The sight of Medusa's head makes the spectator stiff with terror, turns him into stone. But this is reassuring to the male subject, Freud avers: "for becoming stiff means an erection," and thus the spectator is consoled to find himself "still in possession of a penis."[27]

So, too, Petrarch professes and no doubt feels terror at the sight of a mutilated Italy; at the same time, however, he is both inspired and consoled by his own powers of poetic expression in the face of that terror. In fact, Freud has not only denied the terror he originally ascribes to the voyeuristic viewing of the female genitals *as* mutilation, he has also deleted the frame of the Medusa story, as told by Ovid, for example, in which the telling of the tale is necessitated by the metamorphosis, not of men into stone, but of a woman into a monster as a result of a rape, that of Medusa by Neptune. Medusa's powers derive (ironically) from Minerva's punishment of this offense, but these powers in turn are stolen by Perseus, who uses her severed head to turn his enemies into stone. Equally important to our discussion of Petrarch is the fact that Freud also omits the conclusion of the Medusa story, in which the decapitated head (perhaps in a gesture of refusal of the male destructive power wielded by Perseus) delivers two offspring: ". . . and from that mother's bleeding / Were born the swift-winged Pegasus and his brother."[28]

Thus, figurations of female blood, in the Medusa myth and in Petrarch's "Italia mia" as well, can be seen to symbolize both the female powers of creation and the male fear of castration. The spectre of castration associated with images of blood and loss urges the male poet to his compensatory speech, since these two systems of symbolization are intimately linked. Here it bears reiteration that, by the logic of the figural exchange system established in "Italia mia" (and shared by many other texts), female bodily members purchase male speech. Petrarch thus reproduces in this political poem the explicitly heterosexual poetics found throughout the *Rime sparse*. A myriad of other literary topoi could be called upon to support this nexus of associations between wound and disfiguration, and the production of blood and speech. In the wood of the suicides of Dante's *Divine Comedy*, *Inferno* XIII, Pier delle Vigne is the hybrid plant-man whose leaves are torn off and who then vents his pain in blood-language. The sources for this episode include the story of Polydorus in the *Aeneid*, as well as several of Ovid's *Metamorphoses*. While this particular episode in Virgil and Dante features the connections between mutilation and speech, many of the Ovidian myths explicitly link issues of gender with those of mutilation and speech.

Indeed, the myth of Philomela inscribes another fascinating variation on this theme, in that it is the mutilation of the mouth—the severing of the tongue (a displaced castration)—which leads to the narration of the story, this narration being a literal interweaving rather than mere voice. And the story that Philomela tells is that of her own violation. A history can indeed be inscribed without voice (or tongue, or without phallic implement, that is), then; its sine qua non is, however, the mutilation of the female body.[29] If there exist modes of narration other than phalloscripture, they must be purchased by severance and loss. Indeed, Philomela's tale may illustrate an ironic return of the repressed; the prelapsarian mother-tongue is lost at birth; within the postlapsarian domain of the father-tongue, all speech is patriarchal until mutilation and loss return us once again to body language.

As Gayle Rubin's now classic essay "The Traffic in Women" suggests, woman's cultural position has always been that of a commodity in the traffic between men.[30] The profound implication of this insight, which accords with, indeed is based on, the work of structuralist anthropologists such as Claude Lèvi-Strauss, is that the fundamental alliances in culture are those that unite or bond male to male—alliances in which the female is coined as the lucre to purchase such alliances. If, as it would appear, cultural alliances are "homosocial" in nature,[31] is it any wonder that female sexuality presents not only a political and an erotic threat, but an economic one at that? The reproductive function of the female suggests nothing less than the economic, hence political, anarchy made possible by infinite minting of coin, or counterfeiting.

It is to Machiavelli that we owe the most brilliant figuration of this threat, which is at once erotic, political, and economic. In his *Discourses*, Machiavelli relates the tale of the Renaissance heroine Caterina Sforza.[32] The enemies of Caterina's husband had killed him and taken her prisoner along with her six children. Her castle having been taken, Caterina persuaded the guards to let her go inside and order her castellan to surrender; she offered to leave her children outside as hostages. Once inside, however, she refused to surrender, and standing on top of the fortress walls, she bared "her genital members" to the enemy, declaring that she "still had the means for producing more children."

It has been pointed out by Hannah Pitkin that this representation conflates terrifying images of the Medusa's head as symbol of castration, and woman cross-dressing, as it were, in male *virtù*. Pitkin states, "A woman with enough *virtù* to sacrifice her children, it seems, gains a fierce and fascinating power, for she inverts the conventional role of nurturance, and makes manifest what fearful men have always suspected lies hidden beneath it."[33] Besides figuring woman as murderer rather than as nurturer, this representative anecdote presents woman as the potentially anarchic source of endless reproduction and coinage, revealing female fecundity to be the only way to undermine the male system of commodity exchange. We need to highlight the fact that under Freud's apparently simplistic description of the fear of castration lies an apprehension of the complex intertwinings of the political and economic bases of civilization and its discontents. Thus it is that female genitalia symbolize both the loss of the penis in the woman and her possession of the Lacanian phallus—since the Law of the Father surely rests on its powers of economic control as well as on its power of interdiction.[34]

Petrarch's "Italia mia," impassioned plea for peace though it may be, rests finally on an act of verbal-sexual violence. Fully consonant with the techniques of *sparagmos* or dispersion of the female body evidenced in his love lyrics to Laura, Petrarch's canzone to his beloved body of Italy participates in that gendered commodity system wherein the fetishized parts of the generative female become lucre to buy a patriarchal song: a tender lament for the once and future Law of the Roman Father.

Notes

1. Dante Alighieri, *The Divine Comedy*, trans. Charles S. Singleton (Princeton: Princeton University Press, 1973), *Purgatorio*, VI, 76–78.

2. This essay initiates a larger investigation of the figure of the female body of Italy in three canonical Italian poetic texts, by three canonical male authors (Petrarch's "Italia mia," 1344–45; Ugo Foscolo's "Dei sepolcri," 1806; and Giacomo Leopardi's "All'Italia," 1818). While the three poems construct slightly different scenarios, all involve the metamorphosis of the "female principle" into male statehood and selfhood.

3. Teresa de Lauretis, *Technologies of Gender: Essays on Theory, Film, and Fiction* (Bloomington: Indiana University Press, 1987), 1. See especially the chapter entitled "The Violence of Rhetoric," 31–50.

4. The following critics, taken together, have provided new and insightful readings of the love poems to Laura, stressing a "poetics of fragmentation" and a "poetics of idolatry" or fetishism/reification: Robert Durling, "Petrarch's 'Giovene donna sotto un verde lauro,' " *MLN* 86 (January 1971): 1–20; idem, *Petrarch's Lyric Poems* (Cambridge: Harvard University Press, 1976), especially the "Introduction," 1–33; John Freccero, "The Fig Tree and the Laurel: Petrarch's Poetics," *Diacritics* 5 (Spring 1975): 34–40; Giuseppe Mazzotta, "The *Canzoniere* and the Language of the Self," *Studies in Philology* 75 (Summer 1978): 271–96; Nancy Vickers, "Remembering Dante: Petrarch's 'Chiare, fresche et dolci acque,' " *MLN* 96 (January,

1981): 1–11; idem, "Diana Described: Scattered Woman and Scattered Rhyme," *Critical Inquiry* 8 (Winter 1981): 265–79.

5. An exception is Robert Durling, who, in his introduction to *Petrarch's Lyric Poems*, recognizes the crucial placement of "Italia mia" within "the central group of canzoni in the first part, 125–129, most of them explorations of different aspects of the dominance . . . of the image of Laura" (21). Durling describes these canzoni in terms of their Augustinian dialectic of dispersal and reintegration, and their erotic, orgasmic imagery, and then offers this highly suggestive comment: "That 'Italia mia,' Petrarch's most important patriotic poem, is part of this group is not accidental: surrounded by the great love canzoni, with which it has many structural and poetic similarities, it is meant to be related to the critical psychological insights of these poems" (24). See also Peter Hainsworth, *Petrarch the Poet: An Introduction to the "Rerum vulgarium fragmenta"* (London: Routledge, 1988), 148. Hainsworth points to the placement of "Italia mia" "amongst four of the most erotic canzoni in what is more a variation or another demonstration of uncertainty than a progression." He refers primarily to the issue of whether or not there is development in the *Canzoniere*. Neither Durling nor Hainsworth develops the implications of his comment into an analysis of the gendered nature of Petrarch's representation of Italy.

6. Kenelm Foster, *Petrarch, Poet and Humanist* (Edinburgh: Edinburgh University Press, 1984), 58–59.

7. All quotations and translations from Petrarch's *Canzoniere* are from the Durling edition of *Petrarch's Lyric Poems*.

8. In another famous poem, *Metricae* III, 24, Petrarch praises Italy in terms of its feminine attributes: bounteousness, fertility, and beauty. This poem concludes with a salutation to Italy as "Mother, Glory of the World."

9. Several critics have discussed the relationship between subjugation and subjectivity: see, for example, Patricia Parker, *Literary Fat Ladies* (London and New York: Methuen, 1987), 61–62. Parker speaks of the vogue of Petrarchism in Elizabethan England, pointing to the fact that Elizabeth's courtiers related to the queen as Petrarch to his cruel mistress. Parker quotes here the insight of Nancy Vickers that Petrarch reverses the danger of subjugation by scattering the body of Laura. See also Peter Stallybrass's discussion of Renaissance practices of enclosing, mapping, and containing the female body as a political/erotic/economic space in "Patriarchal Territories: The Body Enclosed," in *Rewriting the Renaissance: The Discourses of Sexual Difference in Early Modern Europe*, ed. Margaret W. Ferguson, Maureen Quilligan, and Nancy Vickers (Chicago: University of Chicago Press, 1986), 123–42.

10. For an insightful study of the relationship between the figure of *sparagmos* and the body politic, see Patricia MacKinnon, "The Analogy of the Body Politic in St. Augustine, Dante, Petrarch, and Ariosto" (Ph.D. dissertation, University of California, Santa Cruz, 1988). I am especially indebted to her chapter on Petrarch's "Italia mia."

11. Commenting on Petrarch's use of the Ovidian myths of Actaeon and Daphne, Durling also suggests that sexual fear may subtend the creation of poetry: he describes "the deepest preoccupations" of the *Rime sparse* as "dismemberment

or scattering versus integration; poetic immortality versus death; the creation of poetry as the expression of the impossibility of speech resulting from sexual fear" (*Petrarch's Lyric Poems*, 19).

12. In his translation-paraphrase, Durling renders "la patria" as "fatherland." This is a correct translation of one meaning of the Italian term into contemporary English idiom. In classical Latin, the feminine "patria" (= "one's native land, city, etc., . . . the place of origin [of things])" contrasts with masculine "patrius" (= "of or belonging to one's father, . . . of or natural to a father, . . . inherited from one's father, . . . belonging to one by reason of birthplace; natural by reason of one's species or race"). The rendition of Petrarch's term "la patria" as "fatherland" thus tends to obscure the female connotations of the term. "Homeland" is more consistent with the sense and the female imagery of the stanza than "fatherland." Compare the entries for "patria" and "patrius" in the *Oxford Latin Dictionary*, ed. P. G. W. Glare (Oxford: Clarendon, 1988), 1310.

13. Durling's translation of Petrarch's "vertù" as "manhood" does not convey the ambiguity of the kind of strength being invoked. For Petrarch, probably more than for Machiavelli, "vertù" implies spiritual virtue as well as physical strength and intellectual prowess.

14. Niccolò Machiavelli, *The Prince*, ed. and trans. Mark Musa (New York: St. Martin's, 1964), chap. 26, pp. 222–23.

15. Erich Auerbach's "Figura," in his *Scenes from the Drama of European Literature: Six Essays* (New York: Meridian Books, 1959), 11–76, is perhaps the classic exposition of this biblical and medieval exegetical practice.

16. Stephanie Jed, *Chaste Thinking: The Rape of Lucretia and the Birth of Humanism* (Bloomington and Indianapolis: University of Indiana Press, 1989), 2.

17. Ibid., 2.

18. Annette Kolodny, *The Lay of the Land: Metaphor as Experience and History in American Life and Letters* (Chapel Hill: University of North Carolina Press, 1975) and *The Land Before Her: Fantasy and Experience of the American Frontiers 1630–1860* (Chapel Hill: University of North Carolina Press, 1984). Page duBois, *Sowing the Body: Psychoanalysis and Ancient Representations of Women* (Chicago: University of Chicago Press, 1988). See also duBois, *Centaurs and Amazons: Women and the Prehistory of the Great Chain of Being* (Ann Arbor: University of Michigan Press, 1982), for an analysis of the myths that construct sexual, racial, and species binary systems in the Greek city-state.

19. For an excellent discussion of the symbolic in the French feminists, see Judith Butler, *Gender Trouble: Feminism and the Subversion of Identity* (New York: Routledge, 1990), esp. sections 2 and 3. Butler points out that while Kristeva, Irigaray, and Cixous propose a specifically feminine dimension of writing, Monique Wittig claims that language is neither masculinist nor feminist, but rather an instrument employed for political purposes. Whether one subscribes to the former position or the latter, these feminist critics share the conviction that practices of discourse come to be appropriated in gendered ways in service to political goals.

20. Kolodny also points to this male configuration of the mother/lover/victim in the metaphors of the American frontier: "To the initial fantasy of erotic discovery and possession, settlement added the further appeal of filial receptiveness. The

American husbandsman was cast as both son and lover in a primal paradise where the maternal and the erotic were to be harmoniously intermingled" (*The Land Before Her*, 4).

21. See MacKinnon's dissertation for an extended discussion of this symbology.

22. On the relation of language to wounding, see Geoffrey H. Hartman, *Saving the Text: Literature/Derrida/Philosophy* (Baltimore: Johns Hopkins University Press, 1981), the chapter entitled "Words and Wounds," 118–57.

23. Umberto Bosco, *Francesco Petrarca* (Bari: Laterza, 1968), 164.

24. Northrop Frye, *Anatomy of Criticism* (New York: Atheneum, 1969), 192.

25. Francesco de Sanctis, *Saggio critico sul Petrarca* (Bari: Laterza, 1955), 68.

26. Sigmund Freud, "Medusa's Head," in *Sexuality and the Psychology of Love*, ed. Philip Rieff (New York: Macmillan, 1963), 212–13.

27. For a fascinating discussion of the Medusa figure as both a political and a sexual threat, see Neil Hertz, "Medusa's Head: Male Hysteria under Political Pressure," in his *The End of the Line: Essays on Psychoanalysis and the Sublime* (New York: Columbia University Press, 1985), 161–92.

28. Ovid, *Metamorphoses*, trans. Rolfe Humphries (Bloomington: Indiana University Press, 1983), book IV, ll. 186–87, p. 106.

29. See Patricia Kleindienst Joplin's discussion of how Philomela's mutilation places her outside the gendered commodity system, "The Voice of the Shuttle is Ours," *Stanford Literature Review* 1 (1984): 35–36.

30. Gayle Rubin, "The Traffic in Women: Notes on the 'Political Economy' of Sex," in *Toward an Anthropology of Women*, ed. Rayna R. Reiter (New York and London: Monthly Review Press, 1975), 157–210.

31. This theory is developed in Eve Kosofsky Sedgwick, *Between Men: English Literature and Male Homosocial Desire* (New York: Columbia University Press, 1985).

32. Compare Hannah Pitkin, *Fortune is a Woman: Gender and Politics in the Thought of Niccolò Machiavelli* (Berkeley and Los Angeles: University of California Press, 1984), 250.

33. Ibid.

34. This topos finds its most brilliant and horrifying incarnation in Shakespeare's *Titus Andronicus*, in which again the violation of the female body is narrated, if you will, by blood and member, rather than by lexeme or voice. Here the *sparagmos* is at its most graphic, since the stage is strewn with limbs. The dismembered, fetishized body part is both signifier and signified; here wound and word are indissolubly joined in a Satanic inversion of the Logos.

Linda Lomperis

Unruly Bodies and Ruling Practices: Chaucer's *Physician's Tale* as Socially Symbolic Act

Looking closely at the representation of the body in Chaucer's *Physician's Tale*, one discovers contradiction. On the one hand, the tale seems to focus on matters pertaining to the attractiveness and the attractions of bodies. Besides drawing attention at several points to the "excellent beautee" (8) [1] of Virginius's virginal daughter, the narrative also features the lecherous desires of Apius, the judge-governor who, "caught with beautee of this mayde" (127), intends from that point onward "to make hire with hir body synne" (138). On the other hand, however, the *Physician's Tale* seems to eschew everything having to do with the body, embracing instead metaphysical considerations of virginity and morality. Virginius's daughter, we are told, is chaste "as wel in goost as in body" (43); she is also a veritable mirror of all "that longeth to a mayden vertuous" (109). Similarly, the Physician himself is preoccupied by spiritual matters, as his concluding emphasis on the tale's moral meaning indicates (277–86).

Recent scholarship on the *Physician's Tale* has concerned itself mainly with one side of this contradiction, namely with the nonbodily, metaphysical orientation of the narrative. Derek Pearsall, for example, calls the *Physician's Tale* an "exemplum of virginity," while Ann Middleton reads it as a kind of aesthetic exemplum, a tale that displays in short space Chaucer's routine interrogation and complication of ethical absolutes. [2] Useful as these and related studies have been in making sense of a text that to many has often seemed senseless, they also have left in place certain problematic assumptions about gender-body relations. For in privileging the metaphysical at the expense of the physical, critics of the *Physician's Tale* behave in the same manner as Virginius: they, like him, respond to the tale's representation of bodily considerations by effectively cutting them off. In this regard, both Virginius and the critics can be said to produce and sustain (albeit in different ways) a split between mind and body, a split, moreover, that bears the weight of long-standing gender associations and hierarchies: the "masculinized" claims of the mind work to master, subsume, and finally—in the case of the tale, at least—do away with the "feminized" claims of the body.

In an effort to repair this sort of mind-body split, therefore, the following essay attempts, quite simply, to think the *Physician's Tale* through the body, that is to say, to bring critical attention to bear on the (often ignored) bodily aspects of the tale in order to make them precisely into sites of knowledge, modes of thought—in short, into thinking bodies.[3] The essay as a whole, in other words, stages a feminist undoing of those gender oppositions and hierarchies underwritten by the mind-body split, and at the same time, it seeks to reveal the explicitly political stakes of this kind of feminist critique. For the critical project of thinking through the body, as we shall see, necessarily moves through specific locations of embodiment, that is, through various historical specificities, especially those fourteenth-century British institutions and sociopolitical groupings that establish the discursive contours and ideological investments of Chaucer's writing. In the last analysis, then, this essay points the way toward an understanding of the *Physician's Tale* as both a complex embodiment of and a politically charged commentary on various social forces in its late medieval British environment.

Let us begin, therefore, by examining the intersection in the *Physician's Tale* of questions of the body and questions of power. The first part of the narrative, I would argue, focuses in large part on the Physician's efforts to draw attention away from and thereby gain power over the maid's sexuality, a phenomenon that his own descriptive comments introduce: "This mayde of age twelve yeer was and tweye, / *In which Nature hadde swich delit*" (30–31; italics mine). As this statement implies, Nature, the divinely authorized, procreative force of the universe, delights in the maid precisely because she is a pubescent and, hence, fully sexual and potentially procreative young woman. There is every reason to believe, moreover, that given the maid's marriageable age, she will indeed soon "lerne loore / Of booldnesse" (70–71), as the Physician later laments. And yet, however clear these allusions to the maid's own sexuality might be, the description as a whole finally insists with even greater clarity on the Physician's narratorial attempts to avoid all such reference. In the lines immediately following the reference to the maid's age, the Physician mentions only very briefly the maid's physical characteristics, her "lymes fre" (35) and her "tresses grete" (37), before upping the ante, as it were, for her spiritual qualities: "And if that excellent was hir beautee, / A thousand foold more vertuous was she" (39–40). The next twenty-six lines of the description detail the maid's virtuous qualities and abstemious tendencies, thereby effectively muting, if not simply drowning out, the earlier allusions to her sexuality. A similar erasure of the physical takes place shortly after this when once again the maid's sexuality comes clearly into focus: as soon as the Physician gives clear expression to the fact that the maid is indeed wife material (cf. 70–71), he immediately turns away from this recognition by means of his infamous and lengthy diatribe on parental control of children (72–102). Here once again, the effort on the part of the Physician seems to be one of bridling, containing, or shall we say, policing the physical aspects of the maid through a set of rhetorical strategies designed to focus attention instead either on sexual abstention or on metaphysical virtues, that is, on matters that actively point away from bodily activities.

On the whole, however, the tale actually records the Physician's failure to contain and control the bodily, the sexual. A hint of this failure occurs early in the narrative in the Physician's account of the part played by Nature in the creation of the maid:

> For Nature hath with sovereyn diligence
> Yformed hire in so greet excellence,
> *As though she wolde seyn,* 'Lo! I, Nature,
> Thus kan I forme and peynte a creature,
> Whan that me list; who kan me countrefete?
> Pigmalion noght, though he ay forge and bete,
> Or grave, or peynte; for I dare wel seyn
> Apelles, Zanzis, sholde werche in veyn
> Outher to grave, or peynte, or forge, or bete,
> If they presumed me to countrefete.
>
> (9–18; italics mine)

As the italicized phrase makes clear, the Physician's attempt here is to speak for Nature, to assert his own control over her speech, to play her part, as it were—in short, to counterfeit Nature herself. And yet, as the passage also makes quite clear, Nature cannot be counterfeited. Those who attempt to do so "werche in veyn." The Physician's rhetorical counterfeit-ing gestures are thus at odds with themselves; their value as a means of asserting the Physician's own power to dominate is cast in doubt. Further-more, as the subsequent lines of the speech explain, Nature's own subject position defies an earthbound location. As the "vicaire general" of "He that is the formere principal" (19–20), Nature herself cannot be separated from the godhead: "My lord and I been ful of oon accord" (25). In view of these statements in particular, the Physician's efforts to assert a measure of control over the workings of Nature appear forever outstripped not only by the transcendent positioning of Nature herself, but also, by implication, by those divinely authorized sexual, bodily forces that Nature represents.

Indeed, the entire first part of the *Physician's Tale* seems both consis-tent and unequivocal in its display of the way in which the sexual and the bodily always exceed the Physician's strategies of control. The re-marks addressed to "ye maitresses . . . / That lordes doghtres han in gover-naunce" (72ff.) make this point quite clear. Ostensibly, the aim of this speech is to warn governesses to be vigilant in teaching children virtuous behavior and in protecting them from sexual involvement. What the speech actually winds up doing, however, is insisting on the potentially uncontrollable sexuality of the governesses themselves. In the first part of the speech, for example, the Physician acknowledges the fact that gover-nesses qualify as teachers of virtue either because they themselves are vir-tuous, or because they "knowen wel ynough the olde daunce, / And han forsaken fully swich meschaunce / For everemo" (79–81). Yet despite this categorical dismissal of sexuality, the Physician's subsequent remarks do not in fact suggest the governesses' complete abandonment of "swich meschaunce":

> A theef of venysoun, that hath forlaft
> His likerousnesse and al his olde craft,
> Kan kepe a forest best of any man.
> Now kepeth wel, for if ye wole, ye kan.
> Looke wel that ye unto no vice assente
> Lest ye be dampned for youre wikke entente;
> For whoso dooth, a traitour is, certeyn.
> And taketh kep of that that I shal seyn:
> Of alle tresons sovereyn pestilence
> Is whan a wight bitrayseth innocence.
>
> (83–92)

The obsessively repetitive hortatory statements in this passage, "Now kepeth wel," "Looke wel that ye unto no vice assente," and "And taketh kep" indicate the likelihood, from the Physician's perspective, of the governesses' own sexuality getting out of hand. Taken together, these lines convey a sense both of the governesses sexuality as an ongoing, ineradicable phenomenon, and of the Physician's own desperate attempt to put an end to such unabashedly bodily behavior. A similar sense of the stubborn persistency of sexual, bodily acts also emerges in the Physician's subsequent address to fathers and mothers. Advising them as to how they can best protect their children from sexual involvement, the Physician says, "Beth war, *if by ensaumple of youre lyvynge,* / Or by youre necligence in chastisynge, / That they ne perisse" (97–99; italics mine). Before parents can set an example for their children, it seems, they must abstain from their own manifestly sexual mode of "lyvynge." As all of these examples demonstrate, the Physician's long apostrophe to governesses and parents finally turns into the opposite of what it was originally designed to be: starting out as a discourse that would *ward off* sex, the Physician's remarks instead turn into a discourse *about* sex, a certain kind of "body talk."

If the excessiveness and ungovernability of the body, especially of sexuality, are what emerge from the Physician's speech on parental governance, his subsequent return to the topic of the maid's virginity would seem to suggest the reestablishment of an area in which his own sense of power and control reigns secure. However, by emphasizing as he does the maid's need for no other governance structure than her own (105–6), and by comparing her to a book wherein is written "every good word or dede / That longeth to a mayden vertuous" (108–9), the Physician effectively casts the maid as her own author, the writer of her own text—a text, moreover, whose temporal unfolding leads once again to the realm of the physical: "the fame out sprong on every syde, / Bothe of hir *beautee* and hir bountee wyde" (111–12; italics mine). Although the narrative at this point seems to draw attention away from this situation, in part by reinscribing an authoritative perspective—"The Doctour maketh this descripcioun" (117)—it also exposes, I would argue, the unstable bases of such authorial control precisely by alluding to the "doctor of physik" himself, and thereby designating his own authorial project, his own rhetorical moves, as simply one more element of the fiction.[4] Neither simply inside nor simply outside, the Physician is as much controlled by as he is controlling of the tale he tells. Here as before, the attempt to do away with the maid's "excellent beautee" is something the narrative both posits and continually erodes.

In its representation of a narrator who consistently tries and fails to exercise control over bodily activity, the *Physician's Tale* can be said to press upon, even exacerbate, the precarious power base of physicians in late fourteenth-century England. On the one hand, physicians at that time were accorded little social prestige. The challenges that the Black Plague presented to the late medieval medical community dealt a particularly severe blow to physicians who, unlike other contemporary practitioners (e.g., surgeons, barber-surgeons, and local village leeches), were not themselves clinicians. Physicians, on the contrary, were principally academicians, university-based theoreticians who had no formal training in dealing with actual bodies.[5] Hence, when called upon to deal with plague victims, physicians not only revealed their incompetence as healers; they also established the very conditions out of which their own professional marginalization could take place.[6] On the other hand, however, medicine in fourteenth-century England was also increasingly becoming a distinctly *professional* activity. More and more, that is to say, the practice of medicine was becoming the province of individuals who were part of self-regulating, publicly recognized, and sometimes high-status social organizations.[7] In this climate, physicians actually found themselves in a rather advantageous position: their location within the university put them in contact with other important professional groupings, notably lawyers and members of the higher clergy, and thus gave them the opportunity to forge politically advantageous alliances.[8] Indeed, throughout the century, there were a number of noteworthy connections between physicians and the king's household. Both Edward II and Edward III, for example, employed a number of court physicians, both from England and from abroad, and besides providing medical services especially in the context of military campaigns, some of these physicians also became trusted royal advisors.[9]

Although the *Physician's Tale* does not explicitly cast its narrator as a court advisor, the long speech on the governance of "lordes doghtres" does indeed turn our attention in this direction. Throughout the narrative, moreover, specific class interests are at stake in the handling of body-power relations: the maid's father, after all, is nothing less than a knight who is both "strong of freendes and of greet richesse" (4). Viewed from this perspective, then, the *Physician's Tale* certainly encourages one to reflect upon the workings of sexuality—especially female sexuality—within the context of the late medieval English aristocracy. How, one wonders, did the daughters of knights actually conduct their sexual lives? Within prevailing social constraints was there any room at all for the notion of female sexual autonomy, or rather, were both women and men simply controlled by the political designs of the male-dominated power structure, designs that invariably determined the marital arrangements, and hence the bodily dispositions, of the late fourteenth-century English nobility? To be sure, recent scholarship on medieval marriage focuses considerable attention on questions of voluntarism: historians have pointed to the increasing importance in the later Middle Ages of a church-based model of marriage which rendered marriage quite simply a matter of mutual consent, and which presumably gave both sexes a good deal of personal freedom when it came to choosing a spouse. And yet this church-based model of marriage, it seems, never entirely supplanted another model of marriage, dominant in aristocratic contexts, which made marriage largely a question of political interests and heir production.[10]

Still, the contemporary existence of two different two models of marriage leads us quite naturally to ask about their relationship. In any given set of circumstances, how exactly did these two models of marriage function together? Was their coexistence harmonious, or did it sometimes provide the occasion for practices that resisted or subverted dominant modes of behavior? Recent evidence for the presence of an antimatrimonial sentiment among women of the nobility in late medieval England also suggests that courtly women may have translated such sentiments into actions: these women may have actively opposed or, at the very least, resisted the institutional control of their sexuality.[11] A hypothesis such as this makes us wonder further whether in some instances these same women may have even orchestrated their own marriages, may have found ways, that is, of circumventing the male-dominated political structure and effectively disposing of their own bodies as they themselves wished.

In this respect, and especially in the context of a tale about a sexually desirable noble "mayde," one thinks readily of the marital history of Joan the "Fair Maid of Kent," who also became, in the latter stages of her life, wife of the Black Prince and mother of Richard II.[12] In 1341 Joan of Kent married William Montacute, the son of the earl of Salisbury. In 1347 Sir Thomas Holland, the steward in Montacute's household, contested the marriage, claiming that he and Joan in fact married, via mutual consent and sexual consummation, in 1340. Modern interpreters of these events have wondered why Holland waited until six years after Joan's marriage to Montacute before finally mounting his own claim. The explanation usually adduced is that Holland needed that much time in order to amass the money required in litigating the matter before the higher clergy and, eventually, before the Pope. Joan and he are reported to have claimed in public testimony, moreover, that their marriage was held secret for so long because of Joan's fear that her kinsmen would disapprove.

Another explanation, however, seems equally plausible: Joan of Kent and Thomas Holland actually "married" sometime after 1344, which was the year Holland became Montacute's steward; together, then, the two proceeded to fictionalize an earlier clandestine marriage. In a society in which marriages were routinely arranged and divorce upon demand was simply not an option, such marital complicity and fiction making would have given both women and men a certain degree of autonomy in shaping their own lives, allowing them at the same time to remain both within and outside of oppressive social constraints. Natalie Zemon Davis's account of the sixteenth-century marriage of Arnaud de Tihl and Bertrand de Rols certainly suggests as much.[13] In the case of the allegedly clandestine marriage of Joan of Kent and Thomas Holland, Joan herself, we might reasonably speculate, may have simply wanted to change husbands. Why else would she not have spoken against Holland's claim (which she did not)? Moreover, if we are to believe those medieval accounts of Joan of Kent's own "excellent beautee,"[14] it certainly seems possible—perhaps even likely—that Joan had plenty of opportunities to pick and choose among potential candidates for a husband. And here it is also worth noting that in this allegedly antimatrimonial age, Joan of Kent married publicly three times and is reputed to have attracted the attention and affections of a number of men in high places, including, rumor has it, Edward III himself.[15]

However one might finally assess the "facts" of Joan of Kent's marriages, her story as a *story*—that is to say, this particular critical reconstruction of her story—underscores in the *Physician's Tale* the historicizing aspects of the representation of the Physician's failure to control the body of the maid. Legible in each of these narratives is the sense of English aristocratic women as having been more successful than not in asserting the claims of their own sexuality, their own bodily desires, over and against the various sociopolitical constraints designed to control them.[16] At the same time, however, we would be mistaken, it seems to me, to regard the *Physician's Tale* as a narrative simply *about* female sexual autonomy, for the body of the maid, after all, is not the exclusive focus of the fiction. Indeed, in the second half of the tale, the maid's body virtually disappears as the story turns its attention wholeheartedly to a situation in which men engage in power relations with each other. Apius, we learn, conspires with the churl Claudius, who in turn publicly opposes Virginius over the ownership and possession of his daughter. Virginius himself is represented as an individual more concerned with getting back at Apius than he is with preserving the life of his daughter: no sooner does Virginius perform the beheading of his daughter than he proceeds to shove that fact quite literally in the face of Apius. Once Apius is dead, moreover, Virginius intervenes on behalf of Claudius who has been sentenced to death, a gesture whose primary narrative function seems to be nothing more than the cultivation of male bonding. Male homosocial relations, in short, are dominant right to the end of the tale.[17] The maid's own body, her own sexuality, becomes in this instance little more than the space across which these power relations move.

And yet, far from simply reaffirming a male-dominated power structure, the last half of the *Physician's Tale* actually works to unsettle this structure by displaying its cracks, fissures, and internal tensions. Apius, as Paul Strohm points out, is himself "an agent of social dislocation, setting a 'cherl' against a worthy 'knyght.'"[18] Claudius, moreover, is no docile plowman figure, but rather a churl who is "subtil" and "boold" (141). His conduct in Apius's court, moreover, casts in stark relief the lines of a class-based power struggle. Publicly charging a "knyght, called Virginius" (180) in a paternity suit—"she nys his doghter nat, what so he seye" (187)—Claudius openly launches a churlish threat to Virginius's patrimony, a situation that not only exposes the bodily anxieties surrounding aristocratic lineage,[19] but also reminds one of the specific threat to aristocratic security posed by the events of 1381.[20] In response to Claudius's challenge, Virginius, we learn, is determined to prove his side of things "as sholde a knyght" (193). Immediately after Apius pronounces his judgment, "the cherl shal have his thral" (202), the narrative once again reaffirms Virginius's class-based superiority, that is, his status as a "worthy knyght" (203). In short, what this section of the tale displays is not only the unity of the patriarchal world of power politics—the interactions and conspiracies between men—but also its internal divisions. Relations between men in the space of this narrative are far from smooth. Apius tells Claudius that he must preserve secrecy, lest "he sholde lese his heed" (145). Men can literally damage each others' bodies, fragment them, sever them, and by implication, also fragment and sever the solidity and unity of the male-dominated body politic.

Equally significant is the fact that the *Physician's Tale* translates the public conflict of the courtroom into a private, domestic setting: only in Chaucer's version of the story does Virginius go home to kill his daughter. By mixing the public and private in this manner, Chaucer's writing not only effectively politicizes the domestic space; it also makes public—indeed, it publicizes—what Virginius does in private, focusing attention especially on the speech Virginius delivers to his daughter before he actually beheads her. Ostensibly this speech stands as a testament to Virginius's status as a powerful ruler, as one who governs and controls the lives of others. As many readers have noted, its tone is sententious, and it is marked overall by a sense of godlike, immovable resolve: even though Virginius feels "fadres pitee stikynge thurgh his herte / Al wolde he from his purpose nat converte" (211–12). And yet, at the same time, this speech also brings up a certain set of sexual, decidedly bodily concerns. Virginius, one notes, just like Apius, delivers to the maid his own "diffynytyf sentence" (172):

> "O gemme of chastitee, in pacience
> Take thou they deeth, for this is my sentence.
> For love, and nat for hate, thou most be deed;
> My pitous hand moot smyten of thyn heed."
>
> (223–26)

By tacitly allying Virginius's own judgmental behavior with the legalistic conduct of the lecherous Apius, Chaucer's writing highlights the sexual implications of the entire scene: for in taking off the *maiden's head*, Virginius quite literally accomplishes Apius's own explicitly sexual desire, his desire, that is, to take the daughter's *maidenhead*. At the very moment when the narrative appears to be guided by disembodied, metaphysical perspectives (references to theological categories abound: "mercy" (231), "grace" (236), and "Goddes name" (250), Chaucer's writing reveals the fundamentally ruling force of bodily, sexual, even incestuous considerations. In short, this entire scene can be said to expose the sexual basis of Virginius's own actions, to pull down the pants, so to speak, of the male-dominated forces that rule the social order.

It is worth pondering further the significance that such a revelation might have had in the context of late fourteenth-century England where the sexual lives of the nobility—rulers, in particular—were hardly matters of secrecy. Edward III's fecundity, for example, was well known: not only did he produce twelve legitimate children with his wife Phillipa, but record has it that he also produced several bastard children, some of whom he apparently doted upon.[21] The last decade and a half of his reign, moreover, was characterized by his very public, and often publicly bemoaned, involvement with his mistress, Alice Perrers.[22] Furthermore, as the marriage between Joan of Kent and the Black Prince makes clear, incestuous relations within the English nobility also were not immune from public scrutiny. The union between Joan and the Prince was deemed by the church to be incestuous on two separate counts: not only was the Prince the godfather to Joan's child by her first marriage to Thomas Holland, he was also her second cousin once removed insofar as both Joan and he were grandchildren of Edward I.[23] Canon law bearing on matters of consanguinity required that the couple obtain a papal dispensation—which they did—in order to marry.

But besides their eminently public character, the sexual practices of the fourteenth-century British nobility were also typically tied to specific political concerns. Indeed, as W. R. Ormrod has argued, one of the hallmarks of Edward III's reign was his effective commingling of familial sexual relations and royal dynastic interests. For the better part of the forty-three years that he held the throne, Edward III was successful in orchestrating within the ranks of his large family a series of politically advantageous marriages, unions that not only solidified the power of the crown within the British Isles, but also fostered English colonialist endeavors on the Continent.[24] Corroborating further this sense of a connection between marriage and politics in fourteenth-century England is the coincidence that occurs in the last quarter of the century between England's dynastic decline and marriages within the royal family that evidently eschewed political considerations. Both of Edward's eldest children, when they were in their thirties, married, it seems, primarily for love: the Black Prince to Joan of Kent in 1361 and Princess Isabella to the French noble Enguerrand de Coucy in 1365. Neither of these unions appears to have fostered the crown's dynastic goals. Having originally come to England as a hostage, Enguerrand eventually returned to France without Isabella. Their marriage apparently ended with this separation. Although the marriage of the Black Prince and Joan of Kent provided the English throne with an heir, it did not serve to establish any continental political ties, something the English crown sorely needed in order to repair the loss of its footholds in Spain and France during the 1370s and 1380s. Edward III himself is thought to have opposed their marriage—perhaps, one wonders, because of its manifest disregard for his own dynastic concerns. Bearing witness to the dissociation of sexual and political considerations, both of these royal marriages point to the likely familial sources of England's dynastic collapse in the last decades of the century. In this regard, then, the sexual practices of Edward III's family seem to have contributed to the demise of its own ruling practices, the demise, that is, of its identity as a stable and powerful ruling body.

In the narrative fiction of the *Physician's Tale*, one finds a striking supplement to this kind of historical interpretation.[25] For as we have already observed, themes of sex, death, and political power are conjoined in the beheading scene, a moment in the tale that signals the death of the father-ruler, Virginius, as much as it does that of the daughter: "'O deere doghter,'" laments Virginius, "'endere of *my* lyf'" (218; italics mine). Distinguished merely by a difference in case ending, the identities of father and daughter are not easily separable one from the other.[26] Even when the daughter speaks for herself, she does so only to echo the metaphysical register of her father: "'Blissed be God that I shal dye a mayde! / Yif me my deeth, er that I have a shame'" (248–49). By placing us before this sort of confusion of bodies, Chaucer's writing prevents us from regarding this scene as simply an assault on a specifically *female* body. Indeed, the threat posed here to the male body is perhaps the more obvious one: Virginius's act of beheading does indeed recall the castration anxiety earlier invoked by Apius's own threatened beheading of Claudius.

Even more important to recognize are the specifically political consequences of this confusion of bodies. For if the beheading scene is indeed Virginius's attempt to resolve the crisis brought about by the churlish assault on his power, this resolution, let us note, never achieves representation in terms of the actions of one particular ruling body. Chaucer's writing at this point of the tale obscures the solidity and singularity of the ruler's own body, insisting instead on a set of shifts, transformations, and reralliances within the body politic. The beheading and Apius's subsequent death work to pave the way for a newfound alliance between Virginius and Claudius. The very fact that the narrative no longer mentions their respective social standings suggests a change in social relations. Indeed, there seems to be a leveling of class distinctions, a democratizing of social strata taking place within the final moments of the narrative. The people themselves now come to take the place of Apius. They are now the ones who pass judgment on the whole affair; they now come to play the part of "juge-governour":

> The peple anon had suspect in this thyng,
> By manere of the cherles chalangyng,
> That it was by the assent of Apius;
> They wisten wel that he was lecherus.
> (263–66) [27]

Interestingly, the Physician's own response at the end of the tale is an attempt, once again, to erase the body—in this case, the shifting and newly organized social body—by focusing attention on metaphysical and moral issues: "Heere may men seen how synne hath his merite" (277–86). Predictably enough, however, as we have already seen in previous moments of the tale, the Physician's attempt here to master the body through metaphysical/moral abstractions once again issues in failure. Bodily considerations reemerge immediately through Harry Bailly's very body-oriented response to the tale: "Algate this sely mayde is slayn, allas! / Allas, to deere boughte she *beautee*! . . . / Hire *beautee* was hir deth, I dar wel sayn" (292–93, 297; italics mine). As these lines suggest, the body in the *Physician's Tale* is that which cannot be contained, that which exceeds the frame of the tale proper, that which incenses and incites the tale's audience. The tale as a whole ultimately attributes to the body an uncontainable, boundary-breaking force, one that is explored further in the other half of this fragment, which focuses on the Pardoner's own socially outcast, transgressive body.

Try as he may, the Physician-narrator cannot make bodily concerns, or their political implications, simply go away. On the contrary, the *Physician's Tale*, I would argue, finally reveals these and all such gestures of control for what they are: band-aid gestures amidst the forces of bodies, unruly bodies, that will not simply be governed by the prevailing institutionalized ruling practices; bodies that are themselves the driving forces of such practices, and that left to their own devices, will inaugurate a transformation from one set of ruling practices to another. In this regard, thinking the *Physician's Tale* through the body leads not only to one of the long-standing insights of feminism—the personal is political—but also to a greater appreciation of the way in which Chaucer's writing participates in both the body-oriented politics and the volatile body politic of late fourteenth-century England.

Notes

1. All citations are from *The Riverside Chaucer*, ed. Larry D. Benson, 3d ed. (Boston: Houghton Mifflin, 1987). The numbers in parentheses refer to lines.

2. Derek A. Pearsall, "*The Canterbury Tales*," in *The Middle Ages*, ed. W. F. Bolton (London: Barrie and Jenkins, 1970), 177; and Anne Middleton, "The *Physician's Tale* and Love's Martyrs: 'Ensamples Mo Than Ten' as a Method in the *Canterbury Tales*," *Chaucer Review* 8 (1973): 9–32. Although Pearsall sees the *Physician's Tale* as succumbing to the ethical and moral imperatives of conventional pious narratives, whereas Middleton stresses Chaucer's complication of these very imperatives, both essentially agree in seeing the tale as being principally *about* these sorts of concerns.

3. Here and elsewhere, my thinking has been influenced by the excellent feminist reflections on the mind-body split in Jane Gallop's *Thinking Through the Body* (New York: Columbia University Press, 1988), and also by the wonderful discussion of dance and kinesthesiology provided by Mabel E. Todd in *The Thinking Body* (New York: Dance Horizons, 1937).

4. A number of readers, including C. David Benson, editor of the *Physician's Tale* for *The Riverside Chaucer*, gloss the reference to "the Doctor" in line 117 as a reference to Saint Augustine. Plausible as it may seem, such an interpretation is certainly not the only one possible. In all the extant manuscripts, the *Physician's Tale* is attributed to the "doctor of physik." Hence, there is certainly evidence to suggest that the "Doctor" of line 117 is none other than the tale's narrator, an individual who, according to Harry Bailly, is also a "maister" and "lyk a prelat" (301, 310). For further discussion of the semantic range of the term *doctor* in the late Middle Ages, see Vern L. Bullough, "The Term 'Doctor,'" *Journal of the History of Medicine* 18 (1963): 284–87.

5. On the various obstacles preventing English university medical education from functioning as a training ground for clinical practice, see Robert S. Gottfried, *Doctors and Medicine in Medieval England 1340–1530* (Princeton: Princeton University Press, 1986), 9–18. For information about the life and work of a well-known fourteenth-century British physician, see C. H. Talbot, "Simon Bredon: Physician, Mathematician, and Astronomer," *British Journal for the History of Science* 1 (1962): 19–30.

6. In his *Black Death, Natural and Human Disaster in Medieval Europe* (New York: Free Press, 1983), 104–28, Robert S. Gottfried discusses the ways in which the advent of the plague in medieval Europe actually stimulated the professional growth of surgeons, practitioners who performed operations and set bones, whereas it had little to no effect on the social prestige of physicians who, according to Gottfried, "often never touched their patients" (108).

7. My comments here are indebted to the discussions of this phenomenon

in both Gottfried, *Doctors and Medicine*, and Vern L. Bullough, *The Development of Medicine as a Profession: The Contribution of the Medieval University in Modern Medicine* (Basel: S. Karger AG, 1966).

8. Bullough, *Development of Medicine*, 108.

9. On the royal patronage of physicians, see Gottfried, *Doctors and Medicine*, 91–129, esp. 107–111, and also George Gask, "The Medical Staff of Edward III," in his *Essays in the History of Medicine* (London: Butterworth, 1950), 77–93.

10. The standard discussion of these two models of marriage in the Middle Ages is Georges Duby, *Medieval Marriage, Two Models from Twelfth-Century France* (Baltimore: Johns Hopkins University Press, 1978).

11. William Askins, "Licking the Honey Off Thorns: Antimatrimonial Sentiment among Women in Late Fourteenth Century England," a conference paper delivered at the Twenty-Fifth International Congress on Medieval Studies, Western Michigan University, 11 May 1990. I am very grateful to Professor Askins for sharing this unpublished manuscript with me.

12. Much of my discussion here comes from the account of Joan of Kent's marriages given in Chris Given-Wilson and Alice Curteis's *Royal Bastards of Late Medieval England* (London: Routledge and Kegan Paul, 1984), 15–17, 29–30. Although every scholar I have read on this subject mentions Joan of Kent's designation as the "Fair Maid of Kent," no one, as far as I can tell, is able to identify the exact source for this label or to verify its specifically medieval origin. See, in this regard, the comments of M. le Colonel Babinet, "Jeanne de Kent, Princesse de Galles et d'Aquitaine," *Bulletin de la Société des Antiquaires de l'Ouest* 6, ser. 2 (1894), 438–60, esp. 439 n. 1.

13. Natalie Zemon Davis, *The Return of Martin Guerre* (Cambridge: Harvard University Press, 1983).

14. Froissart calls Joan of Kent "one of the most beautiful young ladies in the world." This and other medieval evidence for Joan of Kent's extraordinary beauty are detailed on page 14 of Margaret Galway, "Joan of Kent and the Order of the Garter," *University of Birmingham Historical Journal* 1 (1947): 13–50.

15. After the Pope granted Joan a divorce from Montacute in 1349, the Pope publicly pronounced her the lawful spouse of Holland, with whom she remained married until his death in 1360. In 1361 she married the Black Prince, and remained married to him until his death in 1376, nine years before her own. On the rumored involvement between Joan of Kent and Edward III—a man who, interestingly enough, occupied the position of her father insofar as Joan herself, her real father having been executed when she was two years old, spent her childhood in Edward's royal family, effectively as one of his children—see Galway's discussion of Joan as Edward's "garter countess" in her "Joan of Kent."

16. An interesting topic of investigation in its own right—one that remains outside the scope of the present study—is the extent to which female sexual autonomy in late medieval England may have affected—even guided—the political concerns that typically dominated in the arrangement of aristocratic marriages.

17. The term *homosocial relations* is, of course, Eve Sedgwick's designation of same-sex relations that are not themselves explicitly homosexual, though they do indeed exist on the same continuum as explicitly homosexual relations. For further

discussion, see Sedgwick's *Between Men: English Literature and Male Homosocial Desire* (New York: Columbia University Press, 1985).

18. Paul Strohm, *Social Chaucer* (Cambridge: Harvard University Press, 1989), 159.

19. In *The Daughter's Seduction, Feminism and Psychoanalysis* (Ithaca: Cornell University Press, 1982), Jane Gallop makes the following comments about the position of the father in the classic Freudian familial setting: "It is only the law—and not the body—which constitutes him [i.e., the father] as a patriarch. Paternity is corporeally uncertain, without evidence. But patriarchy compensates for that with the law which marks each child with the father's name as his exclusive property" (77).

20. My attempt here to establish a connection with the events of the Peasants' Rebellion correlates well with other critical speculations surrounding the date of this tale. Many scholars, following a suggestion made earlier in John S. P. Tatlock, *The Development and Chronology of Chaucer's Works* (Gloucester, Mass.: P. Smith, 1963), believe the *Physician's Tale* to have been written around 1386; their assessment is based largely on the similar dating of the *Legend of Good Women*, a text which the *Physician's Tale* appears to resemble.

21. As Given-Wilson and Curteis point out (*Royal Bastards*), because the births of bastard children often escaped the normal routes of recordkeeping, it is difficult to decide with any certainty just how many bastards any given monarch may have had. On page 179, they suggest that Edward III produced at least three, and possibly four, bastard children. For further discussion of the favors Edward III bestowed on a man who was apparently one of his bastard children, see Margaret Galway, "Alice Perrer's Son John," *English Historical Review* 66 (1951): 242–46.

22. For further information on Alice Perrers, see F. George Kay, *Lady of the Sun* (New York: Barnes and Noble, 1966).

23. As Given-Wilson and Curteis point out in *Royal Bastards,* page 30, the term *incest* in the late Middle Ages applied to a broad set of relations. It referred not only to sexual relationships in the first degree (for example, between brother and sister, or parent and child), but also to sexual relationships in the fourth degree (i.e., between third cousins) and to sexual relations between individuals united by affinity (i.e., by connection to a previous sexual partner, or to a previously intended sexual partner) or by spiritual ties (e.g., sexual relations between parents and godparents).

24. W. R. Ormrod, "Edward III and His Family," *Journal of British Studies* 26 (1987): 398–422. In his discussion, Ormrod elaborates on the various political motivations that guided the marriages of the British monarchy in the late fourteenth century. The betrothal in 1342 of Edward's four-year-old son, Lionel of Antwerp, to Elizabeth de Burgh, daughter and heiress of the deceased earl of Ulster, for example, was apparently part of an attempt to foster the imposition of royal authority over the colonial administration of Ireland. The arranged marriage of John of Gaunt to Blanche of Lancaster in 1359 seemed to have had a similar colonialist purpose, providing an important power base in the north from which a royal invasion of Scotland could someday be launched. Threatened in 1360 with the loss

of English control over the northern provinces of France, Edward tried, albeit unsuccessfully, to negotiate marriages between his fourth son, Edmund of Langley, and Margaret of Flanders, and between his eldest daughter, Isabella, and the Gascon lord of Albret. In other instances, though, he was more successful in establishing British-Continental ties through marriage: Lionel eventually married Violante Visconti, heiress of Milan, in 1368, and John of Gaunt married Constanza, heiress to the throne of Castile, in 1371. The overall profile of Plantagenet marriages in the late fourteenth century does indeed give credence to what Ormrod designates as Edward III's deployment of dynastic, expansionist interests in the mode of a "family firm" (415).

25. I use the word *supplement* here in order to highlight my sense of the *Physician's Tale* as a rewriting, rather than a reflection, of fourteenth-century British political history, which itself has no simple or simply factual existence. My thinking about questions of supplementarity has been influenced by Jacques Derrida's essay ". . . Ce dangereux supplément . . ." in his *De la grammatologie* (Paris: Editions de Minuit, 1967), 203–34, and also by Dominick LaCapra's designation of historical documents themselves as "texts that supplement or rework 'reality' and not mere sources that divulge facts about 'reality.'" See his *History & Criticism* (Ithaca: Cornell University Press, 1985), 11.

26. The name Virginia, which critics typically assume has a referential function, seems rather to have, I would argue, a simple diectic function: it points critical attention away from the demise of the maid and toward the demise of the father.

27. I disagree with Sheila Delany, who in "Politics and the Paralysis of Poetic Imagination in the Physician's Tale," *Studies in the Age of Chaucer* 3 (1981): 47–60, argues that Chaucer's version of the Apius-Virginia story is "depoliticized" because it leaves out all sense of a popular rebellion. The analysis I present here suggests otherwise. Moreover, I disagree with what I take to be a fundamental assumption of Delany's essay, namely, that the only criterion on which to judge political investment in the *Physician's Tale* is that of either the inclusion or the exclusion of a popular rebellion.

Peggy McCracken

The Body Politic and the Queen's Adulterous Body in French Romance

Political metaphors that describe the state as a human body are prominent in the Middle Ages: theories of the king's two bodies attempt to account for the immortal yet human nature of royal sovereignty, while the concept of the entire society as a body whose head is the king reflects the hierarchy of social and political relationships in the medieval world.[1] These abstractions usually leave aside the office of the king's consort; since her official function is not to govern, it is absent from models of political structure that attempt to explain the sovereign's relation to his office, his state, or his subjects. Although a few queens did inherit a throne in medieval Europe, in political theory they were assimilated into the structure of kingship, and although a queen sometimes reigned during the king's absence or a son's minority, her power was based on a relationship to the male ruler and his place in the body politic.[2]

In contrast to the perceived gap between the enduring nature of the king's office and his human, mortal body, the queen consort's political role in the medieval court is entirely located in her physical body: the major duty of her office is to produce heirs in order to guarantee succession and political and social stability. This role is curiously absent from representations of the king's wife in medieval romance, however. In the major literary traditions surrounding Guenevere and Iseut, and in other less celebrated stories, the queen is barren. Moreover, she is adulterous, and her lack of progeny is most certainly linked to a sexuality that both transgresses moral and civic law and, perhaps more importantly, potentially interrupts proper dynastic succession. Georges Duby notes that in medieval literature, "adultery, though consummated, was barren. Bastardy was too serious a matter to be treated lightly even in literature. People were too afraid of it to use it as a subject for a tale."[3]

This essay takes Duby's observation as a starting point in order to interrogate the romance poet's refusal to confront the chaos of disputed paternity, and to explore how the "fear" that Duby identifies appears in the rituals of taboo and transgression surrounding the female body. In medieval romance the queen is portrayed as entirely corporeal, defined by a body shared between her husband and her lover. At the same time, the queen is divorced from any political power that might originate in her own body through maternity. I will ask how a shift from the reproductive sexuality that characterizes historical queens to the transgressive sexuality associated with queenship in romance might work to situate an understanding of the narrative construction of women's bodies in medieval French literature. More specifically, I will explore how the metaphors used to represent the queen's adulterous body participate in the displacement of women's agency from the potentially influential office of mother of the king's heir to a marginalized position as a woman whose authority is used in the service of adultery.

The figure of the adulterous queen in twelfth-century romance is not without historical models. Several queens were charged with adultery in the Middle Ages, and during the period marked by the rise of romance, a prominent example was provided by Eleanor of Aquitaine, queen of England and France.[4] Eleanor was accused of an adulterous liaison with her uncle and was subsequently divorced from Louis VII on grounds of consanguinity after producing two daughters in fifteen years of marriage. Her life illustrates the problematic configuration of adultery, marriage, succession, and power that we will see in romance representations of queenship. Yet unlike her fictional counterparts, Eleanor was not barren nor was the legitimacy of her children disputed. Her subsequent marriage to Henry II produced three daughters and five sons on whom Eleanor staked claims to increased political power.

The grounding of women's political power in succession had prominent models in medieval Europe, and as Eleanor's example demonstrates, that power had potentially disruptive and violent consequences for the orderly succession that it was intended to guarantee. Yet as Duby notes, in the romance literary genre that appears and flourishes during this period, the queen's role in dynastic reproduction is resolutely suppressed, and she is routinely characterized as an adulteress. The most striking consequences of the overt disassociation of the queen from succession in medieval romance is that adultery itself takes on a particularly ritualistic function. The obvious physical result of sexual transgression, a child of disputed paternity, never appears. Though dynastic concerns may be implicit or displaced in the story of a queen and her lover, the interdiction of adultery with the queen seems to focus on the act itself, independent of its possible results. Illegitimacy is not always absent in medieval literature; examples of children conceived outside wedlock include Lancelot's son Galahad and Gauvain's son, who appears in later romances in quest of his own name. Yet the adulterous queen, the female figure on whose bodily integrity the proper succession of stability and power depends, never conceives nor is she shown to consider the possibility. It is not surprising that in the courtly genre of romance the queen and her lover are not shown to discuss pregnancy; however the queen does not mention the subject with her confidantes nor does she raise the possibility in the monologues in which she extols the difficulties and pleasures of the liaison with her lover. Even in their accusations of adultery against the queen, her enemies do not mention the threat to proper succession that would be posed by the son of an adulteress.

Divorced from the reproductive consequences of sexuality, adultery is characterized by secrets and betrayals, judgments and subverted judgments, reconciliations and renunciations, which all work to characterize the liaison of the queen and her lover as forbidden, but at the same time sanctioned, by the romance narrative.[5] Adultery by any woman is of course prohibited by religious and civic law in the Middle Ages, but the interdiction of the queen achieves the status of a social taboo—a ritual restriction on which the integrity and well-being of the society depend—through the repetition of the violation of the law in accusations within individual romances and in the many romances that recount it, and because of the way in which adultery threatens the entire court and its political stability. The physical integrity of the queen is construed as independent of its historically political importance, which is to guarantee succession, and becomes an end in itself. As the condition of the queen's fidelity subsumes the goal of proper succession, reproductive sexuality, through which the queen is empowered, is displaced by a transgressive sexuality, through which she loses status and influence at court.

In speaking of sexuality, adultery, or even courtly love in romances, it is not enough to scrutinize the motivations for liaisons within the individual stories, nor can an analysis be limited to the narrative or symbolic consequences of the adulterous relationship or of its discovery if we wish to understand how woman is constructed in medieval romance through the metaphoric representation of her body. What has been neglected in studies of adultery in the literary text is precisely an interrogation of how the adulterous female body defines and is defined by the social and symbolic orders in which it participates.[6] Rather than asking how adultery structures a narrative, this essay seeks to ask how adultery structures the representation of the female body; rather than taking the queen's body as a pretext for adultery, it interrogates the location of transgressive sexuality in the adulterous female body and asks why the female body, invested with what might be called the collective anxiety of medieval society about stability and order, is a barren body. As we noted above, concerns about succession and legitimacy that might logically be raised by a knowledge of the queen's adultery are suppressed and displaced in social rituals of restriction and violation that focus on the queen's sexual body, but not on reproduction.

This study of romance representations of the queen's body begins by using an anthropological framework to establish the relation of the body and social systems as one in which anxieties about social boundaries are ritually and rhetorically figured in the human body. Moving from the general consideration of the body as a symbol of society, I will use Julia Kristeva's extension of this relationship into the symbolic order to explore the participation of the female body in systems of signification in which it is invested with meaning and through which it generates meaning. Though Kristeva posits an ahistorical psychoanalytic reading of taboos and restrictions surrounding the body, I will use her positioning of the body itself in the symbolic order, in which it is constituted through language, to speak of the body in a historically specific symbolic order, that of medieval romance. The second half of the essay demonstrates the working out of this dynamic in *Cligés*, a romance in which the queen's adulterous body is described through metaphors of dismemberment and doubling. In this twelfth-century romance by Chrétien de Troyes, an empress's sexuality is explicitly linked to a refusal of dynastic reproduction. Moreover, the question of how to name the adulterous female body is debated in opposition to a metaphoric representation of Queen Iseut's body, providing a twelfth-century reading and rewriting of the adulterous queen's body. In *Cligés*, Chrétien challenges the narrative conventions that characterize and determine the representation of adultery in romance, and he speaks this challenge through the voice of the very woman who is defined by them, revealing the rhetorical grounding of the imperative association of women and transgressive sexuality that is a basic structure of the poetics of courtly romance.

The present essay seeks to extend recent feminist studies of medieval romance in two ways. First, by using the place of the queen's body in medieval political systems of hereditary monarchy as the starting point for an analysis of romance representations of the queen, it continues the definition of the place of woman in the rhetorical structures of medieval literary texts from a historically informed perspective. Second, by going beyond the reading of the woman's body as a figure, symbol, or metaphor, to an examination of the metaphors used to describe the female body itself, it contributes to the explication of the relationship between medieval misogyny and the rhetorical conventions of twelfth-century literary language.[7] The metaphors used by romance authors to describe the queen's adulterous body work to define the queen as both excess and lack, as a simultaneously fragmented and doubled subjectivity that is objectified through adultery. The fiction of the queen's body participates in systems of meaning that refuse self-referentiality and narrative presence to the woman's body, defining it as other and as effaced. By privileging the place of the feminine and by questioning how woman is constituted in discourse, a feminist approach to the body revises and enriches our perspective on the rhetorical construction of the body in medieval romance by setting it in the context of other symbolic structures that work to define the feminine through containment, exclusion, and restriction. A reading of the adulterous queen's body in the context of the queen's political function in dynastic reproduction will also add a historical specificity to theories about the place of the female body in the symbolic order and demonstrate one of the nuances that medieval romance can provide to the project of historicizing concepts of the body.[8]

The Body as Symbol

In her analysis of rituals of pollution and taboo that take the human body as their object, Mary Douglas has suggested that the body stands as a model for social systems, that the body itself is a symbol of society.[9] According to Douglas, in its particular configuration of interior and exterior, the body figures in itself the margins of any social system: "The symbolism of the body's boundaries is used . . . to express danger to community boundaries" (122). Concepts of pollution and taboo work to keep the limits of society intact through their symbolic enactment in the boundaries of the body (128).

Douglas's study provides a useful framework through which to read medieval romance. As is well known, in this highly stylized genre the virtues and vices of characters are often reflected in their physical appearance: good and brave knights are always beautiful, for example.[10] Thus, on one level, the body is clearly associated with a symbolic system. More pertinent to an anthropological reading of the body in the context of the society represented in romance, threats to the political stability of the court and to the boundaries that establish and maintain it are figured in the ritualized restriction and transgression of the body. In medieval literature, that prohibition is focused on the queen's body.

The romance character of the queen is defined by her sexuality: she is a woman who accepts—and implicitly demands—two lovers. The sexual voracity that is merely suggested in the actions of courtly queens like Guenevere and Iseut is more forcefully shown to be the motivation for seductions initiated by characters like Queen Eufeme in *Le Roman de Silence* or the duchess in *La Châtelaine de Vergi*.[11] Furthermore, the king's political authority at court is shown to be compromised by his (un)knowing complicity in the adulterous relationship between his wife and her lover. Intrigues against the king are staged through an accusation of the queen's transgressive sexuality, as in the following passage from Béroul's *Tristan*:

> Li roi Marc ont a raison mis,
> A une part ont le roi trait:
> "Sire," font il, "malement vet.
> Tes niés s'entraiment et Yseut,
> Savoir le puet qui c'onques veut;
> Et nos nu volon mais sofrir."
> Li rois l'entent, fist un sospir,
> Son chief abesse vers la terre,
> Ne set qu'il die, sovent erre.
> "Rois," ce dïent li troi felon,
> "Par foi, mais nu consentiron;
> Qar bien savon de verité
> Que tu consenz lor cruauté,
> Et tu sez bien ceste mervelle.
> Q'en feras tu? Or t'en conselle!
> Se ton nevo n'ostes de cort,
> Si que jamais nen i retort,
> Ne nos tenron a vos jamez,
> Si ne vos tendron nule pez.
> De nos voisins feron partir
> De cort, que nel poon soufrir.
> Or t'aron tost cest geu parti:
> Tote ta volenté nos di."[12]

(Then they took King Mark to one side and said: "Sire, things are going badly. Your nephew and Iseut love each other, and anyone who wants to can find out. We will not tolerate this any longer."

The king heard this, sighed and bent his head. He walked up and down, not knowing what to say.

"King," said the three villains, "we will not consent to this any longer, for we know it is true that you are conniving at their wickedness. You know all about this extraordinary thing. What are you going to do about it? Now be advised! If you do not banish your nephew from court so that he never returns, we shall no longer support you nor keep peace with you. We shall make our neighbours leave the court, for we cannot put up with this. We can set out the problem for you quickly; now tell us your wishes.") [13]

The barons invoke the violation of a restricted access to the queen's body; the transgression of that restriction is the focus of and the pretext for the threats against the king's power. As we noted above, the question of disputed paternity for the king's heirs is not openly addressed in the accusation. In this context the barons may be suggesting that the king send Tristan away so that the queen might produce heirs of undisputed paternity, yet this imperative, like any warning of anticipated succession disputes, remains suppressed. Accusations of adultery focus on the sexual rather than the dynastic, and although the terms of the accusation in the above-cited passage concern Tristan and the queen equally, the separation suggested as a solution to the social and political dilemma aims to restore the queen's monogamous sexuality by re-restricting the access to her body that she granted to Tristan. The liaison of Tristan and some other woman, even another married woman, would not raise the same political concerns, since only Iseut is in a position to produce the king's heirs. [14]

It is not surprising that female sexuality and political stability should be conjoined in the queen's body, since she plays an obvious role in succession. [15] But in medieval romance the predictable combination of the feminine and the political is thoroughly subverted in a division of sexuality and reproduction: the adulterous queen is a barren queen. Iseut has no children; Guenevere is usually childless. In the *Perlesvaus*, a thirteenth-century continuation of Chrétien's *Conte du graal*, Loholt, the son of Guenevere and Arthur, is briefly mentioned, but he is a sketchy character and his major role in the story seems to be to die young. [16] Moreover, his paternity is not disputed within the romance, even though the story does recount the adulterous relationship of Lancelot and Guenevere. [17]

The characterization of the adulterous queen as childless is linked to her own lack of political authority, and the sexual nature attributed to the queen is based on a separation of the queen's personal desires and dynastic necessity: though she is married to a king, any influence she might have wielded at court is used in the service of adultery. An episode from *Cligés* serves to illustrate this displacement and to emphasize that the queen's consent is always implicit in the representation of her adulterous sexuality. The queen controls access to her own body, and the moment of agency that marks her consent to take a lover paradoxically works to restrict, or even to efface her status as a subject.

Cligés recounts the story of an empress who wishes to escape from her marriage to the emperor of Constantinople in order to live with the emperor's nephew, Cligés, whom she loves. The empress Fenice conspires with her nurse to trick her husband by staging her own death: Fenice will drink a potion that will give her a deathlike appearance, she will be pronounced dead and entombed, Cligés will steal her from her tomb, and the lovers will live together in hiding. In preparation for the pharmacologically induced "death," Fenice pretends to be ill, and in an effort to ensure the effect of her feigned illness she forbids access to her body. By the empress's own desire, the court doctors are not allowed to examine her (vv. 5598–99, 5627–33). They believe she is ill and pronounce her dead after she drinks the potion that gives her a lifeless appearance. The success of the ruse is threatened only by the arrival of three physicians from Salerno who demand to see and examine the "dead" body. Suspecting that the empress is still alive, the physicians violate her interdiction of her own body: they touch her, undress her, beat her, and torture her. The empress's vocal consent is clearly at stake in this scene, since the physicians attempt to make her *speak* the deception.[18] The transgression of the woman's interdiction of her body in the graphically violent assault of her body by the physicians stands in contrast to Fenice's voluntary consent to open her body to Cligés as her lover. Yet the effect of both acts is narratively similar; Fenice's body is objectified as her subjectivity is suppressed.

If the interdiction of the queen's body functions as a ritual restriction that is always broken, the transgression is located in the queen's consent to take a lover. The woman is shown to invite and accept the transgression of taboos surrounding her own body, an act that idealizes her lover, weakens her husband, and marginalizes the queen herself in the resulting political struggle, as in the following passage from *La Mort le roi Artu* in which Arthur explains to Gawain that he cannot credit the accusations against Lancelot because he is such a worthy knight:

Certes voirement est il li plus preudom del monde et li mieudres chevaliers qui vive. Et se j'eüsse creü Agravain vostre frere, ge l'eüsse fet ocirre; si en eüsse fet grant felonnie et trop grant desloiauté, si que touz li mondes m'en deüst honnir . . . [Agravains] vint l'autre jor a moi et si me dist que il se mervelloit moult conment j'avoie le cuer de tenir Lancelot entor moi qui si grant honte me fesoit comme de moi vergoignier de ma fame; et si me dist outreement que Lancelos l'amoit de fole amor par de jouste moi et que il l'avoit conneüe charnelment.[19]

(Certainly it is true that he is the bravest man in the world and the best knight alive. And if I had believed your brother Agravain I would have had him killed and thus would have committed a great crime and such a great disloyalty that the whole world should have held me to shame . . . [Agravain] came to me the other day and told me that he marveled at the way I could keep Lancelot in my entourage while he insulted me by shaming me with my wife. And he further told me that Lancelot loved her passionately despite me and that he had known her carnally.)[20]

The charge against Lancelot implicates the king's honor and thus his position and authority at court; at the same time, it firmly establishes the knight's own honor and prestige as an ideal lover in stories of the Round Table. What is lost to view is the queen's consent to take a lover. Read in the context of the courtly love tradition of which they form an important part, the stories of Guenevere and Iseut, particularly in the passages cited above, demonstrate a marked reversal of the usual fiction of the lady's power, which is located in the withholding of her (sexual) favors. Lyric poets constantly lament their ladies' refusal to grant them the "sorplus" that they seek, and indeed, power (like desire) is maintained through denial, through the withholding of consent. Yet the structure of adultery is fundamentally grounded in an assumption of the woman's inevitable consent to grant access to her body, a moment of agency that works to efface its subject.[21]

In both of the passages cited above, the queen is barely present; reduced to an adulterous body, she does not seem to wield any power. The founding moment of the liaison that defines her sexuality—her consent to take a lover—is disregarded; even though the sexual transgression is narratively located in her body, any agency on the queen's part is attributed to her lover in the accusation (and admiration) of his seduction.

Dismemberment and Doubling

We have seen above that the representation of the adulterous queen's body may be used to symbolize anxieties and tensions about social stability in medieval romance, but that it is curiously divorced from the most obvious concerns about proper succession. In order more fully to understand the logic of literary descriptions of the female body, however, it is necessary to go beyond an analysis of how adultery creates narrative structures and to examine how it participates in the symbolic order of medieval romance, to discover how the representation of the queen's transgressive sexuality and the metaphors of fragmentation and doubling that describe her body dictate and create each other. Adultery is constructed within the narratives by discourse (request, consent, promises, threats) and above all, by discovery. Indeed, if an illicit liaison cannot remain hidden in medieval romance it is because adultery can only be described within a narrative structure in which signification is linked to transgression.[22]

In a study of the objectification of women in the symbolic order constituted by language systems, Christine Brooke-Rose has recently suggested that the story of an adultery may be inherent in linguistic structures themselves.[23] Positing the triangulated relationship as "an elementary structure of signification" that presumes woman as object and man as possessor, she points out that a familiar double standard (adultery is acceptable for men, forbidden for women) permeates even semiotic models of social and cultural relations.[24] With provocative examples of how the objectification of woman as a possession is always already present in narrative structures as an intertextual referent, Brooke-Rose suggests that semiotics itself may be marked by a nostalgia for "deep, ancient, phallocratic, elementary structures of significance" (315).

A specific focus on the rhetorical description of the adulterous body may avoid the possible prejudice of examining literary representations of adultery through a critical language that presumes the woman's position in the triangulated structure of adultery as a fundamental signifying mode. Moving from a consideration of the effacement of the queen's agency in adultery to the question of how the literary account of adultery is related to the figurative representation of the body, the analysis of the way in which rituals of interdiction and transgression of the queen's body figure anxieties about social integrity in medieval romance might be extended to account for the way in which the adulterous body participates in other systems of significance. Acknowledging that the pretext, object, and subject of adultery are conflated in the body of the queen, it is possible to examine how the female body itself is constructed in and by a particular symbolic order: how does the fictional body participate in the meaning of the narrative that recounts it?

In an important section of *Powers of Horror*, Julia Kristeva has extended Mary Douglas's work on ritual pollution and taboo with a psycho-analytic perspective that may be helpful in formulating a framework through which to read the body of romance. Kristeva observes a distinction in Douglas's analysis between the body *in* a symbolic system and the body as a prototype for the society/symbolic system.[25] She categorizes this split in terms of *syntax* (pollution as an element related to the limits or margins of a social order) and *semantics* (the *meaning* of this element of limit in other systems). For Kristeva the split between the syntax and the semantics of the body can only be resolved by placing it in the symbolic order (as opposed to a symbolic system), that is, in its relationship to language (67).

This relocation completes the syntactic view of the body as a conflation of the sexual and the political by providing a vocabulary with which to pose questions about its *semantic* value: how does the location of the female body within a symbolic order generate meaning, and how can the narrative structure that is symptomatic of this be interpreted in a way that allows it to speak in its specifically medieval context? In the second half of this essay I will explore these questions in the context of a twelfth-century romance in which the heroine poses the question of how to name the adulterous queen's body. Chrétien de Troyes's *Cligés* provides a rich example of the metaphoric description of the adulterous female body as illusion and presence, as dismembered and doubled, as excess and lack. Moreover, *Cligés* is a romance in which the protagonists themselves debate the relation of the adulterous body to dynastic succession and to sexual integrity.

As we have seen, in *Cligés* the heroine Fenice is married to the emperor of Constantinople and in love with his nephew Cligés. She repeatedly laments her situation and discusses possible ways to unite herself with Cligés. Citing the example of Queen Iseut, who loved both King Mark and Tristan, she rejects the possibility of taking Cligés as her lover because of the dismemberment it implies. According to Fenice, Iseut split her body between two men:

> Mialz voldroie estre desmanbree
> Que de nos deus fust remanbree
> L'amors d'Ysolt et de Tristan,
> Don mainte folie dit an,
> Et honte en est a reconter.
> Ja ne m'i porroie acorder

A la vie qu'Isolz mena.
Amors en li trop vilena,
Que ses cuers fu a un entiers,
Et ses cors fu a deus rentiers.
Ensi tote sa vie usa
N'onques les deus ne refusa.
Ceste amors ne fu pas resnable,
Mes la moie iert toz jorz estable,
Car de mon cors et de mon cuer
N'iert ja fet partie a nul fuer.
Ja mes cors n'iert voir garçoniers,
N'il n'i avra deus parçoniers.
Qui a le cuer, cil a le cors,
Toz les autres an met defors.

(vv. 3105–24)

(I'd rather be torn limb from limb than have people in referring to us recall the love of Iseut and Tristan, about whom such nonsense is talked that I'm ashamed to speak of it. I couldn't reconcile myself to the life Iseut led. With her, love was too debased, for her body was made over to two men, whilst her heart belonged entirely to one. In this way she spent her whole life without ever rejecting either one. This love was unreasonable, but mine is firm and constant, nor will my body or my heart ever be shared under any circumstances. Never will my body be prostituted between two owners. Let him who has the heart have the body. I reject all others.)[26]

Situating herself with respect to an adulterous queen, Fenice states her refusal to follow Iseut's example in metaphors of dismemberment: a shared body split between two lovers, a heart possessed by one man while another holds her body. She chooses a course of action that technically preserves the integrity of her body: using the drugs prepared by her nurse, Fenice doubles her body through pharmacological illusions.[27] A first potion, administered during the wedding feast, makes the emperor Alis dream that he possesses his wife, though he never touches her; a second induces the false death intended to help Fenice escape her marriage. In Chrétien's romance, the fragmented body of the adulterous queen claimed by two men simultaneously is displaced by the illusion of a doubled body: Fenice creates the fiction of two bodies possessed by two men. The empress's story ends when her two bodies are united into one: the lover of Cligés (again) becomes an empress when Cligés inherits the throne after his uncle's death.[28]

Following Mary Douglas's suggestion that the body may symbolically contain social anxieties, we might suggest that within the romance Fenice's adulterous and illusory doubled body reflects the doubled claim to the throne by Cligés and Alis. The first claim, by Cligés, is a legitimate one agreed on by Cligés's father and uncle: Alis, a younger brother who claimed the throne based on false rumors of his older brother's death, will hold the title of emperor until his own death, but he agrees not to marry so that the throne will pass to Cligés in a rightful succession to the elder brother's son. The second claim to the throne, by Alis, is fraudulent and contrary to the agreement that established Cligés's succession, since Alis had undertaken never to marry and produce heirs (vv. 2531–38). Fenice of course figures in the conflict, since her role as empress is to guarantee the succession of the throne through Alis, and the tricks she uses to dupe her husband might be seen as part of an effort to rectify the potentially unjust exclusion of Cligés from his inheritance. But Fenice's references to Iseut move her motivation for doubling her body from inside the recounted political dilemma that her doubled body might reflect, to an intertextual space, replacing the deliberation about how to escape her husband's embraces with the question of how to represent her own adultery.

Chrétien's romance is often called an anti-*Tristan* story written to revise and refute the distasteful legend of Queen Iseut and her two lovers with the example of the queen who refuses to share her body,[29] but Fenice's repeated condemnation of Iseut's actions invites interrogation: what exactly is the difference between a body split between two lovers and a body that (through illusions) is possessed by two men and yet only by one? Fenice's repugnance for Iseut's example suggests that at least initially there is a difference between the fragmented body and the doubled body. That difference is based on illusion: while Iseut gives her body to two men, Fenice manages to keep her body intact before she lives with Cligés. The integrity preserved through illusion may prove illusory, as we will see below: through rhetorical oppositions of presence and absence, and of truth and rumor, the body of Fenice is revealed to be no less fragmented and no more intact than the dismembered body she attributes to Iseut.

Mary Douglas has noted that "a desire to keep the body (physical and social) intact" is inherent in notions of sexual pollution, and in her analysis of the internal contradictions that may arise in a social system around rituals of taboo, she poses the question of why pollution fears "do not seem to cluster around contradictions which do not involve sex" (140, 157). The kind of problematic that Douglas sets forth may be explored in *Cligés*: what sort of desire is figured in Fenice's wish to preserve her intact body, and why is the sexual drama so closely linked to the political, yet so consistently divorced from the political role of the queen's body in succession?

Integrity and Excess

It is perhaps worth emphasizing the obvious fact that fragmentation and doubling are metaphors that represent the adulterous queen's body. What I am seeking to discover is how the figural representation of the female body creates or sustains the notion that a woman who has two lovers is not whole. In *Cligés*, Thessala's potions allow the creation of two bodies through pharmacological illusion, preserving Fenice from her husband's embraces and providing her with a way to live with Cligés in a sort of monogamous adultery.[30] A scrutiny of her stated motivations for the deception reveals that although Fenice initially explains her desire to avoid intercourse with her husband in terms of proper succession, her motivation is quickly shifted to a concern for her reputation and, in part, for the representation of her body. Although she has not, like Iseut, split her body between two men, she fears that this will also be the story told of her. In the constantly renewed reasoning about her body, Fenice moves through a series of explanations and justifications of her acts that gradually collapses any difference between Fenice's body and Iseut's body, between the fiction of a doubled body and the metaphor of a dismembered body.

Initially, Fenice states her desire to avoid her husband's embraces in terms of dismemberment, as we have seen: she does not want to split her body between two men and above all she does not want to separate the possession of her heart from the possession of her body. But her refusal of the emperor is also firmly stated as a desire to avoid maternity. She thus explicitly addresses the anxiety suppressed in the accounts of adultery cited above: "Ja de moi ne puisse anfes nestre / Par cui il soit desheritez" ("May there never be born to me a child who causes him to be disinherited").[31] The refusal of motherhood contrasts with the model set forth earlier in the romance by the story of Cligés's mother who promptly produced an heir after her marriage (vv. 2336–44). More importantly, it introduces maternity into the construction of the adulterous love relationship. The two motivations—to save the sexual integrity of her body and to save the throne—are strikingly different when first pronounced. The second seems to come to mind as a justification of the first, which is based on a refusal to take two lovers, not on dynastic or political considerations. Ultimately, the two seemingly contradictory desires converge and result in the same goal: to preserve Fenice's virginity. The control of (reproductive) access to her own body subverts the social restriction of the queen, a restriction that is intended not to exclude her own husband, but simply to guarantee legitimate succession. The ritualized sexual containment of the queen is both an isolation and a penetration, simultaneously a closing of her body to other men and an opening to her husband. The political role of the queen is defined by a fundamental lack of distinction between dynastic and personal desire: her function at court is primarily reproductive. This distinction breaks down in Fenice's speeches of desire, which are divided between the sexual and the dynastic and between the personal and the political. Her motivation for keeping her body intact is thus put into question, and its logic is further undermined when Fenice abandons her virginity to live with her lover.

The question of the integrity of the female body is posed on several levels in the representation of the queen as an adulteress. The dismemberment of her body between two lovers evokes a horror of sexual fragmentation that Fenice tries to avoid by doubling her body through the effect of drugs. Yet the doubled body is also dismembered, split between presence and absence and between plenitude and lack. In the Middle Ages the female sexual body is necessarily seen as fragmented in contrast to the prominent patristic ideal of physical *integritas*. The virginal body is an ideal female body, a body which repudiates a sexuality that is always transgressive because of its association with Eve.[32] The virgin's body is intact, complete, and integral; since the state of the body may reflect the state of the soul, the body's integrity counters spiritual disintegration.[33]

The idea of virginity as a state of salvation and of a pure spirituality began in the first centuries of Christianity. The ideal and idealized female body (it is *female* virginity that is most emphasized by the church fathers)[34] marks the containment of women's sexuality; in its narrative construction the intact body is sufficient to itself, and as a body that does not lack it does not desire. Although the virgin's body may still be an *object* of desire, the virgin herself, as complete, integral, and without desire, is always object.[35] In contrast to the pure, contained body of the virgin, the adulterous queen's dismembered and doubled body always escapes containment, and it is defined by that very transgression. Moving between narrative spaces as a sexual excess, the adulterous queen's body simultaneously establishes and breaks restrictions and taboos by its very presence and by its nature as a conflation of the personal and the political.

To speak of the adulterous female body as fragmented or doubled is to posit two different ways of naming the body and two different ways of describing adultery. The opposition is established by Fenice when she creates the second alternative to avoid the first. As we have seen, the logic of this opposition begins to break down as Fenice continues to state the reasons for her deception. The difference between dismemberment and doubling is a rhetorical one, since these are metaphors when used to describe an adulterous body, and in what follows I will suggest that in the representation of the female body all boundaries are shown to be rhetorical in nature; the possibility of opposing versions of a woman's body is put into question with the blurring of the rhetorical difference between the virgin and the adulteress, between fragmentation and doubling, between excess and lack. This rhetorical subversion occurs as Fenice undermines the very distinction she claims to establish between Iseut and herself. As Fenice and Cligés consider how the empress might be taken away from her husband so that the lovers might live together, Cligés proposes that they steal away to Arthur's court. Fenice adamantly refuses because in spite of the complicated pharmacological ruses that she used to preserve her virginity, she would be equated with Iseut, a woman with two lovers:

> Ja avoec vos ensi n'irai,
> Car lors seroit par tot le monde
> Ausi come d'Ysolt la Blonde
> Et de Tristant de nos parlé;
> Quant nos an serïens alé,
> Et ci, et la, totes et tuit
> Blasmeroient nostre deduit.
>   (vv. 5250–56)

(I shall never go away with you like that; because then, once we had left, people throughout the world would speak of us as of the fair-haired Iseut and Tristan; and on every side one and all would heap blame on our enjoyment of our love. [164])

In Fenice's decision to stage her own death rather than to flee the country with her lover, her desire to preserve the integrity of her body is subsumed in a desire for secrecy. Her concerns about disrupting Cligés's succession to the throne of Constantinople have notably been left behind, and the possibility of having a child with Cligés is not discussed. The difference between dismembering her body and doubling it is a rhetorical choice dictated on the one hand by the unspeakable nature of her virginity and the ruse that preserves it, and on the other by the eminently speakable nature of adultery which would immediately be named and named by the very (proper) name that Fenice seeks to avoid:

> Se je vos aim, et vos m'amez,
> Ja n'en seroiz Tristanz clamez,
> Ne je n'an serai ja Yseuz,
> Car puis ne seroit l'amors preuz,
> Qu'il i avroit blasme ne vice.
>
> (vv. 5199–203)

(If I love you and you love me, you shall never be called Tristan nor I Iseut, for then this would be no honourable love. [164])

Fenice will only award her body to Cligés if they can live together in secret so that she can preserve the illusion of an intact, sealed body (vv. 5204–11). Whereas the success of the first pharmacological deception arranged by Fenice and her nurse, the emperor's sexual possession of his wife, depends on the illusion of sexual pleasure, the second, the false death, works to create an illusion of sexual containment. Fenice will not flee Constantinople to live with Cligés at Arthur's court because it would be said that she opened her body to two men. To counter this accusation, she creates the fiction of the body sealed in its tomb, and she escapes the grave to live secretly with Cligés in a sealed tower that has no visible entrance.[36] The architectural integrity figures the intact body. Both are violated when a hunter leaps over a wall of the hidden garden and discovers the two lovers lying naked under a tree. Once seen and identified, Fenice's adulterous body is named in the reports of her presence in the garden and opened to the accusations that her doubled body was intended to help her to avoid.

Moreover, it seems that Fenice's doubled, excess body is no less fragmented, no less lacking, than the body of Queen Iseut.[37] In a passage describing the effect of the first potion that replaces the empress's body with an imaginary presence, Fenice's absent body is doubled by "nothing":

Tenir la cuide, n'an tient mie,
Mes de neant est a grant eise,
Car neant tient, et neant beise,
Neant tient, a neant parole,
Neant voit, et neant acole,
A neant tance, a neant luite.

(vv. 3316–21)

(He thinks he holds her but he does not. But he finds great enjoyment in nothing at all, embracing nothing and kissing nothing, holding nothing and caressing nothing, seeing nothing and speaking to nothing, struggling with nothing and striving with nothing. [137])

In the play of substitution and illusion and in the alternation of presence and absence, the "nothing" that is the double of Fenice's body puts into question the nature of the original: if "nothing" can stand as its substitute, where is the body itself located and of what does it consist?

The apparent reunion of Fenice's bodies at the end of the romance—the lover of Cligés (again) becomes empress—only serves to underscore the lack, the fragmentation, and the dismemberment of the empress's body as it is constructed in the romance. While Fenice herself avoids any adverse consequences from the ruse of the doubled body, she leaves a legacy for the empresses who will succeed her on the throne of Constantinople. After Fenice's example, the emperor's wife is firmly removed from the public and confined to private spaces, a displacement that is designed to maintain the integrity of her body.

Einz puis n'i ot empereor
N'eüst de sa fame peor
Qu'ele nel deüst decevoir,
Se il oï ramantevoir
Comant Fenice Alis deçut,
Primes par la poison qu'il but,
Et puis par l'autre traïson.
Por ce einsi com an prison
Est gardee an Constantinoble,
Ja n'iert tant haute ne tant noble,
L'empererriz, quex qu'ele soit:
L'empereres point ne s'i croit,
Tant con de celi li remanbre.

(vv. 6645–57)

(Never again has there been an emperor who was not afraid of being deceived by his wife, once he had heard tell how Fenice deceived Alis, first by the potion he drank and then by that other ruse. For this reason the empress, whoever she might be and however rich and noble, is guarded in Constantinople as in a prison; for the emperor does not trust her so long as he remembers this other lady. [183–84])

Cligés is the story of the subversion and reinstatement of proper (male) succession. At the same time as female sexuality is defined in relation to questions of dynasty, succession, and power, woman, as a manipulator of meaning and perception, is defined as a threat to the order of the court, an order guaranteed through proper lineage and succession. This threat is not explored in the form of the questioned legitimacy of a royal heir but in the questionable integrity of the queen's adulterous body.

Figure and Fiction

As representative of fragmentation, the body of the adulterous queen in medieval romance represents a threat to notions of unity: the union of a married couple, the uninterrupted succession of a dynasty, the wholeness of a body restricted to one lover. The adulterous female body introduces instability into a symbolic order that is founded on unitary institutions, putting into question the legitimacy of the entire order along with the social and political systems that it creates and supports. Political, institutional, and social boundaries and limits of the romance world are figured in restrictions and taboos surrounding the queen's body, and the transgression of sexual interdiction is assigned to the queen herself, who controls access to her own body. In the metaphoric link between the state of the queen's body and the state of the body politic, the threat of disputed succession posed by adultery is suppressed in the accusations against the queen as the threat of adultery becomes rhetorical rather than dynastic—rumors of the queen's liaison threaten the king's standing in his court. The possible physical result or manifestation of the adultery—an illegitimate child—is displaced in and onto accusations of impropriety.

Rumors about the queen demonstrate the theoretical nature of both adultery and power, and we have seen above that the political function of the queen's body is subsumed by its figurative representation. In a further effacement of the queen's reproductive body, the implied consequences of speech about the royal consort suggest a displacement of restriction and taboo from the queen's body to the king's name, as the king's political authority is attacked through rumors of his wife's sexuality. Julia Kristeva notes an analogous shift in the ritual taboos listed as Leviticus: "Impurity moves away from the material register and is formulated as profanation of the divine name. . . . Defilement will now be that which impinges on symbolic oneness, that is, the sham, substitutions, doubles, idols" (104). To name the queen's adulterous body is to speak fragmentation and lack, a rhetorical act that resituates the body in the symbolic order as a challenge to its wholeness and its unity.

Feminist scholars have shown that universalizing myths in the Western philosophical tradition have consistently posited the feminine as inferior or subordinate to the masculine.[38] In romance, metaphors of fragmentation and doubling extend the perception of the female body as an incomplete (male) body, as a personification of lack, or as a split being. These characterizations are found in the medical writings of Aristotle and Galen and are the basis for most medical treatises written in medieval Europe.[39] It is not surprising then to find the same sort of characterization in medieval literature. As the implicit contrast to the intact, closed virginal body suggests, political and rhetorical stability depend on closure, on an intact, closed system that guarantees univocal meaning and wholeness of consensus. That woman opposes that unity in medieval romance is not unexpected, since she is excluded from its founding moment, marginalized in its maintenance by her lack of political power, and instrumental in its destruction.[40] Thus, the characterization of woman as subversive of social, religious, and natural order is both reflected in and created by the narrative tradition produced by a society strongly marked by overt misogyny. I have attempted to re-pose the question of how woman is described in these narratives and to question why the threat to stability, to unity, is figured in transgressive female sexuality without reference to maternity, and what this equation suggests about the poetics of the feminine in medieval romance.

The importance of an analysis of the female body in medieval romance does not lie in placing the genre (yet again) within the tradition of medieval misogyny, nor is an understanding of romance descriptions of the body significantly advanced by pointing out that the rhetorical interdependence of the feminine, the sexual, and the corporeal is inherent in literary conventions. Based on Fenice's characterization of Iseut's adultery and her attempt to rewrite that representation only to repeat it, we might ask whether within the logical and rhetorical structures of romance narrative Chrétien could have written her story differently. *Cligés* participates in a system of signification in which female sexuality is always transgressive and is always described metaphorically in terms of excess and lack; in turn, the female sexual body metaphorically figures other kinds of threats to the social, political, or symbolic unity from which it is excluded because of its fragmentary nature. The physical being that can be doubled by "nothing" is a body that is always absent as a subject; it is an objective, figurative presence that is constantly displaced by the metaphors that name it. The narrative construction of the queen depends fundamentally on the idea of an agency that acts to efface itself. In the position of the woman as object in adultery, she is a subject who invites her own objectification through the opened access to her body, and although the queen controls access to her body, that fiction of agency is deconstructed by the way the act itself displaces the agent: once opened, the body is possessed by an other.[41]

Rather than simply pointing out its consequences, an analysis of the convergence of gender, sexuality, and corporeality must go beyond its (re)discovery to uncover its grounding in literary language and the political import of such a grounding.[42] In its debates about how to speak and in its manipulations and subversions of representational traditions, literature does not merely reflect medieval misogyny, it exposes its rhetorical foundations, the linguistic and literary conventions that create and sustain it. If, as Christine Brooke-Rose has suggested, the double standard of adultery is always already at work even in the critical vocabulary through which its structure is exposed, it is perhaps only through the examination of the construction of its object—the female body—that it is possible to go beyond the interpretive program inherent in the semantic and narrative structures of the romance institution of adultery.

In this essay I have focused on a set of metaphors used to name the queen's adulterous body in one medieval romance in order to examine how female sexuality is associated with narrative impropriety. Possessed by two men, the queen's adulterous body challenges the notion of property and, implicitly, of proper succession. It is perhaps precisely in the absent but always present question of legitimacy that the tensions and anxieties of the aristocratic society of late twelfth-century France are to be read. In the idealized self-representations in which it celebrates courtly love, any consideration of dynastic reproduction is suppressed. Fenice's justifications of the ruses that permit her adultery suggest that this omission is a highly conscious one that not only seeks to maintain an idealized view of love outside of marriage, but that forcefully works to displace women's agency from dynastic reproduction to the act of consent to commit adultery. The physical act through which the woman might gain authority and influence is subsumed in a linguistic act that effaces her agency or deflects it into the service of adultery.

In its sterile, multiple, and vanishing forms, the body of the queen is both the product and the support of a network of power relations founded on a linguistic system which, through fictions and metaphors, celebrates love within rituals of interdiction and transgression, and in which culpable agency is assigned to the woman in the form of her consent to adultery. That brief moment of agency is immediately effaced as the adulterous woman's voice is subsumed into her body-as-object, doubled and split between two men.

Notes

1. For a brief discussion and overview of the political use of body metaphors from Antiquity through the Middle Ages, see Jacques Le Goff, "Head or Heart? The Political Use of Body Metaphors in the Middle Ages," in *Fragments for a History of the Human Body*, ed. Michel Feher, with Ramona Naddaff and Nadia Tazi, 3 vols. (New York: Urzone, 1989), 3:12–27. For a more detailed study, see Ernst Kantorowicz, *The King's Two Bodies: A Study in Mediaeval Political Theology* (Princeton: Princeton University Press, 1957).

2. Kantorowicz notes that the corporate body of the ruler is sexless because women rulers were gendered as masculine in medieval political rhetoric, but he suggests that when women are excluded from succession "the king's 'Body corporate' could probably not claim sexlessness" (*King's Two Bodies*, 80, 394). On the historical stereotyping of the "wicked queen" as a response to power wielded by a woman, see Susan Mosher Stuard, "Fashion's Captives: Medieval Women in French Historiography," in *Women in Medieval History and Historiography*, ed. S. M. Stuard (Philadelphia: University of Pennsylvania Press, 1987), 16–17.

3. Georges Duby, *The Knight, the Lady and the Priest: The Making of Modern Marriage in Medieval France*, trans. Barbara Bray (New York: Pantheon Books, 1983), 222.

4. See Janet L. Nelson, "Queens as Jezebels: The Careers of Brunhild and Bathild in Merovingian History," in *Medieval Women*, ed. Derek Baker (London: Basil Blackwell, 1978), 36–39; Pauline Stafford, *Queens, Concubines, and Dowagers: The King's Wife in the Early Middle Ages* (Athens: University of Georgia Press, 1983), 86–92, 115–74. On Eleanor of Aquitaine, see Duby, *The Knight*, 189–96; E.-R. Labande, "Pour une image véridique d'Aliénor d'Aquitaine," *Bulletin de la Société des Antiquaires de l'Ouest*, 4th ser., no. 2 (1952): 175–234, 187–88, 190–91, 206–7. On fabrications created about Eleanor after her death, see Frank McMinn

Chambers, "Some Legends Concerning Eleanor of Aquitaine," *Speculum* 16 (1941): 459–68.

5. R. Howard Bloch notes that "a certain medieval (and peculiarly modern) notion of poetry is implicated in what seems to be an obsession with transgression" ("The Lay and the Law: Sexual/Textual Transgression in *La Châtelaine de Vergi*, the *Lai d'Ignauré*, and the *Lais* of Marie de France," *Stanford French Review* 14 [1991]: 182).

6. Recent studies of the place of the female body in society permit us to recast the kinds of questions we ask about the body and the symbolic order that constructs it in medieval romance. See, for example, the essays in *The Female Body in Western Culture: Contemporary Perspectives*, ed. Susan Rubin Suleiman (Cambridge: Harvard University Press, 1986), and in *Fragments for a History of the Human Body*, ed. Feher et al. Volume 3 of the latter is particularly concerned with political metaphors using the body.

7. Joan M. Ferrante's *Woman as Image in Medieval Literature: From the Twelfth Century to Dante* (New York: Columbia University Press, 1975) remains the most important general study of the symbolic treatment of women in medieval literature. A more historically oriented approach is that of Roberta L. Krueger, who juxtaposes romance representations of women with the female audience of romance in order to question the complicity of historical women in the representations of female characters in medieval stories. (See especially "Love, Honor, and the Exchange of Women in *Yvain*: Some Notes on the Female Reader," *Romance Notes* 25 [1985]: 302–17.) The present essay attempts to combine elements from both of these projects: by reversing Ferrante's terms in order to inquire what kind of symbolic language names the feminine, and by setting the romance construction of the queen in relation to role of historical queens, I will attempt to show how constructions of the queen's sexuality in medieval romance work to restrict woman from the political order.

8. This is the project of the three volumes entitled *Fragments for a History of the Human Body* (see n. 1 above). Essays from volume 3 that relate to the topic explored here include Le Goff's above-mentioned "Head or Heart?" and Thomas Laqueur, "The Social Evil, the Solitary Vice and Pouring Tea" (on the nineteenth-century belief that prostitutes are barren), 335–42; Florence Dupont, "The Emperor-God's Other Body" (on the deification of Roman emperors), 395–419; Luc de Heusch, "The Sacrificial Body of the King" (on the location of ritual pollution in the king's body in African societies), 386–94; and Guilia Sissa, "Subtle Bodies" (especially the section entitled "The Seal of Virginity"), 143–56. For a study of the female body and mystical discourse using Kristeva's theory of abjection, see Karma Lochrie, "The Language of Transgression: Body, Flesh, and Word in Mystical Discourse," in *Speaking Two Languages: Traditional Disciplines and Contemporary Theory in Medieval Studies*, ed. Allen J. Frantzen (Albany: State University of New York Press, 1991), 115–40.

9. Mary Douglas, *Purity and Danger: An Analysis of the Concepts of Pollution and Taboo* (New York and London: Routledge and Kegan Paul, 1966), 115.

10. Alice M. Colby-Hall, *The Portrait in Twelfth-Century Literature* (Geneva: Droz, 1965).

11. Heldris de Cornuälle, *Le Roman de Silence*, ed. Lewis Thorpe (Cambridge: Heffer, 1972), vv. 3711–42; *La Châtelaine de Vergi*, ed. Gaston Reynaud, rev. Lucien Foulet (Paris: Champion, 1921), vv. 43–102.

12. Béroul, *Le Roman de Tristan*, ed. L. M. Defourques (Paris: Champion, 1947), 19–20, vv. 604–26.

13. *The Romance of Tristan by Beroul and the Tale of Tristan's Madness*, trans. Alan S. Fedrick (New York: Penguin, 1970), 60–61.

14. The liaison of Tristan and Iseut differs from that of Lancelot and Guenevere in that the queen's lover is also the king's heir; the liaison of Mark's wife and his nephew constitutes the double sin of adultery and incest. Cligés is also the nephew and heir of his lover's husband, who is his paternal uncle. According to Donald Maddox, the paternal line in *Cligés* and the maternal one in *Tristan* provoke different moral problems ("Kinship Alliances in the *Cligés* of Chrétien de Troyes," *L'Esprit Créateur* 12 [1972], 5). Maddox concentrates on the nephew-uncle relationship. A focus on the queen's agency rather than on the motivations of her lover or the implications of his betrayal of his paternal/maternal uncle lends a different perspective to the moral and political implications of adultery. Adultery of a vassal with his lord's wife is also a crime of treason, and John F. Benton sees the treasonous potential of courtly love as evidence that it was a purely literary phenomenon. I am suggesting that the representation of treasonous adultery against the king, as a conflation of sexual, dynastic, and political anxieties, may be read as an exploration of notions of women's power and the place of women in government. See Benton's "Clio and Venus: An Historical View of Medieval Love," in *The Meaning of Courtly Love*, ed. F. X. Newman (Albany: State University of New York Press, 1968), 24–28.

15. Duby, *The Knight*, 195; 212–213; Nelson, "Queens as Jezebels," 38–39. On the question of adultery, illegitimacy, and royal succession in early fourteenth-century England and France, see Charles T. Wood, "Queens, Queans, and Kingship: An Inquiry into Theories of Royal Legitimacy in late Medieval England and France," in *Order and Innovation in the Middle Ages*, ed. William C. Jordan, Bruce McNab, and Teofilo F. Ruiz (Princeton: Princeton University Press, 1976), 385–400.

16. *Le Haut Livre du Graal, Perlesvaus*, ed. William A. Nitze and T. Atkinson Jenkins (Chicago: University of Chicago Press, 1932), vol. 1, branche 8, §180, branche 9, §272–73. This is one of only two texts that explicitly name Loholt as the son of Guenevere, though Arthur is commonly named as his father. For a comparative discussion of Loholt in medieval literature, see Keith Busby, "The Enigma of Loholt," in *An Arthurian Tapestry: Essays in Memory of Lewis Thorpe*, ed. Kenneth Varty (Glasgow: French Department of the University of Glasgow, 1981), 28–36.

17. Although the chaos of disputed paternity for the queen's son is consistently refused in medieval romance, it is fully exploited in the stories of the king's illegitimate children, the most famous example being Arthur's son Mordred, who enacts the destruction of his father's kingdom. See *La Mort le roi Artu: Roman du XIIIe siècle*, ed. Jean Frappier (Geneva: Droz, 1964), 211.

18. "Bien savons que vos estes vive, / Ne parler a nos ne daigniez; / Bien savons que vos vos faigniez, / Si traïssiez l'empereor" ("We know well enough that

you're alive and don't deign to speak to us. We're quite sure you are shamming and deceiving the emperor" (Chrétien de Troyes, *Cligés*, ed. Alexandre Micha [Paris: Champion, 1957], vv. 5888–91; see also vv. 5841–43, 5882–84; translations from Chrétien de Troyes, *Arthurian Romances*, trans. D. D. R. Owen [London: Dent, 1987], p. 173).

19. *La Mort le roi Artu*, 29.

20. My translation.

21. It is notable that when the roles in seduction are reversed, men do not consent to grant sexual favors. In both *Le Roman de Silence* and *La Châtelaine de Vergi*, for example, the man resists seduction, a refusal that ultimately empowers him in the stories. (In *Le Roman de Silence*, the object of seduction is Silence, a woman disguised as a man.)

22. See my "Poetics of Silence in the French Middle Ages" (Ph.D. dissertation, Yale University, 1989, 91–128; and Bloch, "The Lay and the Law," 181–210.

23. Christine Brooke-Rose, "Woman as Semiotic Object," in *The Female Body in Western Culture*, ed. Suleiman, 305–16.

24. Ferrante comments on the double standard and its spiritual and political dangers in medieval poetry, contrasting the way that the woman is represented as almost compelled to commit adultery, while a man who loves two women usually escapes betrayal and sometimes even manages to marry both women (*Woman as Image*, 92).

25. Julia Kristeva, *Powers of Horror: An Essay on Abjection*, trans. Leon S. Roudiez (New York: Columbia University Press, 1982), 81.

26. P. 135. I have sometimes modified the translation of *Cligés* to reflect the language of the original more literally.

27. Queen Iseut is also doubled in the character of Iseut aux Blanches Mains, but these are two different characters, and the doubling is located in Tristan's wish to duplicate the object of his love, not in the woman's desire to avoid adultery. Susan Dannenbaum suggests that the doubling in *Tristan* is a narrative reflection of the internal contradictions in the story, while Terrence Scully sees the doubling of Iseut as a way to "split the personality of the heroine," the first Iseut representing carnal love and the second, sentimental, chaste love (Dannenbaum, "Doubling and Fine Amor in Thomas' *Tristan*," *Tristania* 5 [1979]: 1–14; Scully, "The Two Yseults," *Medievalia* 3 [1977]: 34). We will see that Fenice appears to understand the split in more disturbing terms and that her plan to double her body is motivated by an explicitly expressed desire to avoid such a split.

28. On paired narrative structure in the romance, see Patricia Harris Stablein, "Transformation and Stasis in *Cligés*," *Arthurian Tapestry*, ed. Varty, 155–56. Stablein suggests that change in the romance is only illusory, that its structure is one reflective stasis. I will return to the question of how effectively Fenice "changes" her body through its illusory doubling.

29. Wendelin Foerster first posited the "anti-*Tristan*" reading of *Cligés* in the introduction to his edition of the romance (Halle: Niemeyer, 1901). In his review of Foerster's edition, Gaston Paris suggested a view of *Cligés* as a "nouveau *Tristan*" and suggested its origins in the protests of twelfth-century women, who objected precisely to the "partage de la femme entre l'amant et le mari" in the Tristan

story and demanded a story in which the woman would belong only to her lover ("*Cligés*," *Journal des savants*, ser. 3, vol. 67 [1902], 443–44).

30. Gaston Paris faults Fenice for her refusal to accomplish her marital duties and cites her deception as support for his reading of *Cligés* as a "nouveau *Tristan*," a more refined version of the Tristan story, but not one that promotes an ideal of love in marriage ("*Cligés*," 444–45). Marie-Noëlle Lefay-Tourry locates Fenice's fault not in preserving herself from her husband's embraces but in making him think that he possessed her. She situates this "amoralisme" in a progressive degradation of female characters in Chrétien's romances, and does not interrogate the premises (largely established by the tenets of courtly love) on which she evaluates the behavior of the women ("Roman breton et mythes courtois: L'évolution du personnage féminin dans les romans de Chrétien de Troyes," *Cahiers de civilisation médiévale* 15 [1972]: 202).

31. Vv. 3152–53; p. 135. See also vv. 3185–86: "Garder cuide son pucelage / Por lui sauver son heritage" ("She believes that she saves her virginity to save his inheritance").

32. Jo Ann McNamara points out that this renunciation is even celebrated as a masculinization of the feminine in patristic literature ("Sexual Equality and the Cult of Virginity in Early Christian Thought," *Feminist Studies* 3 [1976]: 145–58, esp. 153–54).

33. Jane Tibbetts Schulenburg, "The Heroics of Virginity; Brides of Christ and Sacrificial Mutilation," in *Women in the Middle Ages and the Renaissance: Literary and Historical Perspectives*, ed. Mary Beth Rose, (Syracuse: Syracuse University Press, 1986), 31–32; John Bugge, *Virginitas: An Essay in the History of a Medieval Ideal* (The Hague: Martinus Nijhoff, 1975), esp. 37, 49–50; Marina Warner, *Alone of All Her Sex: The Myth and the Cult of the Virgin Mary* (New York: Vintage, 1983), esp. 72–74.

34. Schulenburg, "Heroics of Virginity," 31.

35. See R. Howard Bloch, "Chaucer's Maiden Head: 'The Physician's Tale' and the Poetics of Virginity," *Representations* 28 (1989): 113–34, esp. 114–16.

36. "Encor i a de tex reduiz / Que nus hom ne porroit trover . . . Ne ja l'uis trover n'i porrez / Ne antree de nule part" ("There are still more hidden places that no one could find . . . you'll not be able to find a door or entrance anywhere") (vv. 5508–9, 5522–23; p. 168).

37. Rita Lejeune describes Fenice as "faussement vertueuse" in "La Femme dans les littératures française et occitane du XIe au XIIIe siècle," *Cahiers de civilisation médiévale* 20 (1977): 213.

38. See especially Luce Irigaray, *Speculum of the Other Woman*, trans. Gillian C. Gill (Ithaca: Cornell University Press, 1985).

39. Vern L. Bullough, "Medieval Medical and Scientific Views of Women," in *Marriage in the Middle Ages*, *Viator* 4 (1973): 485–501. Of course the idea of woman as an incomplete man is a tenet of Freud's theories of female sexuality, which have elicited various elaborations and refutations. See, for example, Jacques Lacan, *Encore* (Paris: Seuil, 1975); Irigaray, *Speculum of the Other Woman*; Sarah Kofman, *The Enigma of Woman: Woman in Freud's Writings*, trans. Catherine Porter (Ithaca: Cornell University Press, 1985). In his account of the construction of

the one-sex body, Thomas Laqueur notes that "boundaries between male and female are primarily political; rhetorical rather than biological claims regarding sexual difference and sexual desire are primary" (*Making Sex: Body and Gender from the Greeks to Freud* [Cambridge: Harvard University Press, 1990], 19).

40. Exclusion is illustrated in Fenice's and Soredamors's absence from the succession agreement between Alis and Alexandre in *Cligés* (vv. 2518–56); Mordred's desires for the crown and for Guenevere are intertwined in *La Mort le roi Artu* (171–72).

41. In spite of the complicated ways in which she seeks to control access to her own body, Fenice describes it as the possession of her lover: "Qui a le cuer, cil a le cors" ("Let him who has the heart have the body") (v. 3123; p. 135).

The agency of the woman who controls access to her own body is also obscured in critical readings of adultery. For example, in an opposition of the power to orient and control their own passions accorded to lovers by Chrétien and the troubadours, and the potion-induced passion of Tristan and Iseut, Pierre Jonin seems to suggest that passion and consent are inevitably linked for women (*Les Personnages féminins dans les romans français du Tristan au XIIe siècle* [Aix-en-Provence: Ophrys, 1958], 180–81).

42. For a theoretical study that seeks "to locate the political in the very signifying practices that establish, regulate, and deregulate identity," see Judith Butler's *Gender Trouble: Feminism and the Subversion of Identity* (New York: Routledge, 1990), 147.

Theresa Coletti

Purity and Danger: The Paradox of Mary's Body and the En-gendering of the Infancy Narrative in the English Mystery Cycles

The biblical narrative of Christ's conception, birth, and infancy offered medieval dramatists challenging and intractable material. Taxing the technical ability of medieval stagecraft to devise convincing incarnational stage mechanics, these moments in Christian history called for dramatic representation of corporeal mysteries that medieval theologians had struggled to describe even in metaphoric terms. The central Christian mystery that God had become man through a human mother who remained a virgin after his conception and birth furnished a dramatic situation that was theatrically complex, theologically sensitive, and socially resonant.

The English mystery cycles draw on all the problematic moments of the scriptural infancy narrative, making that story a locus for dramatic conflict and robust comic energy.[1] Central to their adaptations are the plays of Joseph's Troubles, in which Joseph returns home after a long absence to find Mary pregnant; unbeknownst to him, the Incarnation has occurred. Recent interpretations give their comedy its due, finding in the plays dramatic strategies that subsume their folkloric and fabliau impulses within a redemptive scheme large enough to embrace puns on typological exegesis and portraits of moral goodness. Efforts to recuperate the unsavory and contentious elements of the scenes of Joseph's Doubt have highlighted their theological emphases: earthy play is regenerated in the cosmic comedy of salvation history.[2]

Yet the pious and harmonious outcomes of the scenes of Joseph's Troubles, indeed of all the fractious moments of the infancy narrative, may also be read in terms of the substantive conflicts they labor to resolve. In their efforts to tease out the implications of Christian theology and miracle, the plays dramatize the challenge to the patriarchal household posed by what seems to be incontrovertible evidence of Mary's adultery. As Joseph says in the York Troubles play, "Thy wombe allway it wreyes thee / That thou has mette with man" (p. 121, ll. 165–66).[3] The infancy plays develop this challenge through spirited representations of sex and gender roles and meanings, which transform the biblical story of Christ's conception, birth, and early life into a prominent site of domestic struggle and social critique in the mystery cycles.

At the center of this en-gendering of the infancy story is the dramatic image of the pregnant, virginal body of Mary. If, as Johan Huizinga puts it, the "union of Joseph and Mary always remained the object of a deplorable curiosity in which profane speculation mingled with sincere piety," that curiosity grew out of an inevitable human puzzlement over the idea of a virginal maternity that paradoxically defied nature and logic.[4] While Christian doctrine called for belief in Mary's virginal maternity, every element of the Incarnational narrative conspired to implicate that story in the earthly elements that were at once so essential and yet so inimical to it.

This essay examines the meanings of Mary's paradoxical corporeality in the English infancy plays and in late medieval culture. Challenging idealist interpretations of the English mystery cycles that emphasize the theological and formal dimensions of the ironic comedy of the Incarnation, I argue that dramatic representations of Mary's anomalous body make biblical story available for a diverse and highly developed social inscription that is singularly responsive to the ideological concerns and daily practices of the late medieval sex and gender system. My analysis suggests that representations of Mary in the infancy plays serve not simply or mainly to reinforce dominant ideologies but rather to expose contradictions and instabilities within the sex and gender system.

I am aware of the potential for controversy in arguing that Marian representations may contest rather than simply reproduce traditional gender roles and meanings, particularly in light of the prominent view that the medieval Marian cult had a negative impact which underlined "the weakness, inferiority, and subordination of real females" and hence only served to reinforce patriarchal ideology.[5] To be sure, the Middle Ages present ample and incontrovertible evidence that the images and themes of the Mary cult provided symbolic and social mechanisms for control of women. But rather than seeing the Virgin Mary exclusively as the subject of an impossible idealization, one term of a binary opposition of good women and bad, I propose that the dramatic image of the pregnant Virgin

should be viewed as a complex sign in which the mysteries of divine reproduction also reproduce social relations. Besides inspiring the daring
comedy of the mystery cycles at one of the most important moments in
Christian history, the spectacle of the pregnant virgin enabled cycle dramatists simultaneously to deploy and to undercut traditional discourses of
gender. They placed the reverent cultic image in a refashioned biblical
story that exploits highly charged topics such as age and sexuality in marriage, adultery, cuckoldry, and illegitimacy, and that explores the interaction of domestic and economic relationships.

Marian representations and meanings in the Middle Ages in fact appear to have had widely varying purposes and effects. While it seems likely,
as Margaret Miles states, that conceptions of Mary "played an important
role in shaping real women's subjectivity and socialization," the form of
such influence is far from clear.[6] Miles's discussion of images of the nursing
Virgin in fourteenth-century Tuscan painting, for example, shows the
multiple significations that such an image could have for different people
within the Christian community.[7] Moreover, evidence from late medieval
culture suggests a reciprocity of influence: Marian meanings and representations also incorporated important aspects of women's subjectivity and
social behavior.[8]

Clearly, late medieval representations of Mary stand in extremely
complex relationship to historical women and to cultural discourses and
social practices.[9] For this reason, they are an especially apt subject for a feminist critique. Marian invocations in late medieval society and culture are
profoundly connected to perceptions of the female body and assumptions
about the nature(s) of women, the naturalness of sexuality, and the essen-
tiality of gender roles. An analysis of the complex en-gendering of Mary
in the infancy plays illustrates the relevance of texts of the past to contemporary theorizing about the construction and contingency of sex and gender meanings.

From the perspective of literary history, another issue raised by a
feminist critique of the mystery cycles involves these plays' relations to the
communities and individuals by and for whom they were produced. The
particular contours of these relationships, from our present vantage point,
are extremely difficult to recover. Our understanding of the social and
symbolic function of dramatic activity in specific communities, for instance, is hampered by scarce knowledge about auspices and authorship
that might permit a fuller contextualization. Only recently have interpretations of the mystery plays as bearing a dynamic and productive relationship

to cultural meaning begun to challenge earlier views, which saw the plays as primarily reflecting and reinforcing dominant ideologies.[10] Although women play an extremely important role in the salvation history the cycles present, the plays have customarily proved resistant to oppositional readings focusing on gender and political interpretations of various sorts.[11]

The analyses offered here recognize that the cycle dramatists, in taking advantage of opportunities to develop and exploit gender issues in the infancy story, were to an extent simply expanding upon meanings already present in Scripture and the apocryphal infancy gospels of James and Pseudo-Matthew. These had been passed on to the later Middle Ages thoroughly mediated by centuries of interpretation, vernacular redactions of Scripture, pictorial iconography, and the thematic and ideological concerns of popular vernacular writing.[12] The gendering of action and discourse in the infancy plays distinguishes these dramatic appropriations of Scripture from other nondramatic late medieval versions. In particular, the narrative lives of Christ, which are often cited as sources for the plays themselves, shy away not only from the risky comedy of the cycles but also from the thematic and discursive focus on gender, family, and society.[13]

Purity and Danger: Unstable Margins

From the early Christian centuries the fathers had debated about the physical nature of Mary's body. Numerous ancient cultures had upheld a belief in virgin birth, but Christianity was unique in attributing to Mary a perpetual virginity.[14] The idea of Mary's inviolate maternity provided the foundation for all Marian hermeneutics throughout the Middle Ages.

The mystery cycles record their debt to the tradition of Marian interpretation that employed figures of enclosure as consummate signs of Mary's wholeness, integrity, and physical purity.[15] Still, even as they regularly deploy the standard tropes for the sacred enclosure of Mary's womb, the cycles' interest in the ineluctable corporeality of her miraculous maternity does not always settle comfortably in careful and joyous representations of the miracles of Christ's Incarnation and birth.[16] Rather, they focus specifically on Mary's body as an ambiguous site of purity and pollution.

All the cycles articulate the contradictory messages of Mary's body by highlighting the conflict between evidence of her contamination and her avowed cleanness. In the York Annunciation, Mary herself, expressing her requisite incredulity about the imminent Incarnation, comments on her own purity: "I knawe no man that shulde haue fyled / My maydenhode, the sothe to saye" (p. 115, ll. 173–74). Mary in the Coventry Shearmen and Taylors' Pageant assures her husband that "with spott of syn I am not defylde," an assurance the messenger angel repeats to Joseph: "a cleyne meydin ys schee" (p. 5, ll. 124, 146). The N-Town play of the Betrothal of Mary shows Joseph admonishing Mary to "Kepe the clene as I xal me" (p. 104, l. 292); N-Town also contains an entire play, the Trial of Joseph and Mary, that dramatizes accusations of impurity against the holy couple. In the Towneley plays, Mary asserts her innocence: "I know none othere man; / ffor fleshly was I neuer fylyd" (p. 92, ll. 205–206). All these protestations of cleanness offer discursive counterpoint to the spectacle of a swelling womb, which seems more than sufficient testimony that Mary is anything but pure.

The interpretive register of the Virgin Mary's body in the mystery cycles is illuminated by the important work of anthropologist Mary Douglas on pollution beliefs and behaviors and social systems. Douglas argues that the body is not a thing unto itself but a symbol of society and of the powers and dangers that structure social relations.[17] By this formulation the body is constructed not as a set of natural facts but as a network of social meanings that work expressively and instrumentally in historically specific cultural contests.[18] Since, as Douglas points out, pollution beliefs express views about the social order, "sexual dangers are better interpreted as symbols of the relationship between parts of society, as mirroring designs of hierarchy or symmetry which apply in the larger social system."[19] The socially constructed body is particularly vulnerable at its margins, the boundary areas where distinct categories of meaning are open to ambiguity and ambivalence. Margins are "dangerous" because "if they are pulled this way or that the shape of fundamental experience is altered. . . . We should expect the orifices of the body to symbolize its specially vulnerable points." Alteration at the margins upsets the social and conceptual order; it pollutes the purity of distinct and bounded categories and introduces the perception of disorder that Douglas defines as dirt.[20] According to the terms of this analysis, the female body in particular is burdened with an exceptionally heavy semiotic load of powers and dangers.[21]

For my present purpose is it important to point out that Douglas's model is thoroughly compatible with medieval scientific and theological thinking, which saw in the female body's openness "breaches in boundaries" that were analogous to its moral character. Commenting on medieval devotional texts, Caroline Bynum observes, "the good female body is closed and intact; the bad woman's body is open, windy and breachable."[22] Because of their openness and temporal instability, the ambiguous boundaries of the female body can only be thoroughly confounded by the idea of a virginal maternity. In the West generally and in the textual and hermeneutic traditions on which the mystery cycles draw, Mary is invested with the powers and dangers of her anomalous body.[23] Its integrity and impermeability identify that body as holy, with holiness understood as chaste marriage and physical purity; its putative signs of sexual pollution— disturbances at the margins—open it up to the "dirt" that accompanies marital disorder—domestic strife, public shame, potential punishment.

When, in the Towneley Annunciation, Gabriel announces to Mary that she "shall conceyue within thi sydys / A chyld of myght" (p. 88, ll. 93–94), she is aptly bewildered by what his message conveys about the ambiguous margins of her body. Adapting Luke 1:34—"Quomodo fiet istud, quoniam virum non cognosco?"—she responds:

> A child to bere thou me hetys,
>   how shuld it be?
> I cam neuer by man's syde,
> Bot has avowed my madynhede,
>   ffrom fleshly gett.
> Therfor I wote not how
> That this be broken, as a vow
>   That I haue hett. . . .
>   (p. 89, ll. 111–18)

Mary's wonder at her putatively "broken" maidenhead (and vow) signals the infancy plays' larger preoccupation with violations of boundaries and shifting of categories, as dramatic representation must come to terms with a body that is supposed to be closed yet gives all the signs of being open, as Joseph says in the York Purification, to "mans pleasoure" (p. 154, l. 207).

The infancy plays dramatize the ambiguity that issues from the disturbed boundaries of the socially constructed female body. Joseph's discovery of a pregnant Mary redefines her virginal body in terms of a corporeal sexual nature, attesting to the dangerous margins of both body and household. In the Towneley Annunciation, Joseph becomes an anthropologist of sorts, critiquing the fluid boundaries of cultural categories that he holds to be stable. The play follows a tradition, originating with Pseudo-Matthew, in which Joseph, having discovered Mary's pregnancy, is told by her handmaidens that she has been visited only by an angel. Joseph's usual response, adopted by many vernacular versions of the episode, is to say that Mary has been beguiled by someone who only looks like an angel.[24] But here Joseph emphasizes a different point:

> Shuld an angell this dede haue wroght?
> Sich excusyng helpys noght,
>   ffor no craft that thay can;
> A heuenly thyng, for sothe, is he,
> And she is erthly; this may not be,
>   It is som othere man.
>   (p. 94, ll. 293–98)

According to his understanding of the bounded categories that define Mary, Joseph takes pains to distinguish the behaviors appropriate to a "heuenly" nature from those of an "erthly" woman: the two should not mix. Yet it is precisely the mingling of "heuenly" and "erthly" natures that the anomalous boundaries of Mary's body signify. From the perspective of Douglas's socially inscribed body, the Incarnation itself was a dangerous event.

The Trouble with Mary

The scenes of Joseph's Troubles repeatedly show Mary's husband struggling with the evidence of semiotic and social disorder that her pregnant body signals. The response of York's Joseph, though excessive, is representative: he persists in trying to extract from Mary the name of the father of her child, posing nine different times one of the central anxious questions of patriarchy: "Whose is't Mary?"[25] Joseph's mistaken assumption that Mary is an adulteress and he a cuckold reinforces the dominant sexual stereotypes of patriarchal culture and enables the infancy plays' infusion with the themes and tropes of medieval misogyny.

The many invocations of misogynist and misogamous discourse in the infancy plays reconfigure Mary in terms of sex and gender roles consistent with the evidence provided by her ambiguous body.[26] The disturbing sight of the violated bodily margins of a pregnant virgin turns the traditional conception of Mary's singularity among women into what Joseph believes must be her likeness to them. For example, in the Towneley Annuciation, Joseph claims not to blame Mary for having "woman maners" (p. 92, ll. 209–10), assuming she possesses the appetite of the libidinous woman constructed by misogynist discourse and canon law: "ffor yong women wyll nedys play them / with yong men, if old forsake them, / thus it is sene always" (p. 95, ll. 302–4).[27] The Detractors of the N-Town Trial of Joseph and Mary similarly assess the evidence provided by Mary's ambiguous body; they deem her "such a mursel as . . . / Wolde cause A yonge man to haue delyght" (p. 142, ll. 92–93) and anatomize her in a fabliau idiom:

> Such a yonge damesel of bewte bryght,
> And of schap so comely also
> Of hire tayle ofte tyme be lyght
> and rygh tekyl undyr the too.
> (p. 142, ll. 94–97)

In a harsher vein, these same Detractors associate Mary's condition with the antics of a wife whose "yonge galaunt . . . his leggys to here hath leyd" (p. 142, ll. 87–88), an identity that allies her with "every scowte" whose sins openly declare her guilt and make her a "bolde bysmare" who presumes against God (p. 144, ll. 182–83; p. 148, ll. 298–99). N-Town's Joseph is most loquacious about the problems that a "yonge wench" makes for an "olde cokwold" (p. 125, ll. 49–56). Even at the Betrothal, the satiric complaints of the aged prospective husband proleptically transform Mary into a dominating shrew:

> An old man may nevyr thryff
> With a yonge wyff, so God me saue.
> Nay, Nay, sere, lett bene!
> Xuld I now in age begynne to dote?
> If I here chyde she wolde clowte my cote,
> Blere myn ey, and pyke out a mote!
> And thus oftyntymes it is sene.
> (p. 104, ll. 278–84)

But the categories upon which Joseph depends for his gender dis-tinctions are fundamentally compromised by Mary's ambivalent body. In the Coventry Troubles scene, Joseph acknowledges this confusion when he apologizes to Mary for erroneously interpreting her body's dangerous margins: "I dyd they mys-name" (p. 6, l. 160). "Misnaming," in fact, is the crucial hermeneutic gesture of the infancy plays, as Joseph in all the cycles, the erring midwives of Chester and N-Town, and the N-Town Trial play's Detractors all learn. Critical readings of these hermeneutic errors have focused mainly on the problems of the interpreter rather than on the ambivalent sign herself. But I wish to suggest that in the infancy plays, the sustained interest in adultery, the persistence of misplaced misogynist and misogamous discourse, and the focus on domestic relations and struggles in their own right are all functions of that ambivalence. These features of the infancy plays help to shape representations of Mary that are neither totally commensurate with nor circumscribed by traditional ideologies of sex and gender. Roberta Krueger's observation that "medieval European culture . . . explored the instability of gender roles even as it ordained their innate and divinely sanctioned nature," is instructive here, for it permits us to see how dramatic representations could be at once perfectly consonant with theological tenets and fully cognizant of the impact of the glaring contradictions in the sex and gender system that Christian belief required.[28]

Several post-Nativity plays in the cycles reinforce my contention that the dramatic interest in gender was an inevitable outgrowth of the plays' scrutiny of the marital situation of Joseph and Mary itself. The infancy plays continue to enact the blurring and shifting of sex and gender categories even after Joseph's questions about paternity have been felicitously resolved. In plays such as the Flight into Egypt in the York and Towneley cycles, for example, domestic disorder returns in power struggles between Joseph and Mary.[29] The Coventry Weavers' Pageant of the Purification and Disputation in the Temple also dramatizes gender struggle and the disruption of family norms, more emphatically than any individual play in all the cycles. Joseph's role as head of the household is underscored by his repeated reluctance to accept the duties accorded him by his position. He is more misogynistically garrulous than anywhere else in the cycles, and he must undergo not one but multiple illuminations, since not even the instructions of a series of messenger angels are sufficient to get him on the pious road to assisting his wife. Mary proves a fit match for her stubborn husband, prodding, directing, and holding her ground as he repeatedly rejects her requests and his responsibilities as head of the household.

The play characterizes Joseph and Mary within the discursive tradition that focused on power relationships in marriage, showing the couple struggling to determine who will perform two tasks: obtaining turtledoves to offer at Mary's Purification and retrieving Jesus from the

Temple. Oddly, Gabriel urges Mary to make sure Joseph participates in the sacrifice (p. 45, ll. 379–82, 387–90). Joseph's behavior vacillates between obedient subservience and surly resistance (pp. 46–47, ll. 417, 428–34, 444–49); Mary casts the conflict with him in terms of the respective roles of husbands and wives: "Husebande, these be no womens dedis; / Therefore, Josoff, ye must forthe nedis; / For surely there ys no reymedy" (p. 47, ll. 450–52).

The sustained tension in the Weavers' pageant between Joseph's predictable misogynist complaints and Mary's steady facilitation of biblical story reverses and destabilizes gender roles, because Mary's insistence on fulfilling her subordinate position in the family ("these be no womens dedis") ironically leads to just the opposite. From Joseph's perspective it becomes an act of dominance itself: "Soo full of feyre wordis these wemen be, / Thatt men thereto must nedis agre" (p. 50, ll. 555–56). By the end of the play Mary literally assumes the public role of head of the family as she steps forward, before her husband, to claim her lost child from the Doctors.[30]

Though anticipated by the conflicts between Joseph and Mary in the plays of Joseph's Troubles, the characterization of the holy couple in the Coventry Purification has proved problematic for the few scholars who have commented on the play. V. A. Kolve felt obliged to respond to earlier criticism that the treatment of Joseph was "irreverent and objectionable exploitation." In his view the Coventry Purification's portrait of Joseph contributes to "a delightful dramatic statement" aimed largely at emphasizing the comic and redemptive drama of Christian history.[31] Rosemary Woolf finds in the Play an aberrant and ill-conceived approach to what should be a pious purpose.[32]

In contrast to these views, I submit that in the Weavers' Pageant, Joseph's unwillingness to recognize what Mary elsewhere in the play calls the familial "order" (p. 65, l. 1033) is neither an infelicitous aesthetic move nor a sign of a religious game in which the foibles of "natural" man are at once exposed and forgiven. Rather, I wish to suggest that the play's inversion of gender roles and unsettled portrait of domestic struggle are functions of the gendered symbolism of the Purification itself. If the symbolic and social significance of Mary's ambiguous body provides the impetus for conflict in the infancy plays, it is not surprising that the Purification could emerge as a prominent site of contestation. For the Purification represents the moment in the infancy story in which Mary gratuitously participates in the rites that cleansed and resanctified the female body after the violations of childbirth, rites that were principally dedicated to purifying the female body's dangerous margins.[33]

Despite Mary's exemption from any such violation, the idea of ritual purification was thus inevitably linked to the female body that was, as Joseph states in the York cycle, "fyled" in "mans pleasoure" (p. 154, ll. 207–8). Coventry's Joseph in fact makes a connection between Mary and other women when he responds to her request for help in obtaining turtledoves with "Go thyself, dame . . . Ye, or ellis get the a nev page" (p. 47, ll. 444–49). Raising once more the spectre of adultery that dominates the Troubles plays, Joseph's remark implicitly links his wife with the sexual domain in which getting a "new page" is a viable option. Thus his "trouble" with Mary in the Coventry Purification may be seen as a further reenactment of the dangers that accrue to the socially inscribed female body.

As the mystery cycles exploit the conflict inherent in the gendered meanings of the infancy story, they call attention to the problematic transgressions of natural law and social custom that Mary's ambiguous body lent to her marriage with Joseph: conjugality without sex, conception without intercourse, human infancy without a natural fatherhood. Consequently, Mary's virginal maternity emerges in these plays not as an idealized and exemplary feature of her singular womanhood but rather as one crucial term in an entire system of sexual and social meanings, what Kirsten Hastrup, adapting Douglas, calls the "semantics of biology," in which "the meaning and significance of one single aspect of sexuality and reproduction" are related to other "concepts within the same semantic domain":

> The meaning of specific categories depends on their position within a larger system of cultural categories. . . . The semantic load of [virginity] . . . is defined by its position within a larger semantic field of "female sexuality," and this field . . . is defined in relation to society at large.[34]

Hastrup further explains that social and conceptual order depends upon established boundaries between categories. And, since categories interact with social context, the potential for disorder occurs when "a discrete category within one context" becomes "less ambiguously 'pure' within another context."[35]

The disordered domestic situations of the infancy plays exemplify the violations of social norms that were inherent in the biological semantics of Christian narrative. Facing the prospect of representing an impossible conception and a metaphoric cuckoldry, medieval dramatists in many instances opted to make the metaphoric literal and to show the consequence of such violations in terms that their audiences were likely to understand. Thus the infancy plays exhibit all the themes and tropes of patriarchal society and discourse, relying for their humor and their conflict on the prevailing gender and social arrangements of a male-dominated society in which woman is preeminently inscribed with the ambiguity of her dangerous body. But they also make problematic the structure and discourse of that society because the plot of the Christian story calls for Joseph and Mary to occupy roles that are fundamentally different from what they seem.[36] Joseph and Mary's continual evasion of exemplarity is responsible for much of the dissonance in the infancy plays because the customary roles and rules simply do not apply to them.

The Transgressive Body and Society

The contradictory domestic elements of the infancy story also provided cycle dramatists opportunities to link the divinely authorized disorder of the Incarnation with transgressions germane to their own temporal and material world. In fact, I believe the impulse to make scriptural narrative compatible with the discourses and social practices that comprised the system of sex and gender meanings in late medieval society is one of the signal features of the infancy plays. As they further inscribe the symbolic disorder of Mary's ambivalent body in representations of the social realm, the plays focus on the relationship between violation of the body's boundaries and transgression of social norms.

For example, the infancy plays explore the relationship between economic production and sexual reproduction by imaging the consequences of adultery for domestic arrangements. The mystery cycles' transformation of the infancy story into an adultery plot problematically introduces into the household a child of suspect paternity. Though the Joseph's Troubles scenes otherwise vary widely among the mystery cycles, each of the five versions shows Joseph unambiguously stating his relationship to the expected child: "myin is it noght," as he says in the Towneley Annunciation (p. 90, l. 160).[37] Illegitimacy appears to have had variable significance in the Middle Ages. Barbara Hanawalt observes, for instance, that in medieval peasant communities illegitimacy seems "not to have been heavily stigmatized."[38] Noting the possibility that in the fifteenth century even the child of an adulterous union may have been considered legitimate, she cites the example of the jurist who stated "Whoso bulleth my cow, the calf is mine."[39]

As Joseph's insistence on his lack of involvement in Mary's pregnancy in all the Troubles episodes well attests, this generous view was not exactly shared by the cycle dramatists. In the Towneley Annunciation play, Joseph in fact declares quite the opposite of the jurist's sentiment: "Godys and myn she says it is; / I wyll not fader it; she says amys" (p. 92, ll. 221–22). The N-Town Trial of Joseph and Mary shows how questions about legitimacy were subject not only to the scrutiny of ecclesiastical courts but to the severe derision of neighbors.[40] If evidence for the undesirability of bearing or fathering an illegitimate child is any indication, we can suppose that both Joseph's concern about Mary's pregnancy and the couple's shared distress, in the N-Town Trial, for their undeserved public defamation were consistent with popular practice and sentiment.[41]

Adultery disordered the household because the bastard child could present a drain on resources.[42] The mystery cycles make clear that apart from public shame over illegitimacy, the child of an adulterous union could bring economic distress to the household. Despite Joseph's disclaimer in the Towneley plays about not wishing to "fader" Mary's child, his real life counterpart may have had to accept his wife's children as his legitimate offspring.[43] This is the position Joseph takes in the York Troubles play; he is more concerned about knowing the child's true paternity than about the cost of supporting the child: "Yhitt for myn awne I wolde it fede, / Might all be still. / Tharfore the fadir tell me, Marie" (pp. 121–22, ll. 185–87). The crude material consequences of the adulterous union did not escape dramatic scrutiny. Among the harshest words the Detractors of the N-Town Trial play hurl at Joseph are these barbed comments about the relationship of the supposedly illicit child to his household economy: "Now muste he faderyn anothyr mannys chylde, / And with his swynke he xal be fedde" (p. 142, ll. 100–101).

The infancy plays also dramatize specific social rituals and practices that registered transgressions of the norms and boundaries of the sex and gender system. The York play of Joseph's Troubles, for example, unmistakably establishes the connection between that episode and the ritualized hostilities of charivari. The play was brought forth by the Pewterers and Founders, the makers of metal domestic utensils, the kettles, pans, and dishes through which the "rough music" of charivari was expressed.[44]

In the medieval and early modern period, the situations provoking charivari varied widely, but basically the ritual denunciations and rough music of charivari commented on and registered changes in sexual and matrimonial roles, directing attention, for example, to asymmetrical marriages, husband and wife beaters, second marriages, and adulterous wives.[45] If charivari is a "discordant concert given outside the home" of the social offender, it is easy to see how the Troubles episode could have been deemed an occasion suitable for "rough music," since it focuses particularly on Joseph's return to and departure from the domicile he shares with Mary.[46] I suggest that in the York play, the Pewterers and Founders displayed the usefulness of their wares by serenading Joseph and Mary with the clacking of metal objects, registering the social disorder of their asymmetrical marriage and her suspected adultery. These are, in fact, the interlocking themes that the Troubles episodes consistently develop. In protesting his innocence regarding Mary's pregnancy, Joseph resorts to declarations of the incapacities of his age: "Slike works yf I do wauld, / Thase games fra me are gane" (p. 122, ll. 195–96). At the same time, it is the disruptive marital relationship that the York Troubles play seeks to restore; the angel who appears to Joseph is sent "to say with steven / In lele wedlak thou lede the" (p. 123, ll. 259–60).[47]

While historians advance varying opinions about the social impact of practices such as charivari, it is clear that the public censure of charivari signified the extent to which private and personal relationships were available for community scrutiny in terms of the norms and roles of the society in which the censured couple lived. Had Joseph and Mary been citizens of late medieval York they might well have been subjected to the derisive noise accompanying the Pewterers and Founders' production, which provided the audience with a reminder of the larger realm of informal and formal regulation that affected the far from rare instances of marital and sexual disturbance in late medieval and early modern England.[48]

The social regulation of matrimonial, especially sexual, behaviors is the focal point of still another play that registers with unusual specificity the relationship between the ambiguous margins of Mary's body and the system of social meanings inscribed by that body. Based on an apocryphal episode in which Joseph and a pregnant Mary are brought before a high priest to offer evidence of their chastity, the N-Town Trial of Joseph and Mary transforms their ordeal into an ecclesiastical court proceeding, complete with judges, witnesses, and summoner.[49] Although the contemporary resonances of the N-Town Trial of Joseph and Mary have been regularly noted, commentary on the play has more frequently focused on its literary features or moral implications.[50] I am interested here in the play's elision of the theological paradox and corporeal mystery of Mary's body with the social regulatory system that ecclesiastical courts represented.

The Trial weighs the holy couple's protestations of cleanness against the inescapable evidence of Mary's "swollyn" womb. The First Doctor of the Law assesses Mary's condition, assuming her likeness to other women:

> Thu art with chylde we se in syght;
> To us thi wombe the doth accuse!
> Ther was nevyr woman yitt in such plyght
> That from mankynde hyre kowde excuse.
>
> (p. 148, ll. 302–5)

The play emphasizes the unlikely phenomenon that the trial must examine: the impossibility that Mary can be, as she is pronounced near the end, "clene mayd, bothe modyr and wyff" (p. 150, l. 353). Mary's accusers in the play of the Trial assume a role analogous to that of Joseph in the Troubles episodes: their judgment is the public equivalent of Joseph's response in the private domestic realm to the appearance of Mary's paradoxically closed and open body.

The predominance of sex-related cases in ecclesiastical courts in much of late medieval England strongly indicates that the dramatic audience would have appreciated the transposition of Joseph and Mary's problem to the regulatory climate of their own time. According to James Brundage, late medieval society and the courts that served it "seem to have been preoccupied with the norms of sexual behavior." Although the "proportion of matrimonial and sex offense cases varied considerably from one region to another," "in most jurisdictions whose records have been studied, marriage and sex issues accounted for a majority, often a large majority, of the total business of the Church's lower level courts." Brundage cites the following evidence: between 1470 and 1523 at Bridgenorth, sex-related cases comprised three-quarters of the case load; at Lichfield in 1466, 90 percent of persons brought before the court were charged with adultery or fornication; in the Canterbury Consistory court in 1478 nearly 70 percent of ex officio cases involved sex charges; sexual matters also comprised nearly two-thirds of the business of London commissary courts.[51]

The N-Town Trial follows familiar ecclesiastical court procedures for matrimonial and sex-related cases in giving such a prominent role to charges brought by witnesses. The play includes two very nonbiblical figures, the Detractors "Raise Slander" and "Backbiter," who instigate the legal proceedings against Joseph and Mary and are specifically associated with acts of defamation. Defamation suits and sexual misconduct suits, as Richard Wunderli has demonstrated, were intimately related in ecclesiastical court proceedings, comprising what he terms the "warp and weft" of the sexual moral fabric. In late medieval London, for example, cases dealing with sexual offenses and defamations of sexual offenses together represented most of the commissary court's business for entire years.[52]

Although the apocryphal episode on which the Trial of Joseph and Mary is based states that a "rumor" began to circulate that Mary was pregnant, nothing in the biblical account prepares for the role that unruly speech comes to play in the N-Town drama. In N-Town's treatment of the apocryphal episode, suspicions about Joseph and Mary's sexual transgression are consistently linked with public issues of defamation and reputation. This thematic focus is apparent from the first mention of the play in the N-Town Proclamation, where the Trial promises to show how Joseph and Mary "were sclawndryd with trey and tene" (p. 10, l. 185). The first Detractor boasts that he and his brother Backbiter can "more slawndyr . . . arere / Within an howre thorweouth this town / Than evyr ther was this thowsand yere" (p. 140, ll. 45–47). Both the Detractors and Joseph and Mary repeatedly invoke the public, verbal significance of the charges brought against the holy couple, a gesture realized in the play's frequent collocation of the rhyming terms *defame*, *shame*, and *name*.[53] In the Trial, Mary is as much concerned with maintaining her good reputation as defending her chastity (p. 145, l. 210) when she is accused by her kinsman the bishop: "Telle me who hath wrought this wrake. / How has thou lost thin holy name?" (p. 145, ll. 208–9). The Detractor who is nearly leveled by the purgative drink that leaves Joseph and Mary unaffected repents his "cursyd and ffals langage" (p. 150, ll. 366–67) and is forgiven by Mary for his "defamacion" (l. 375). Even one of the play's stage directions characterizes the action taken against Joseph and Mary in these terms: "Hic sedet Episcopus Abizachar inter duos legis doctores et, audientes hanc defam[a]cionem, vocat ad se detractores" (p. 142, after line 105).

The N-Town Trial of Joseph and Mary also stresses the important role of community participation in the judicial proceedings it represents, illustrating the very public quality of the justice system that ecclesiastical courts regulated.[54] Two speeches by Den the Summoner serve in part to define the community—here inseparable from the dramatic audience—for whom these proceedings are enacted, since Den first warns "all the rowte" to appear at the ecclesiastical court (l. 6), and then apparently makes his way through a group of people in order to summon Joseph and Mary specifically: "Awey, serys, lete me come nere" (p. 143, ll. 150–69). The play also emphasizes the public nature of the process of purgation. Mary prays to God "that all this fayr peple my clennes may se" (p. 149, l. 337). When the first Detractor refuses to accept the evidence of Mary's innocence, the Bishop orders him to drink the same draught as she "beforn all this pepyl" (p. 150, l. 361). Celebrating Mary's newly cleared name and her forgiveness of the Detractor, the Bishop offers to accompany her home with a group to serve her with "hyy reverens," an offer that Mary refuses: "I thank yow hertyly of youre benevolens. / Onto you owyn hous I pray yow ye goo / And take this pepyl hom with you hens" (p. 151, ll. 382–84). The people serve to bear witness to the outcome of the false accusations just as the Detractors bore witness to the charges; they participate in the exposure of the defamation and the restoration of Mary and Joseph's reputation, as the couple's "clennesse is knowyn ful opynly" (p. 152, l. 404).

While the linking of sexual and defamation cases may have been a common feature of ecclesiastical court proceedings throughout late medieval England, the emphasis on these elements in the N-Town Trial play may also be illuminated by certain features of East Anglian social practice.[55] Susan Amussen has recently described the social regulatory climate fostered by the ecclesiastical courts, particularly through their jurisdiction over all matters pertaining to sex and marriage. She observes in early modern East Anglia a system of social control and coercion in which appearances before the ecclesiastical court were a principal means of registering the power of public scrutiny of reputation.[56] This structure of social control, Amussen says, was fundamentally connected to the sex and gender system of the communities in which it operated. The roles and norms of sexual behavior as well as specific sexual transgressions (e.g., fornication, bastardy, concubinage) were all subject to a social regulation that relied on the informal controls of gossip and surveillance. Because of their special jurisdiction, ecclesiastical courts were the obvious venue for community interest in reputation that had the larger purpose of elaborating and maintaining gender norms and social order.[57]

According to Amussen, patterns of accusation before religious tribunals for sexual irregularities in early modern East Anglia functioned to mitigate the contradictions between, on the one hand, an ideology of gender that asserted women's natural inferiority and submissiveness, and on the other, the conditions of a social life that both called for women's independence and provided opportunities for it. The aim of such a system,

Amussen states, was to regulate the sex and gender system through public concepts of reputation and to expose flagrant infractions of law, while leaving unremarked the daily transgressions of a rigidly defined official system of sex and gender roles. Accusations before religious tribunals provided compensatory public control on behalf of other transgressions of sex and gender roles that did not reinforce hegemonic models of male dominance.[58]

The N-Town Trial of Joseph and Mary records many features of a social regulatory climate in which gossip about sexual transgression, or "defamation" as it is referred to in the play, had an enormous impact on reputation. The force of public speech is underscored by the power the Detractors have to jeopardize the good reputation of Joseph and Mary.[59] The defamation of the holy couple's good name depends on an erroneous judgment about Mary's sacred body—"thou art with childe eche man may se"—and thus points up the dynamic and potentially dangerous relationship of the profaned body to the society it inhabits. Joseph and Mary's successful purgation accomplishes a critique of the institutional mechanisms of social control that ecclesiastical justice represents, and it enables just as sharp a critique of the patterns of informal regulation of private behavior that were driven by the gossip and surveillance personified in the characters of the Detractors. In the N-Town Trial play, Mary's paradoxical body is deployed in order to upset institutions that order society, showing them to be vulnerable precisely where the boundaries of her own sacred body are not.

Re-presenting Gender

In the infancy plays of the mystery cycles, social imperatives and the claims of the material world interact with sexual ideology and Christian doctrine to produce the Virgin Mary as a complex sign. Marian meanings in these plays are informed by the dynamic relationships of the sex and gender system with which all female bodies were inscribed. Representations of Mary in the infancy plays move, in fact, in two opposing directions. On the one hand, they invoke roles for Mary that directly link her to historical women: she bears, cares for, nurses, and protects her child; she marries, has disagreements with her husband, and observes the division of sex roles within the nuclear family unit. On the other hand, these same representations deploy ideological assumptions about woman's nature and woman's body to emphasize Mary's deviation from those assumptions.

It is the resulting interplay of likeness and difference, I would argue, that fundamentally structures representations of Mary in the infancy plays, much more than an idealized, hierarchically ordered binarism expressing moral values. Problematic relationships of likeness and difference undergird Joseph's efforts to reconcile the very idea of a pregnant Mary with his understanding of what he believes are stable gender categories and meanings. The pregnant virgin challenges his assumptions about what is "'always already' knowable," that is, natural, transparent, essential about women's bodies,[60] demonstrating in that challenge how the significations of the ambiguous female body are not simply given, but rather are susceptible to multiple and contrary interpretations and are thoroughly mediated by the family and larger social institutions.

Neither aloof from nor totally contained by the traditional ideologies of gender, representations of Mary in the infancy plays call attention to contradictions sustained within the sex and gender system. As we have seen, the Marian semiotics of the infancy plays exposes the uncertain authority of misogynist discourse; highlights discrepancies between the mores and practices of the sex and gender system; and emphasizes the conflict between traditional gender roles and the social circumstances that could destabilize them.

My argument—that Marian meanings deployed in the infancy plays have the potential to disrupt traditional ideologies of gender—departs from recent assessments of the impact of the medieval Marian cult in two fundamental ways. First, it challenges the view that sees the cult primarily as having further restricted the conception and status of women.[61] "Rather than deepening an appreciation of the bipolarity of God's creation or female equivalence," the Mary cult is said to degrade women because of her "theological isolation from human femaleness."[62] According to this interpretation, Mary represents at best a dualistic ideal whose exaltation above all women depends upon an androcentric view of "the subordinate, auxiliary, and ultimately inferior character of female personhood relative to the masculine norm."[63] In these terms, emulation of Mary "involves an acceptance of a view of women that regards certain aspects of womanliness as highly undesirable."[64]

Alternatively, I propose that, rather than privileging Mary's inevitably negative exemplary function in relation to historical female subjects, cycle dramatists saw in the complex semiotics of Mary's pure yet dangerous female body the opportunity to read Christian myth as a text about the social order and to create versions of that story that examine gender meanings in relation to canon law, popular belief, and contemporary social mores and practices. Dramatists were less concerned with depicting Mary's exemplarity than they were with exploring the concrete and potentially dangerous implications of Marian significations in the everyday world.

Second, my argument also implicitly contests the position—advanced by some feminist scholars and theorists—that essentializes Mary's difference in terms of a total and unique separation from sexuality and an impossible relationship to historical female subjects. An emphasis on Mary's difference has been of central importance to contemporary assessments of the Marian cult. Kristeva, for example, sees in Mary's virginity a uniqueness that is "attained only through an exacerbated masochism: a concrete woman, worthy of the feminine ideal embodied by the Virgin as an inaccessible goal, could only be a nun, a martyr or, if she is married, one who leads a life that would remove her from the 'earthly' condition and dedicate her to the highest sublimation alien to her body."[65] Similarly, Mieke Bal calls Mary a "sadistic" invention that represents a failed attempt by generations of Christian commentators to resolve the tension between a positive valuation of motherhood and a negative valuation of woman's body and moral inferiority.[66]

To be sure, from the commentaries of the fathers to the vernacular biblical redactions of much later medieval centuries, interpretations highlight the special status of Mary's body and the absolute difference accorded to her through her perpetual virginity and consequent exception from the pains and burdens of the uxorial cycle in which she was nevertheless a full participant. As John Lydgate described her in his *Life of Our Lady*, Mary was "Chosyn of god for to stynte our stryve, / Of all wymen, by hir self aloon."[67] Still, although the history of Marian doctrine and devotion emphasized Mary's separation from sex as the ground of her holiness, late medieval invocations of Mary's virginity tend to focus less on her exclusion from sexual involvement than on the variable and specific significations of her body generally. This tendency is illuminated by recent work on the meanings of virginity and physicality in the Middle Ages and on the multivalence of religious symbols; this work has shown the extent to which the deployment of sex and gender symbols occurs in the context of the social regulation of both male and female sexuality and within the constraints provided by families, communities, and larger social institutions.[68]

Despite the theological and intellectual difficulty that Mary's immaculate but human body presented to the fathers and early theologians of the Church, in symbolic and social practice medieval people seem not to have been terribly troubled by Mary's impossible difference. Rarely do we find them bewailing their distance from the pure and rarified Madonna. Rather, we see them intent on honoring Mary's incarnating mother-flesh and its continual mediation of the distance between body and spirit.[69] At the same time, they brought Marian meanings down to earth, overshadowing the ideology of her singular virginity with a social hermeneutics emphasizing her closeness to historical female subjects. While medieval canon law probed the marriage of Mary and Joseph to determine whether sexual consummation was necessary for the formation of the marriage bond, medieval dramatists, as we have seen, quite comfortably depicted Mary and Joseph in the familiar institutional settings inhabited by ordinary mortals.[70] When the Virgin Mary addressed Saint Bridget in the saint's exceedingly popular revelations, she stressed her likeness to ordinary women, referring to herself as an "earthly vessel," not as an immaculate and unique body.[71] Margery Kempe's *Book* solicits Mary's childbirth, motherhood, and companionability in an account of a life that frequently challenges both the public and the private meanings of gender roles.

But medieval people were also capable of interrogating as well as celebrating and domesticating Mary's virginal mysteries. If the late medieval cult of the Virgin honored her paradoxical maternity and memorialized the saving fecundity of Mary's body in images that concretely and literally depicted such things as the enclosure of the entire Trinity in her womb,[72] still other notices of her corporeal mysteries grappled with the conflicting demands that Christology and the Mary cult placed on formulations about the Virgin's own physiology. As Charles T. Wood has shown, later medieval medico-theology puzzled over the inherent contradiction between belief in Mary's Immaculate Conception, which exempted her from sin and all its tangible effects, and a Christology that required her to have a normal woman's physiology. Interestingly, this dilemma came to focus on the fluids that may have been exuded from Mary's body, on the possibilities of its producing menses and milk. Theologians pondered how an immaculately conceived virginal body could menstruate, and if it could not, how it could possibly produce milk. Still, countless medieval texts and images show the lactating Virgin, extolling the power and benefits of her milk.[73] What seems clear in all of this, as Wood states, is that "for all her remarkable traits, Mary remained imperturbably and ineluctably female, and even though men did their best to rid her flesh of all carnal taint, they were forced in the end to recognize that she, too, had possessed all those sexual attributes which had so often become the target of male abuse in the case of others."[74]

This strand in Christian theology and piety in the later Middle Ages reveals a steady preoccupation with the boundaries and openings of Mary's body and its contact with the world. It provides one important context in which we may understand the cycle dramatists' preoccupation with Mary's ambiguous body and with the "new combinations and strange instabilities" in the semiotic system that Mary's hybrid body inspired.[75] As we have seen, the mixed categories of Mary's body translate into trouble with boundaries in the social realm: the plays dramatize domestic disputes over gender roles, the impact of a transgressed virginity on family and community, and the inevitable links between women's reproduction and the household economy. The infancy plays' interest in the forms of social disorder underwritten by the representation of Mary's body illustrates what Peter Stallybrass and Allon White have observed of the symbolic domains—the human body, psychic forms, geographical space, and the social formation—in which "cultures 'think themselves' in the most immediate and affective ways": "transgressing the rules of hierarchy and order in any one of the domains may have major consequences in the others."[76]

At this distance it is difficult, if not impossible, to determine the practical social force of these transgressive dramatic representations; as Stallybrass and White make clear, the politics of a specific instance of symbolic transgression "cannot be resolved outside of a close historical examination of particular conjunctures."[77] What does seem clear is that infancy play dramatists identified a strong compatibility between the hybrid symbolism of Mary's paradoxical maternity and the symbolic and actual struggles that we know to have characterized the sex and gender system of the late Middle Ages.

The infancy plays' depictions of Mary's ambiguous body and of the differences articulated by gendered conceptions of body, family, and household underscore the differences and contradictions in Christian story itself. The consistency with which dramatists irreverently detail the idea of Joseph's "troubles" may in fact be seen as their attempt to come to terms with what Martin Walsh has called the "essential absurdity of the Virgin Birth."[78] Epitomizing the founding contradictions of Christian story, Mary emerges as a sign of difference, of the irreconcilability of matter and spirit, the human and the divine.

Late medieval reverence for and appropriation of Mary were inextricably tied to her mediation of those irreconcilable differences that her ambiguous body signified. In the infancy plays of the mystery cycles, gender emerges as a crucial category that simultaneously acknowledges the paradox at the heart of Christian story and unflinchingly enables its translation into the realm of everyday life. Under the sign of Mary's purity and danger, the infancy plays exploit the potential to rewrite Christian story. They employ gender as the language through which the basic tensions and incompatibilities of Christian myth and mystery may be expressed and assert at the same time the unsettling differences of gender in their own right.

Notes

1. By the term *infancy narrative*, I understand a story, drawn from Scripture and the apocrypha, of the life of Christ, beginning with the life of Mary and extending through Christ's childhood. The most important episodes in that story, the conception and nativity of Jesus, appear in all the cycles; inclusion of other episodes varies from cycle to cycle. I am concerned here with the infancy plays and episodes from the four complete mystery cycles and the two surviving Coventry plays. Quotations in the text of this essay, cited by page and line numbers, refer to the following editions: *York Plays*, ed. Richard Beadle (London: Edward Arnold, 1982); *Towneley Plays*, ed. George England and Alfred W. Pollard, EETS, e.s. 71 (London: Oxford University Press, 1897; rpt. 1966); *The Chester Mystery Cycle*, ed. R. M. Lumiansky and David Mills, EETS, s.s. 3 and 9, 2 vols. (Oxford: Oxford University Press, 1974, 1986); *The N-Town Play*, ed. Stephen Spector, EETS, s.s. 11 and 12, 2 vols. (Oxford: Oxford University Press, 1991); *Two Coventry Corpus Christi Plays*, ed. Hardin Craig, EETS, e.s. 87, 2d ed. (London: Oxford University Press, 1957). Orthography has been modernized.

2. See, for example, V. A. Kolve, *The Play Called Corpus Christi* (Stanford: Stanford University Press, 1966), 247–53; Rosemary Woolf, *English Mystery Plays* (Berkeley: University of California Press, 1972), 169–74; Gail McMurray Gibson, "'Porta Haec Clausa Erit': Comedy, Conception, and Ezekiel's Closed Door in the *Ludus Coventriae* Play of 'Joseph's Return,'" *Journal of Medieval and Renaissance Studies* 8 (1978): 137–56; Martin W. Walsh, "Divine Cuckold/Holy Fool: The Comic Image of Joseph in the English 'Troubles' Plays," *Proceedings of the 1985 Harlaxton Symposium*, ed. W. M. Ormrod (Woodbridge, Suffolk: Boydell Press, 1986), 278–97; Albert H. Tricomi, "Reenvisioning England's Medieval Cycle Comedy," *Medieval and Renaissance Drama in England* 5 (1991): 18–19. Kolve and Gibson summarize much of the earlier commentary on these plays. Two studies worth mention are Brother C. Philip Deasy, *St. Joseph in the English Mystery Plays* (Washington, D.C.: Catholic University of America, 1937); and Brother Cornelius Luke, *The Role of the Virgin Mary in the Coventry, York, Chester and Towneley Cycles* (Washington, D.C.: Catholic University of America, 1933). The readings cited here move significantly

beyond the simple condemnation of the Troubles plays' putative indecencies; for this view, see Samuel B. Hemingway, ed., *English Nativity Plays* (New York: Russell and Russell, 1909), xviii. One important recent exception to the recuperative reading of the Joseph's Troubles episode is C. Clifford Flanigan's "Liminality, Carnival, and Social Structure: The Case of Late Medieval Biblical Drama," in *Victor Turner and the Construction of Cultural Criticism: Between Literature and Anthropology*, ed. Kathleen M. Ashley (Bloomington: Indiana University Press, 1990), 58–62.

3. Explicit references to Mary's physical condition appear in all the cycles. See *N-Town Play*, pp. 124–25, ll. 25–33; *Towneley Plays*, p. 92, ll. 213–14; *Chester Mystery Cycle*, p. 102, ll. 130–32; *Two Coventry Corpus Christi Plays*, p. 4, l. 111.

4. Johan Huizinga, *The Waning of the Middle Ages*, trans. F. Hopman (Garden City: Doubleday, 1954), 170.

5. See, for example, Eleanor Commo McLaughlin, "Equality of Souls, Inequality of Sexes: Woman in Medieval Theology," in *Religion and Sexism: Images of Women in the Jewish and Christian Traditions*, ed. Rosemary Radford Ruether (New York: Simon and Schuster, 1974), 245–51 (quotation is from p. 246).

6. Margaret R. Miles, *Carnal Knowing: Female Nakedness and Religious Meaning in the Christian West* (Boston: Beacon Press, 1989), 139.

7. Margaret R. Miles, "The Virgin's One Bare Breast: Female Nudity and Religious Meaning in Tuscan Early Renaissance Culture," in *The Female Body in Western Culture: Contemporary Perspectives*, ed. Susan Rubin Suleiman (Cambridge: Harvard University Press, 1986), 99–118.

8. See, for example, David Herlihy's analysis of the relationship between increased veneration of Mary and cultural attitudes toward the function of motherhood in the twelfth century (*Medieval Households* [Cambridge: Harvard University Press, 1985], 121). Susan Groag Bell proposes that the frequent appearance in the late Middle Ages of images of the Virgin Mary surrounded by books or reading can be explained in terms of their artists' intent to portray Mary in relation to the habits of their patrons ("Medieval Women Book Owners: Arbiters of Lay Piety and Ambassadors of Culture," in *Women and Power in the Middle Ages*, ed. Mary Erler and Maryanne Kowaleski [Athens: University of Georgia Press, 1988], 168–77).

9. See the comments by Martha C. Howell on the relationship of literary representations to the lives of historical women, in *Women, Production, and Patriarchy in Late Medieval Cities* (Chicago and London: University of Chicago Press, 1986), 182–83.

10. Flanigan provides a useful summary of these earlier views in "Liminality, Carnival, and Social Structure," 43–47. Other recent interpretations of the social instrumentality of English biblical drama include Kathleen M. Ashley, "Image and Ideology: Saint Anne in Late Medieval Drama and Narrative," in *Interpreting Cultural Symbols: Saint Anne in Late Medieval Society*, ed. Ashley and Pamela Sheingorn (Athens: University of Georgia Press, 1990), 111–30; Peter W. Travis, "The Social Body of the Dramatic Christ in Medieval England," in *Early Drama to 1600*, ed. Albert H. Tricomi, *Acta*, vol. 13 (Binghamton: State University of New York Center for Medieval and Early Renaissance Studies, 1987 [for 1985]), 17–36.

11. Two recent exceptions are Gerald Kinneavy's brief but probing "Portrayal of Women in the York Plays," *Medieval Feminist Newsletter* 9 (Summer 1990):

10–12; and Ruth Evans's forthcoming essay "Feminist Re-enactments: Gender and the Towneley *Uxor Noe*," in *A Wyf Ther Was . . .* , ed. Juliette Dor. I am grateful to Dr. Evans for providing me with a copy of her article and for her very generous and valuable comments on this essay. See also my article "A Feminist Approach to the Corpus Christi Cycles," in *Approaches to Teaching Medieval English Drama*, ed. Richard K. Emmerson (New York: Modern Language Association, 1990), 79–89.

12. For the apocrypha, see *Ante-Nicene Christian Library*, ed. Alexander Roberts and James Donaldson, vol. 16, *Apocryphal Gospels, Acts, and Revelations*, trans. Alexander Walker (Edinburgh: T. and T. Clark, 1870): *Protevangelium*, 1–15, and *Pseudo-Matthew*, 16–52. On the debt of these cycle episodes to traditions of Scripture and its interpretation, see Woolf, *English Mystery Plays*, 169–73; and Walsh, "Divine Cuckold," 280, 285–86. Both Woolf and Walsh cite the work of Albert S. Cook, "A Remote Analogue to the Miracle Play," *JEGP* 4 (1902): 421–51; see also Hemingway, *English Nativity Plays*, 250–53. The similarities between the marital situation of Joseph and Mary and the plights of old husbands and young wives in vernacular literature is discussed by Deasy, *St. Joseph*, 62–83. On the development of Joseph as a comic figure in art, see Erwin Panofsky, *Early Netherlandish Painting*, 2 vols. (New York: Harper and Row, 1971), 1:70, 105.

13. Walsh notes that English vernacular works do not elaborate Joseph's Trouble with Mary ("Divine Cuckold," 286). I am thinking here of works such as the *Meditationes vitae christi*, the *Speculum humanae salvationis*, the *Legenda aurea*, the *Stanzaic Life of Christ*, the Middle English lives of Saint Anne, and John Lydgate's *Life of our Lady*.

14. Michael P. Carroll, *The Cult of the Virgin Mary: Psychological Origins* (Princeton: Princeton University Press, 1986), 6–7; Marina Warner, *Alone of All Her Sex: The Myth and the Cult of the Virgin Mary* (New York: Knopf, 1976), 34–49. For a good overview of Marian theology see Warner and Hilda Graef, *Mary: A History of Doctrine and Devotion*, 2 vols. (London: Sheed and Ward, 1963–65).

15. In the figures of Old Testament poetry and prophecy the fathers of the Church found allegories of Mary's closed womb: she is the *porta clausa* of Ezekiel 44:2, the *hortus conclusus* and *fons signatus* of Canticles 4:12, and the Temple of Solomon of I Kings 6. Famous epithets of Marian praise, these tropes of Marian hermeneutics informed scriptural commentary, liturgy, and Latin and vernacular writings. By the late Middle Ages, images and metaphors of enclosure as figures for Marian purity were commonplaces of dogma and devotion, appearing in pictorial iconography, lyric poetry, and a wide variety of devotional texts. For example, the fifteenth-century Benedictine monk John Lydgate, whose *Life of our Lady* is a compendium of Marian tropes, returns frequently in that work to the figural and the physical meanings of Mary's body; she is the "chaste toure," the "holy tabernacle," the sweet "closet," and the "hous of yvour" (*A Critical Edition of John Lydgate's Life of our Lady*, ed. Joseph A. Lauritis, Ralph A. Klinefelter, Vernon Gallagher [Pittsburgh: Duquesne University Press, 1961]). Gibson discusses figures for Mary's closed womb in "'Porta Haec Clausa Erit,'" 142–50.

16. The N-Town plays show a special preoccupation with Mary's enclosed

body; see, for example, p. 67, ll. 41–48; pp. 122–23, ll. 316, 333; and p. 408, l. 511. See also *York Plays*, p. 394, l. 110; and *Chester Mystery Cycle*, p. 150, l. 556.

17. Mary Douglas, *Purity and Danger: An Analysis of Concepts of Pollution and Taboo* (Harmondsworth: Penguin, 1970). The symbolic significance of Mary generally is aptly characterized by Julia Kristeva, who calls her "one of the most powerful imaginary constructs known in the history of civilizations" ("*Stabat mater*," *Kristeva Reader*, ed. Toril Moi [New York: Columbia University Press, 1986], 163).

18. Douglas, *Purity and Danger*, 13–14. See also Kirsten Hastrup, "The Semantics of Biology: Virginity," in *Defining Females: The Nature of Woman in Society*, ed. Shirley Ardener (New York: John Wiley and Sons, 1978), 49.

19. Douglas, *Purity and Danger*, 14.

20. Ibid., 144–45, 12; see Hastrup's comments on Douglas, "Semantics of Biology," 51–52.

21. On the power and dangers of the female body from the perspective of cross-cultural anthropology, see Peggy Reeves Sanday, *Female Power and Male Dominance: On the Origins of Sexual Inequality* (Cambridge: Cambridge University Press, 1981), 91–92; and Peter Stallybrass, "Reading the Body: *The Revenger's Tragedy* and the Jacobean Theatre of Consumption," *Renaissance Drama* 18 (1987): 142. Also helpful here are the observations by Miles, *Carnal Knowing*, 17–18.

22. Caroline Walker Bynum, "The Female Body and Religious Practice in the Later Middle Ages," in *Fragments for a History of the Human Body*, ed. Michel Feher, with Ramona Naddaff and Nadia Tazi (New York: Zone Books, 1989), part 1, pp. 186, 212 n. 98. See also Karma Lochrie, "The Language of Transgression: Body, Flesh, and Word in Mystical Discourse," in *Speaking Two Languages: Traditional Disciplines and Contemporary Theory in Medieval Studies*, ed. Allen J. Frantzen (Albany: State University of New York Press, 1991), 124–25.

23. Though she tends to see Mary's virginity as influential primarily in negative aspects, the view of Marina Warner is helpful here (*Alone of All Her Sex*, 67). See also John A. Phillips, *Eve: The History of an Idea* (San Francisco: Harper and Row, 1984), 143.

24. See *York Plays*, p. 120, ll. 123–38; *N-Town Play*, p. 126, ll. 67–73; Lydgate, *Life of Our Lady*, bk. 2: 1208–28; *The Middle English Stanzaic Versions of the Life of Saint Anne*, ed. Roscoe E. Parker, EETS, o.s. 174 (London: Oxford University Press, 1928), p. 20, ll. 745–69.

25. *York Plays*, pp. 119–22, ll. 94, 103, 108, 158, 167, 177, 187, 198, and 207. In the N-Town Troubles play, Joseph reports the disturbing evidence three times in the short space of ten lines (pp. 124–25, ll. 26, 30, 35).

26. All the cycles make reference to the imbalanced marital situation of Joseph and Mary; see *Two Coventry Corpus Christi Plays*, p. 5, ll. 133–35; *Chester Mystery Cycle*, p. 102, ll. 125–26; *York Plays*, p. 117, ll. 11–12; *Towneley Plays*, p. 90, ll. 161–66, 170. A good recent work detailing the interplay of misogynist and misogamous discourses is that of Katharina M. Wilson and Elizabeth M. Makowski, *Wykkyd Wyves and the Woes of Marriage: Misogamous Literature from Juvenal to Chaucer* (Albany: State University of New York Press, 1990).

27. See James A. Brundage, "Prostitution in the Medieval Canon Law," in *Sisters and Workers in the Middle Ages*, ed. Judith M. Bennett et al. (Chicago: Uni-

versity of Chicago Press, 1990), 86–87. Joseph's gesture derides an aspect of Mary's nature that the writers of the nondramatic infancy narratives frequently emphasized: that Mary was so pure and free of sin herself that she effected purity in others. See *A Stanzaic Life of Christ*, ed. Frances A. Foster, EETS, o.s. 166 (London: Humphrey Milford, 1926; rpt., New York: Kraus, 1971), pp. 98–99, ll. 2911–20; Lydgate, *Life of our Lady*, bk. 1: 288–94; *Mirour of Mans Saluacioun*, ed. Avril Henry (Aldershot: Scolar Press, 1986), p. 65, ll. 890–902.

28. Roberta L. Krueger, "Constructing Sexual Identities in the High Middle Ages: The Didactic Poetry of Robert de Blois," *Paragraph* 13 (1990): 107.

29. *York Plays*, pp. 164–65, ll. 147–48, 159–72; *Towneley Plays*, p. 164, ll. 131–50.

30. On the similarities between the second part of the Weavers' pageant and the Christ among the Doctors episode in York, Towneley, and Chester, see *Two Coventry Corpus Christi Plays*, xxviii–xxxiv; and *Chester Mystery Cycle* 2:160–72.

31. Kolve, *The Play Called Corpus Christi*, 249, 252.

32. Woolf, *English Mystery Plays*, 200.

33. Similarly, the Digby play of "Candlemas and the Killing of the Children of Israel" juxtaposes the Purification and the Massacre of the Innocents to dramatize gender conflict in relation to both female and male corporeality and social identity. I am presently writing a book on gender and early English drama that discusses this play in relation to the theme of gender struggle in the Innocents' plays.

34. Hastrup, "Semantics of Biology," 50.

35. Ibid., 52.

36. Discussing the Towneley Annuciation in light of cultural models propounded by symbolic anthropology and social theory, Clifford Flanigan makes a similar point in "Liminality, Carnival, and Social Structure." Flanigan argues that the Troubles episode illustrates the potential for late medieval biblical drama simultaneously to reinforce dominant ideologies and to critique social structures and practices. In his analysis, the Troubles episode engages recognized models for ideal conjugal relationships while also hinting at "taboos against marriage across age barriers" (60). The play thus invokes a subversive cultural practice while also appearing to authorize it because the practice is attributed to Joseph and Mary, who, Flanigan argues, otherwise serve an idealized exemplary function. Flanigan's is the only analysis of the infancy plays I have encountered that approaches, albeit from a very different direction, the issues discussed in this essay.

37. See also *York Plays*, p. 118, l. 55; *N-Town Play*, p. 127, l. 108; *Two Coventry Corpus Christi Plays*, p. 5, l. 114; *Chester Mystery Cycle*, p. 102, l. 133.

38. Barbara Hanawalt, *The Ties that Bound* (New York: Oxford University Press, 1986), 103; see also pp. 156 and 196. The frequency of illegitimacy is very difficult to determine; among the English peasantry, states Hanawalt, the number of premarital pregnancies and illegitimate births is "impossible to know" (196), and records from the sixteenth century "suggest that only about 3 percent of the births were illegitimate" (103). Evidence from a slightly later period shows rates changing over the course of the seventeenth century; see Susan Amussen, *An Ordered Society: Gender and Class in Early Modern England* (Oxford: Basil Blackwell, 1988), 132. Rates of illegitimate births of course are thoroughly determined by the

processes and protocols of reporting. On this topic generally, see Peter Laslett, "Long-term Trends in Bastardy in England," in his *Family Life and Illicit Love in Earlier Generations* (Cambridge: Cambridge University Press, 1977), 102–55.

39. Hanawalt, *The Ties that Bound*, 73; the quotation is from R. H. Helmholz, "Bastardy Litigation in Medieval England," *American Journal of Legal History* 13 (1969): 370–71.

40. In the N-Town Trial play the transgression of which Joseph and Mary are accused corresponds to one of the criteria, identified by Peter Laslett, for establishing illegitimacy in early modern England, namely, procreation by avowed celibates ("Introduction: Comparing Illegitimacy over Time and Between Cultures," *Bastardy and Its Comparative History*, ed. Laslett, Karla Oostervenn, and Richard M. Smith (Cambridge: Harvard University Press, 1980), 7.

41. On the efforts of people to avoid accusations or discovery of engendering illegitimate children, see Amussen, *An Ordered Society*, 111–117.

42. Alan Macfarlane, "Illegitimacy and Illegitimates in English History," in *Bastardy and Its Comparative History*, ed. Laslett et al., 75. See also Madeleine Jeay, "Sexuality and Family in Fifteenth-Century France: Are Literary Sources a Mask or a Mirror?" *Journal of Family History* 4 (1979): 340. On the general disordering of the household by illegitimacy, see Amussen, *An Ordered Society*, 111. Hanawalt's remarks on the relationship between bastardy and inheritance suggest a more tolerant view of illegitimacy in relation to economic concerns; see *The Ties that Bound*, 72–73.

43. Laslett, "Introduction: Comparing Illegitimacy," 8.

44. To my knowledge, the direct connection between the York Troubles play and charivari has not been noted; see Beadle's endnotes, *York Plays*, 425. On the striking of pots and pans in charivari, see Claude Gauvard and Altan Gokalp, "Les Conduits de bruit et leur signification à la fin du Moyen Age: Le Charivari," *Annales E.S.C.* 29 (1974): 699; and on charivari generally, see Edward P. Thompson, "'Rough Music': Le Charivari anglais," *Annales E.S.C.* 27 (1972): 285–312.

45. Gauvard and Gokalp, "Les Conduits de bruit," 698–99, 703; Natalie Zemon Davis, "The Reasons of Misrule," in her *Society and Culture in Early Modern France: Eight Essays* (Stanford: Stanford University Press, 1975), 116–117; Amussen, *An Ordered Society*, 118; Thompson, "'Rough Music,'" 301.

46. The definition of charivari is from Gauvard and Gokalp, "Les Conduits de bruit," 693.

47. The York play's linking of the marital situation of Joseph and Mary with the contemporary social ritual of charivari is not unique. Christiane Klapisch-Zuber observes, for example, that Tuscan painters of the fourteenth and fifteenth centuries frequently represented the *Sposalizio*, or Marriage of the Virgin, by referencing contemporary rituals of engagement and marriage that specifically registered intergenerational conflict between young bachelors and old men. They thereby lent to the marriage of old Joseph and young Mary one classical element of the charivari (Christiane Klapisch-Zuber, "Zacharias, or the Ousted Father: Nuptial Rites in Tuscany between Giotto and the Council of Trent," in her *Women, Family, and Ritual in Renaissance Italy*, trans. Lydia G. Cochrane [Chicago: University of Chicago Press, 1985], 178–212, especially 204–6).

48. This characterization of the sexual mores of late medieval society is based on James A. Brundage, *Law, Sex, and Christian Society in Medieval Europe* (Chicago: University of Chicago Press, 1987); R. H. Helmholz, *Marriage Litigation in Medieval England* (Cambridge: Cambridge University Press, 1974); Richard M. Wunderli, *London Church Courts and Society on the Eve of the Reformation* (Cambridge, Mass.: Medieval Academy of America, 1981); and Peter Laslett, *Family Life and Illicit Love*.

49. The Trial of Joseph and Mary is a rare subject in Western art and drama; in English drama it is unique to the N-Town plays. See the commentary on the play by Woolf, *English Mystery Plays*, 174–77; Walsh, "Divine Cuckold," 290–91; Richard Axton, *European Drama of the Early Middle Ages* (London: Hutchinson University Library, 1974), 175–76; and Lynn Squires, "Law and Disorder in *Ludus Coventriae*," in *The Drama of the Middle Ages: Comparative and Critical Essays*, ed. Clifford Davidson, C. J. Gianakaris, and John H. Stroupe (New York: AMS Press, 1982), 277–78. Several late medieval nondramatic texts do include the episode; see the *Life of Saint Anne* found in University of Minnesota Ms. Z. 822, N. 81 (*Middle English Stanzaic Versions of the Life of Saint Anne*, ed. Parker, pp. 21–23, ll. 799–876); and Lydgate, *Life of our Lady*, bk. 2: 1348–1592.

50. Woolf, *English Mystery Plays*, 177; Squires, "Law and Disorder," 277; Axton, *European Drama*, 175–76.

51. Brundage, *Law, Sex, and Christian Society*, 544–45. For a detailed discussion of sexual crimes brought before London commissary courts in the later Middle Ages, see Wunderli, *London Church Courts*, 81–102.

52. Wunderli, *London Church Courts*, 81. Though Wunderli's evidence is drawn largely from London commissary court records, he also observes the more general importance given to concepts of good fame and ill fame in a justice system in which canon law permitted a person "to be accused by ill fame alone" (40). On the important role of witnesses in the execution of canon law, see also Brundage, *Law, Sex, and Christian Society*, 253; and Helmholz, *Marriage Litigation in Medieval England*, 155–56.

53. See lines 106, 108, 141–42, 183, 185, 186, 207, 209, 275, 277–278. See also Wunderli, *London Church Courts*, 40.

54. One Middle English life of Saint Anne containing the trial episode describes circumstances resembling those of the N-Town version, stating that "the folke" who dwelled near Joseph and Mary suspected her pregnancy and brought Joseph to appear before the bishop; *The Middle English Stanzaic Versions of the Life of Saint Anne*, p. 21, ll. 799–807. The *Holkham Bible Picture Book*, an East Anglian work from the early fourteenth century, includes backbiting Jews who provoke the Troubles scene but not the Trial: "Marie est grose ne est pas te tey. / E la fet a contre la ley. / E a fet a tey grant tort / Ele est digne de sufrir mort" (quoted in Walsh, "Divine Cuckold," 284).

55. Apart from the general consensus on the East Anglian origin of the N-Town plays, there is little agreement on their auspices. For one provocative view, see Gail McMurray Gibson, "John Lydgate, Bury St. Edmunds and the N-Town Cycle," *Speculum* 56 (1981): 56–90. My own view is that N-Town is a collection of plays from multiple origins, probably a mixture of community-based

theater and plays from ecclesiastical auspices. The Trial of Joseph and Mary appears to be a freestanding play, perhaps an example of parish drama.

56. Amussen, *An Ordered Society*, 97–104; and see her "Feminin/Masculin: Le Genre dans l'Angleterre de l'époque moderne," *Annales ESC* 40 (1985): 269–87. Though Amussen's evidence focuses on the late sixteenth and seventeenth centuries and hence postdates the N-Town play, I am prompted to pursue her findings in relation to N-Town because of the relative stability of both ecclesiastical and civil regulation of sexual practices in late medieval and early modern England; see Helmholz, *Marriage Litigation in Medieval England*, 3.

57. Amussen, "Feminin/Masculin," 272–73, 280–82.

58. Ibid., 270, 272, 280–82.

59. Like many of their counterparts in real-life defamation cases, the Detractors hurl insults at Joseph and Mary that are largely sexual in nature, insults emphasizing different roles for men and women in the sex and gender system. Mary is a "bysmare" and a "wench" who can "cause A yonge man to have delyght"; called a cuckold six different times, Joseph bears the additional burden of having to "faderyn A-nother mannys chylde." Amussen notes of defamation cases that while sexual insults "predominated for both women and men," the insults directed at men had more social implications, while those aimed at women "had more concrete sexual implications." Thus accusations of cuckoldry also comment on household order, while the label of say, "bysmare" is "more narrowly rooted in sexual behavior" (*An Ordered Society*, 102–3). See also Wunderli, *London Church Courts*, 79.

60. This characterization of the concept of essence is adapted from Diana Fuss, *Essentially Speaking: Feminism, Nature, and Difference* (New York: Routledge, 1989), 21. In formulating this characterization of Marian representations in the infancy plays, I have also found helpful Elizabeth V. Spelman, *Inessential Woman: Problems of Exclusion in Feminist Thought* (Boston: Beacon Press, 1988).

61. McLaughlin, "Equality of Souls," 245–51; Sheila Fisher, "Taken Men and Token Women in *Sir Gawain and the Green Knight*," in *Seeking the Woman in Late Medieval and Renaissance Writings*, ed. Sheila Fisher and Janet E. Halley (Knoxville: University of Tennessee Press, 1989), 76. But see also Charles Wood, "The Doctors' Dilemma: Sin, Salvation, and the Menstrual Cycle in Medieval Thought," *Speculum* 56 (1981): 726–27.

62. McLaughlin, "Equality of Souls," 246. For a slightly different yet compatible view, see the assessment of the late medieval Marian ideal by Kathleen Casey, "The Cheshire Cat: Reconstructing the Experience of Medieval Women," in *Liberating Women's History: Theoretical and Critical Essays*, ed. Berenice A. Carroll (Urbana: University of Illinois Press, 1976), 240–41.

63. McLaughlin, "Equality of Souls," 251.

64. Phillips, *Eve: The History of an Idea*, 146.

65. Kristeva, "*Stabat mater*," 181; see also Kristeva's comments on the construction of Mary in the West, 163–65.

66. Mieke Bal, "Sexuality, Sin and Sorrow: The Emergence of the Female Character (A Reading of Genesis 1–3)," *Poetics Today* 6 (1985): 39. Chris Weedon essentializes the masochism of virginity while arguing for the social production of

the female body (*Feminist Criticism and Poststructuralist Theory* [Oxford: Basil Blackwell, 1987], 23).

67. Lydgate, *Life of Our Lady*, bk. 3: 194–95.

68. Caroline Walker Bynum, *Holy Feast and Holy Fast: The Religious Significance of Food to Medieval Women* (Berkeley: University of California Press, 1987), 29; Ellen Ross and Rayna Rapp, "Sex and Society: A Research Note from Social History and Anthropology," *Comparative Studies in Society and History* 23 (1981): 54–58. See also Beatrice Gottlieb, "The Problem of Feminism in the Fifteenth Century," in *Women of the Medieval World*, ed. Julius Kirshner and Suzanne F. Wemple (Oxford: Basil Blackwell, 1985), 337–74; Natalie Zemon Davis, "'Women's History' in Transition: The European Case," *Feminist Studies* 3 (1976): 90–93; Elizabeth Alvilda Petroff, "Introduction," in her *Medieval Women's Visionary Literature* (New York: Oxford University Press, 1986), 3–53; Ashley and Sheingorn, "Introduction," in *Interpreting Cultural Symbols*, ed. Ashley and Sheingorn, 1–6.

69. This aspect of the Mary cult has been richly set forth by Gail McMurray Gibson, *The Theater of Devotion: East Anglian Drama and Society in the Late Middle Ages* (Chicago: University of Chicago Press, 1989), 137–76.

70. See Penny S. Gold, "The Marriage of Mary and Joseph in the Twelfth-Century Ideology of Marriage," in *Sexual Practices and the Medieval Church*, ed. Vern L. Bullough and James Brundage (Buffalo: Prometheus Books, 1982), 102–17.

71. *The Liber Celestis of St. Bridget of Sweden*, ed. Roger Ellis, EETS, o.s. 291 (Oxford: Oxford University Press, 1987), 1:12, 15.

72. See Gibson, *Theater of Devotion*, 144.

73. Wood, "The Doctors' Dilemma," 717–27.

74. Ibid., 726.

75. I am invoking here the analysis of the transgressive functions of symbolic inversion offered by Peter Stallybrass and Allon White, *The Politics and Poetics of Transgression* (Ithaca: Cornell University Press, 1986), 58.

76. Ibid., 3.

77. Ibid., 16.

78. Walsh, "Divine Cuckold," 297.

Sarah Stanbury

Feminist Masterplots: The Gaze on the Body of *Pearl*'s Dead Girl

One of the most haunting parables of loss is the story of Orpheus, which Ovid tells in Book 10 of *The Metamorphoses*. Looking back in a forbidden glance at Eurydice, Orpheus reaches out his arms to hold on to her retreating shade. Finding he holds nothing, he stares dazed, turned, in effect, to stone:

> When Orpheus saw his wife go down to Death,
> Twice dead, twice lost, he stared like someone dazed.
> He seemed to be like him who saw the fighting
> Three-headed Dog led out by Hercules
> In chains, a six-eyed monster spitting bile;
> The man was paralyzed and fear ran through him
> Until his very body turned to stone.[1]

The simile that Ovid chooses as a figure of Orpheus's gaze on a lost woman is not, as we might expect, one of emptiness, but one of horror and petrification, an image that evokes the story of Medusa. As it is to those who gaze on the Gorgon, the consequence to Orpheus of looking is paralysis, the body's very substance hardened at the spot.

Describing this scene in his famous essay "The Gaze of Orpheus," Maurice Blanchot maintains that the moment Orpheus looks at the shade of Eurydice is the moment of his liberation, the instant that binds inspiration to desire: "Orpheus' gaze is the extreme moment of freedom, the moment in which he frees himself of himself and—what is more important—frees the work of his concern. . . . So everything is at stake in the decision to gaze."[2] What is at stake, that is to say, is poetic inspiration; only through losing a woman (a loss effected by Orpheus's own decision to look) can Orpheus be initiated into poetry. Following the loss of Eurydice, we may recall, Orpheus withholds himself from women and in the glade sings a series of tales that complete the work of mourning by telling stories of love similar to his own:[3] love is lost, and the lover—transformed into tree or flower, as in the tales of Cyparissus, Apollo and Hyacinthus, Cinyras and Myrrha, Venus and Adonis—is metamorphosed into a monument to love.

The figure of the body of the poet turned to stone remains a strange one, however, for it would also seem to imply that Orpheus is so immobilized by his own desiring gaze that he becomes, for a moment, an object, a specular and frozen monument to his own inability to hold the present moment. Freud's reading of the Ovidian tale of Medusa, however, provides an interpretation of the workings of the male gaze that might be applicable as well to the complex interplay of terror and creative power engendered by the gaze of Orpheus. In his essay "Medusa's Head," Freud equates rigidity, being "stiff with terror," with the excitation of the primal look on female mutilation. Being "turned to stone," according to Freud's extraordinary reading of Perseus's confrontation with the Gorgon, actually doubles as an image of male visual desire:

> The sight of Medusa's head makes the spectator stiff with terror, turns him to stone. Observe that we have here once again the same origin from the castration complex and the same transformation of affect! For becoming stiff means an erection. Thus in the original situation it offers consolation to the spectator: he is still in possession of a penis, and the stiffening reassures him of the fact.[4]

In this image, petrification may result in reconfigured sexuality, but hardly in impotence. Freud's male spectator, rigid with the terror at the sight of his own potential emasculation in a replay of the castration drama, is also tumescent, empowered organically by his severance and exclusion from the feminine.[5]

Freud's comments on the ways in which the male spectator's gaze on the Medusa defines his singularity and empowerment through a replay of primal loss can help us understand Blanchot's argument that the gaze of Orpheus is liberating. Like the look on Medusa, Orpheus's stare upon the vanished Eurydice seems to be, Ovid's simile implies, a look of horror on something monstrous—loss figured as presence, a six-eyed monster spitting bile. In this image her disappearing shade is materialized as an action, at once devastating and empowering, on and of his own body. From this moment Orpheus cloisters his sexuality, keeps himself from women; and from the tumescence of that cloistering, he memorializes his loss in poetry.

Freud's—and Blanchot's—argument that male autonomy and creative power derives, in part, from violent or painful separation from a woman has also been central to the arguments of recent studies of the psychoanalytic workings of elegiac poetry. In *The English Elegy*, for instance, Peter Sacks draws on studies of mourning by Freud and others to argue that the work of mourning, which involves repeated and even obsessive meditation on the lost object, achieves its ends by recalling our first loss: the child's severance from the mother. The elegy, a poetic work of mourning that is almost always voiced by a male speaker, also replays the desire and terror of this first or primal loss.[6] The loss of the mother, in turn, gives a distinctive mark to elegiac imagery, such as the frequent images of violent natural metamorphosis and of maimed male sexuality. Because the work of mourning replays the earliest traumas in which the body is inscribed as separate (the incest taboo prohibiting maternal incest; the castration threat that defines the female body as an object of taboo and mutilation and that initiates male autonomy through a potential physical trauma to his own body), the elegy, Sacks implies, is a profoundly material and embodied form, instantiated between substance and absence, between the desiring male body and the absent and even genitally mutilated feminine form.

In his discussion of the work of mourning, Sacks does not discuss the gaze as such, though an embodied elegiac drama is explicit in the Freudian and Lacanian paradigms of loss on which he draws: the mirror stage and the *fort-da* game through which the child comes to identify self and not-self, body and not body.[7] The relationship between a male gaze and female body, a relationship shaped by a paternal symbolic order that designates the maternal body as a site of lack and of ever-displaced desire, has been important, however, to feminist studies of gender identity, and central to feminist work on film theory The lines of sight of Hollywood cinema, as film theorists Laura Mulvey, Mary Ann Doane, E. Ann Kaplan, and others have argued, are monolithically masculine and are structured to replay and disavow originary losses that constitute the male self as separate.[8] The body of woman plays a key role in organizing male lines of sight, Mulvey argues:

> But in psychoanalytic terms, the female figure poses a deeper problem. She also connotes something that the look continually circles around but disavows: her lack of a penis, implying a threat of castration and hence unpleasure. Ultimately the meaning of woman is sexual difference, the absence of

the penis as visually ascertainable, the material evidence on which is based the castration complex essential for the organisation of entrance to the symbolic order and the law of the father. Thus the woman as icon, displayed for the gaze and enjoyment of men, the active controllers of the look, always threatens to evoke the anxiety it originally signified.[9]

This formulation, modeled on work by Freud and Lacan, suggests that the visual assertions of the masculine gaze are structured, at least in part, by castration anxieties; representation of the male gaze, that is to way, is etiologically located in anxieties about the female body. Cinema, according to this feminist "masterplot," enacts a drama of disavowal in which the spectator and camera lens jointly, indeed collusively, watch from a masculine position. This placement defines the woman on the screen through a representational system of absences—a drama of lack—and her form and voice are shaped accordingly. The woman's body on the screen—exposed, objectified, fetishized—is displayed to expose and contain her danger, the threat she projects of castration.

If we return for a moment to the Ovidian underworld, we can bring to Orpheus's visual drama an expanded context for understanding how the singer's poetic gifts originate in his horrified look at the disappearing body of a woman. This paradoxical interplay between grief and danger, and between male visual entitlement and female corporeal loss, may also be useful for understanding the gendered gaze in the medieval dream vision. This genre, which is almost exclusively male in voice, frequently has its origins in the loss of a woman: the dead Beatrice, reincarnated in Dante's *Comedy*; or Chaucer's Blanche (as Louise Fradenburg has pointed out in an essay on the political poetics of loss and as Gayle Margherita describes elsewhere in this volume), mastered through the work of mourning.[10]

Arguments about the psychoanalytic construction of male lines of sight may be particularly applicable to the Middle English *Pearl*. Like Orpheus, a bereaved lover who sings stories of lovers, the *Pearl* narrator comes to his garden to mourn the death of a girl, and there attempts to resolve his loss through repeated encounters with her transformed body. The elegiac *and* spiritual processes of this medieval dream vision are intricately structured by gendered prerogatives and taboos that codify lines of sight. The Dreamer's desire, that is to say, is shaped through tropes that are crucially gendered to play out a visual drama about the loss of a female body. Precisely *what* that lost body signifies and to whom it belongs, however, are central questions I would like to address in this essay. In so doing, I will also question both the phallic premise and the historical grounding of "feminist masterplots" that axiomatically equate loss with castration and locate the origin of male anxieties about female bodies in a genital threat.

The formulation by Laura Mulvey and others that the meaning of woman is sexual difference nevertheless offers a seductively neat masterplot for a psychoanalytic reading of the ocular/bodily poetics of *Pearl*. This highly visual poem, explicitly about female loss (the Dreamer's dead daughter), describes a dramatic bodily displacement similar to the disavowing "epistemological division" that feminist film theorists claim is central to the representation of male vision and female bodies in modern cinematic production.[11] To see his lost daughter in reincorporated form, the Dreamer severs his body from his gaze: his body lies asleep in the garden, the *erber* where she presumably is buried, as his perceptual self wanders in a dream. From his first sight of his transformed daughter, he quickly embarks on a journey of visual discovery. The poem becomes from this point an extraordinary excursus in visual penetration. The Dreamer becomes the true scopophilic, enraptured with sight; even from the beginning when he finds himself in the Otherworld, he yearns to see "ay more and more."[12] The experience of looking in, from without, even doubly removed (his visionary self across the stream; his body, asleep in the *erber*, severed from his dream), is ecstatic, a kind of visual *jouissance* that culminates in his attempt to cross the stream and fracture the divide between his body and the object of his gaze.[13]

The girl who appears in his dream also seems to be shaped through a replay of a drama of disavowal: loss figured as presence. Reading her incarnation through Mulvey's masterplot, we might argue that the male spectator looking at her is adopting both of two alternatives for dealing with the threat posed by the woman's body: the first, according to Mulvey, is "preoccupation with the re-enactment of the original trauma (investigating the woman, demystifying her mystery)," and the second is "fetishistic scopophilia," disavowing castration by turning the woman into idealized object, such as the female movie star.[14] In the *visio* of *Pearl*, the incarnation of the Dreamer's lost daughter seems to conform with remarkable precision to both of Mulvey's options. In the long central debate, which is ordered through his questions about her and her explanations, the Dreamer becomes an inquisitor, seeking to know first who she is, "Art þou my perle þat I haf playned" (242), and then what kind of life she leads (392), whether she is the queen of heaven (423) and how that can be possible (474), who her spouse is (755), and where she lives (936). Throughout, however, the object of his investigation remains the starlet, the lost infant reconfigured as idealized courtly maiden, white as ivory (178), whiter than whale's bone (212), even multiplied, like Warhol's pop fetish Marilyn, into a hundred thousand duplicate images.[15]

If we follow the psychoanalytic paradigm of the gaze of Orpheus—the male gaze that is constructed around a threat of castration—in reading the Dreamer's visual journey, it leads us with an almost uncanny directness to a dramatically new reading for the final, violent moment of the dream. The Dreamer awakens when he tries to cross the stream; he tries to cross (even though he might die in the attempt, "þaȝ I ther swalte" [1160]) because he has seen the maiden, one of the hundred thousand brides of Christ, in the company of the lamb. But this enthroned lamb, a conventional motif in apocalyptic imagery, is endowed with a wound, a bleeding gash torn in its side:

> Bot a wounde ful wyde and weete con wyse
> Anende hys hert, þurȝ hyde torente.
> Of his quyte syde his blod outsprent.
>
> (1135–37)

The bleeding wound, as Rosalind Field has pointed out, is an addition to the Apocalypse source.[16] In her study of forty illustrated apocalypses, Field notes that the image, which appears in only twelve out of the forty manuscripts, is not an artistic commonplace. Of those manuscripts that include the image, in only one, an English Apocalypse dating from 1340, does she find the wounded lamb not only in the early adoration scenes, but also, as in *Pearl*, within the New Jerusalem.

Field's study of the history of the image of the bleeding lamb suggests that its appearance in *Pearl* is highly self-conscious. The location of this image of violence and pity at the end of the Dreamer's visionary quest allows, Field claims, rich possibilities for a meditation on the Passion and the wounds of Christ. The placement of a bleeding lamb within the New Jerusalem also allows the Dreamer's gaze to come to rest on an image that is complexly gendered, shaped by Christological imagery as well as by a feminized iconographic scheme. Not only is the image of the lamb fused with the vision of the girl conceptually through marriage and sequentially through the temporal logic of the Dreamer's gaze, the bleeding lamb is also metonymically allied with her body. Like the white pearl that stands in for the Maiden throughout the text, the lamb is garbed in white "wedeȝ" (1133); blood springs through a rent in his white side.

In his study of the psychoanalytic origins of elegiac form, Sacks describes the displacements that are necessary to the work of mourning: "Just as the child performs a voluntary symbolic castration to avoid death or what he fears as actual castration . . . so, too, the griever wounds his own sexuality, deflecting his desire, in order to erect a consoling figure for an ongoing, if displaced, generative power."[17] The bleeding lamb that the Dreamer sees as the culmination of his elegiac visual pilgrimage offers what Sacks describes as a displaced self-wound, giving us an extraordinarily condensed and materialized image of loss that is male Christologically, but female imagistically. The Dreamer's gaze, severed from his body as it reincarnates his lost daughter, penetrates the walls of the city to see an image of mutilation that is generated by and also productive of his sight and desire for her. His response to this vision, a response that shatters the visionary dream, is one of compassion and desire, what we might speak of as identity and alterity, seeing in the lamb a trauma of his own potential castration, seeing in the girl the Other, the feminine that repeatedly defines the male self as separate. This vision, of course, is *not* her; it is, however, an emblem of primal loss, the escutcheon (the genitalia *manqué*) of all the losses that women represent. The visual text replays that loss again and again, up to the climactic vision of Christ as wounded lamb that fractures the dream and propels the dreamer into a male community.

But Whose Body, Exactly, *Is* Lost?

When Orpheus goes to Hades to recover Eurydice, his lament moves the hearts of the underworld. The terms of her recovery belong also with him: he is not to look. But where, in this, is the gaze of Eurydice? Does she even want to return with Orpheus? And how does his gaze back over his shoulder appear to her? What does *she* see the moment he turns back— appetitive, desiring, hungering to visualize her into flesh?

If we were asked what the *Pearl* Maiden saw when the Dreamer reincarnated her in his vision, however, we could tell a very different story. Unlike Eurydice—about whom we might speculate that she fled, terrified, when she saw him looking at her that way—the *Pearl* Maiden looks at and speaks to the Dreamer with extraordinary visual and verbal authority. Even though we can locate the Maiden—investigated, fetishized by a voyeuristic visual program—within Mulvey's formulation, she is hardly erased. One of the most remarkable features of the Maiden's representation, in fact, is the visual and verbal power with which her embodied form is endowed, a feature she shares with female personifications in other medieval allegorical works. In cantos 30 and 31 of *Purgatorio*, for instance, the gaze of Beatrice is the center of Dante's "thousand desires hotter than flame" ("milli disiri più che fiamma"), and the power of her look, "which had already pierced me before I was out of my boyhood" ("che gà m'avea traffito / orima ch' io fuor di puerizia fosse") (30.41–42),[18] is recalled through his own remembrance and in *Purgatorio* 31 is invoked through the choral refrain, "Turn, Beatrice, turn thy holy eyes on thy faithful one" ("Volgi, Beatrice, volgi li occhi santi . . . al tuo fedele") (31.133–34). In Boethius's *Consolation of Philosophy*, Lady Philosophy also assumes a similar ocular command with her flashing eyes, the first feature Boethius describes. In the first prose she banishes the muses with the glare of her "burning eyes" and so astonishes Boethius that his own look is defeated: "My sight was so dimmed by tears that I could not tell who this woman of imperious authority might be, and I lay there astonished, my eyes staring at the earth, silently waiting to see what she would do."[19]

Similar to these other commanding female figures, the *Pearl* Maiden assumes extraordinary power through her verbal and visual authority. Not only is she seen: she sees him. Their encounter, in fact, first involves a complex series of returned gazes, each making the other a spectacle. After he spots her on the other side of the stream, he gazes on her, muses on her, marvels that she is one who is familiar to him. His appetitive stare—"On lengthe I loked to hyr there"—takes a jolt, however, when she raises her head:

> Þenne vereȝ ho vp her fayre frount,
> Hyr vysayge whyt as playn yuore:
> Þat stonge myn hert ful stray atount.
>
> (177–79)

Suddenly he is paralyzed, stunned by her look:

> More þen me lyste my drede aros.
> I stod ful stylle and dorste not calle;
> Wyth yȝen open and mouth ful close
> I stod as hende as hawk in halle.
>
> (181–84)

What follows is a long, highly ornamental enumeration of the pearls that encrust her clothing, a description that, according to Mulvey's argument, could be said to neutralize the threat of her authoritative gaze (and implicit castrating bodily mutilation) through a protracted, fragmenting, fetishizing blazon. The terms of the subsequent dialogue, however, are set by the Maiden's visual gestures, bowing her head or commanding with her gaze. When she lowers her head and bows womanlike, "in wommon lore" (236), he feels free to address her. That verbal ordering is soon reversed, however, when she rises:

That juel þenne in gemmeȝ gente
Vered vp her vyse wyth yȝen graye,
Set on her coroun of perle orient,
And soberly after þenne con ho say:
'Sir, ȝe haf your tale mystente.'

(253–57)

She replaces her crown, gazes at him with her gray eyes, and chastizes him for believing too literally in what he sees.

Within the formulation of lines of sight and loss provided by psychoanalysis and feminist film theory, how can we account for such visual assertiveness? Stephen Heath, describing the consequences to men of the woman's look, writes that the "reply given by psychoanalysis is from the phallus": "If the woman looks, the spectacle provokes, castration is in the air, the Medusa's head is not far off; thus, she must not look, is absorbed herself on the side of the seen, seeing herself seeing herself, Lacan's feminity."[20] Heath is describing a woman's gaze on a man and the threat projected by her look through its reversal of dominant systems of ocular power. When the Maiden looks in *Pearl*, we can similarly argue, her gaze provokes and initiates the dialogue, galvanizing an inquisitorial, scopophilic investigation that has its culminating moment in a vision of the very "Medusa's head"—female mutilation and lack as signified by the wounded lamb—that incited the investigation.

Yet Heath does not suggest this outcome. In his formulation, as in many of the descriptions of the monolithic cinematic "male gaze" provided by feminist film theory, the woman cannot look with authority: she is, as he says, "absorbed on the side of the seen." The response of Hollywood's classic cinema to the threat of woman's look has been, as Kaja Silverman argues, an ocular castration that excludes her from structures of power:

Thus, the female subject's gaze is depicted as partial, flawed, unreliable, and self-entrapping. She sees things that aren't there, bumps into walls, or loses control at the sight of the color red. And although her own look seldom hits the mark, woman is always on display before the male gaze. Indeed, she manifests so little resistance to that gaze that she often seems no more than an extension of it.[21]

This description, which may aptly describe Julia Roberts in *Pretty Woman* or Ingrid Bergman in the 1944 *Gaslight*, does not describe the girl of the *Pearl* Dreamer's vision, who corrects his speech and commands with her eyes—who challenges, that is to say, the authoritative strictures of his gaze with a focused and steady look.

A chief difficulty in accounting for empowered look within the story Mulvey might construct for the Dreamer about the male gaze and the fetishized female body resides within the difficulties that feminist film theory has in accounting for female subjectivity—and more specifically, for female visual mastery. One explanation, chiefly articulated by Linda Williams in her studies of horror films, is that the woman who looks does so transgressively or masochistically.[22] The threat of her look is neutralized through a masochistic reversal such that she is punished, often through the very unveiling of the taboo object: when Melanie opens the attic door in Hitchcock's *The Birds*, she collapses, disturbingly helpless before the attack of the birds, who stage over her passive body what can only be seen as a symbolic rape.[23] Other accounts of the woman's gaze suggest that she participates in a masquerade in which the positions she adopts oscillate between the seer and the seen, the appetitive male viewer and the object of his look.[24] Playing this masquerade, Mulvey claims, she occupies an unstable and oscillating position in which she takes on the masculine gaze, adopting a "phantasy of masculinization at cross-purposes with itself, restless in its transvestite clothes."[25]

Underlying these descriptions of feminine lines of sight is the assumption that they are shaped by a male norm, an assumption that is, as a growing number of critics are arguing, deeply problematic for feminism. The essentialized male gaze, a construct of a Freudian/Lacanian model of personality development that assumes culture is instituted in Lacan's third term, the Law of the Father or paternal prohibition of mother/son incest, leaves little room for a spectatrix.[26] According to Jackie Byars, writing in a volume that addresses the complex position of the female spectator,

within a theory based on Freudian psychoanalysis, as Mulvey's is, the male/masculine is active and normative, and there is no way to explain the female/

feminine except through this "norm." . . . A primary difficulty is the dominance in feminist film theory of Freudian and Lacanian theories of psychoanalysis, which describe personality development from a position which favours the masculine, and as such, operate conservatively to extend and naturalize the repression of women, defining "woman" in terms of aberrance and deviance and effectively obscuring any variant "voice."[27]

Byars and other film theorists, most notably Teresa de Lauretis and Kaja Silverman,[28] as well as feminist literary critics such as Patricia Waugh and philosophers such as Jane Flax and Judith Butler, have developed challenges to Freudian and Lacanian analytic theory, which locates the child's entry into language and culture in the discovery of the anatomical difference between the sexes—in the highly visual and bodily drama of the castration complex—rather than in earlier separations.[29] The limitation of the meaning of castration to the absence of a penis, Silverman suggests, is itself a project of disavowal that protects the male subject from acknowledging his own lack:

> Freud's emphasis upon the delayed nature of the castration crisis can be read . . . as a device for protecting the male subject from a painful and culturally disruptive confrontation with his own insufficiency. By granting a retroactive status to the little boy's "recognition" of woman's lack, and by making that recognition the effect of prohibition and threat, Freud implies that the idea of lack is so alien to male consciousness that it must be installed through paternal admonition.[30]

Applying her critique of Freud to the visual and auditory regimes of mainstream cinema, Silverman does not challenge the importance for feminist film studies of an ideology of lack or absence; what she *does* challenge is the location of lack specifically in the moment of discovery of anatomical difference. The castration complex, that is to say, offers a kind of masterplot for reading cinematic lines of sight, one that has evolved in tandem with what I have called the feminist masterplot of American literary and cinematic criticism of the last few decades: woman is the cultural Other; woman is the repressed and disappearing zone of narrative.

In the Middle English *Pearl*, the complex figurations of loss seem to replay the cinematic masterplot with remarkable precision. I would like to suggest, however, that it might be productive to follow the lead of Silverman, Waugh, Byars, and others in challenging the essentialized, ahistorical assumptions of an ego psychology based on the castration complex when we encounter the text's moments of resistance. In other words, I would like to reexamine the phallic model of spectatorship that Mulvey offers.

For while one might argue persuasively that the Maiden's authoritative gaze and voice are registered within the program of the Dreamer's attempt to master her through a complex voyeuristic and fetishizing visual itinerary, that reading subtly muffles her voice, screens her gaze, in essence absorbs her very presence within the drama of the Dreamer's story.

It is difficult, of course, to talk about her outside of that story: she is, after all, *his* dream. Yet within his fiction, her representation, up to the climactic moment in which she is yoked in marriage to the bleeding lamb, suggests desire for union rather than threat. Indeed, the image of the lamb, even as it evokes the female wound of the castration plot, is perceived as an image of desire, one that holds no resonance of damage to the Dreamer's own body. Whereas Orpheus's gaze on the loss of Eurydice evokes terror and petrification, being "turned to stone," the Dreamer's gaze on the lamb, the poem's central image of loss and desire, is tender and compassionate. When he sees the lamb, immediately before he sees the girl in its company, the Dreamer grieves,

> "Alas, þo3t I, who did þat spyt?
> Ani breste for bale a3t haf forbrent
> Er he þerto hade had delyt.
>
> (1138–40)

One might argue, of course, that the terror of the bleeding lamb is simply displaced; a less convoluted reading of the image, however, invites us to account for its evocation of a constellation of emotions that seem centered not in danger to the self but in empathy: grief, compassion, joy, and desire.

One explanation for the dual resonance of mutilation and desire in this image is provided by Nancy Chodorow's theories about the development of female gender identity. While Chodorow's work is based on Freud, she critiques his highly corporeal and androcentric drama for its elisions of preoedipal attachments. The primary loss, her ground-breaking work implies, is social rather than biological; this loss (structured in *Pearl* through the Dreamer's elegiac replay) is experienced not only as a potential loss to the self, the fear of genital mutilation through paternal admonition implied by the castration complex, but also as loss of union with the mother, the highly ambivalent primary severance that establishes separation and independence as central components of masculinity.[31]

Chodorow's etiology of sexual difference thus suggests that the castration complex recapitulates rather than initiates the recognition of sexual difference. It also implies that the image of the "castrated" woman would evoke first the pain of severance from a primal union, and only secondarily a fear of severance of one's own penis.[32] Freud's restriction of the image of castration explicitly to the absence of the penis rather than to the absence of the mother, however, disavows the power of that union and the pain of its loss.[33]

Chodorow's formulation seems particularly applicable to the description of the Dreamer's gaze on the wound in *Pearl*, for the wounded lamb that evokes the Dreamer's compassion quite clearly stands in for other feminine or at least feminized losses: the lost daughter that precipitates the visionary journey and the passionately desired courtly Maiden that the Dreamer immediately spots in the Lamb's company. The desire for union with an often metaphoric feminine is in fact central to medieval Christian imagery. As Caroline Walker Bynum's studies of medieval religious texts and iconography have shown, a complex system of feminizing epithets describe the body of Christ in the Middle Ages: his body on the Cross, an image of pain and desire, is passive, rent, exposed; his blood becomes milk in the chalice.[34]

Highly gendered language expressing a yearning for union also appears repeatedly in medieval Apocalypse cycles and in their commentaries, both of which, as scholars have shown, served as important sources for the final scenes of *Pearl*.[35] For instance, the Berengaudus Commentary, which often accompanied the illustrated Apocalypse cycles, explains that John worships the angel in Revelation at those moments when he has seen the union of Christ with his Church.[36] As I have argued elsewhere, this moment has remarkable parallels with the Dreamer's attempt to join the Maiden in *Pearl*.[37] For both John and the Dreamer, spiritual apotheosis is conflated and even confused with desire for a corporeal presence close at hand.

Pearl's Maiden, the lost little daughter who is allegorized in an image of a feminized Church, fused with the sacrificial Christ, is materialized through a drama that is both devotional and familial. One of the most remarkable features of this fourteenth-century text, in fact, and a feature that has not been sufficiently recognized by critics, is its focus on the loss of a two-year-old girl. With the exception of the infant Christ, very young children seldom appear in medieval fictions, particularly in such central positions; when they do, it is rarely as the object of elegiac mourning.[38] Indeed, a study of children in Western literature claims that *Pearl* gives

English its first "true child figure."[39] That the source of the Dreamer's highly formalized, even eulogizing grief should be the loss of a girl child seems even more exceptional. Studies of family life in the Middle Ages indicate that disappointment at the birth of daughters was common. Documents from early fifteenth-century Italy even express—in terms that seem particularly resonant for *Pearl*'s insistence on the girl's stainless-ness—the common belief that the birth of a daughter, as Christiane Klapisch-Zuber puts it, was occasioned by a "conjugal act stained by some impurity, sickness, debauchery, or broken taboo."[40] The poet's choice of an infant girl as elegiac subject thus would seem to centralize a normally marginal familial and gender category to evoke poignantly a female-centered family drama.

That the wounded lamb in this dream vision evokes or stands in for a spectrum of female losses at least as fully as it stands in for a genital wound is also supported by late medieval iconographic traditions equating the wound in Christ's side with the nourishing maternal breast. Illustrations from the visual arts assembled by Caroline Walker Bynum demonstrate that the wound in Christ's side (in *Pearl*, the wound in the lamb) and Mary's breast are explicitly paralleled as like sources of nourishment.[41] Psychoanalytic arguments by Michael Carroll and Julia Kristeva similarly can help account for the relationship of the maternal or the female to images of male sacrifice in late medieval devotion. Medieval Christianity, Kristeva claims, celebrated maternity and even incestuous union with the mother as an alternative to what she describes as its own murderous filial plot. Prior to the Renaissance repression of maternity and incest, Kristeva argues, "Christianity celebrates maternal fecundity and offsets the morbid and murderous filial love of paternal reason with mother/son incest."[42] The lost daughter in *Pearl* initiates such an incestuous plot: in an extraordinary fracture of familial categories—first as the daughter, then as the desired courtly lady—she is also the mother, the one who looks at him, knows his faults, and teaches him.

When the Dreamer awakens and then, retrospectively, attempts to explain how he has learned resignation through Christ, the poem moves to a formally balanced closure: the narrator returns to the waking world and explains that he has given over (byta3te, 1207) his Pearl into the blessing the memory of Christ, which the priest reveals daily through the Eucharist.[43] Yet in spite of the consolation that the poet promises in the last stanza, the imperative memorial image in the poem is one of loss—loss registered through the feminine, even as an entire category: daughter/ lover/mother. The feminist masterplot might allow us to read this ending as a silencing or denial of the feminine through a move away from her to Christ, a fracture and turn that follows immediately on the Dreamer's confrontation with an image of woman's primal threat. The powerful evocation of desire and empathy in the vision of the wounded lamb argues against the exact application of the masterplot to this fourteenth-century text. The ending of *Pearl*, I would argue, gives us not a simple resolution of a threatening feminine, but a conflicted recognition, through the elegiac work of mourning, of a complex and recapitulating series of severances. The narrator's claim that he finds consolation at the ritual table of Communion is even hauntingly apt; severed from the feminine body, a condition not only of a particular and singular death but of his gender, he still seeks sustenance in a material ritual of nurturance.

The question we must return to, in conclusion, concerns the central tension between loss and desire: whose body, in this poem, is lost? If we read *Pearl* as a Hollywood drama through Mulvey's visual script, we would argue that the lost girl replays a story that originates in the castration complex, and that the fourteenth-century dream vision describes a masculine investigation of that loss, its recapitulative work of mourning led by a investigation of a fetishized Lady, up to the point where the primal trauma, which threatens a loss to the man's own body, is unveiled and ultimately mastered. If, however, we argue that loss is situated before, rather than in, the recognition of anatomical difference between the sexes, we can shape a more complex story for Mulvey's statement that "the meaning of woman is sexual difference." Sexual difference in her terms is a threat that must be contained. Sexual difference, in the terms of feminist object relations theorists who have challenged the Freudian paradigm, registers not only as threat, but also as lost plenitude and fusion. This paradigm seems to offer a more persuasive explanation for the various and often contradictory expressions of medieval Mariological devotion than does the Victorian phallocentric plot. "If the woman looks, castration is in the air," not simply, as Heath implies, because the eye, equated with the genitals, portends sexual mutilation. The woman's directed gaze also recasts maternal power, both desired and disavowed. When the *Pearl* Maiden looks, her gaze does not submit to the Dreamer's visual mastery but rather oscillates with his look. It is through her transformed and shifting incarnations—daughter, lover, mother—

that the Dreamer confronts what he has lost, not only a threat to his own body of mutilation, but also a memory of union that remains beyond his grasp. He collapses in the garden mourning an infant daughter; he sees a graphically embodied woman, powerful, articulate, infinitely desirable, who dares to stare back.[44]

Notes

1. Ovid, *The Metamorphoses*, trans. Horace Gregory (New York: Viking Press, 1958), 275.

2. P. Adams Sitney, ed., and Lydia Davis, trans., *The Gaze of Orpheus, and Other Literary Essays* (Barrytown, N.Y.: Station Hill Press, 1981), 104.

3. As part of the work of mourning, the mourner repeatedly and seemingly endlessly replays the loss; see, for example, Sigmund Freud, "Mourning and Melancholia," in *Collected Papers*, trans. Joan Riviere (London: Hogarth, 1948), 4:167.

4. Sigmund Freud, *Sexuality and the Psychology of Love*, ed. Philip Rieff (New York: Collier, 1963), 212.

5. For a lucid introduction to feminist arguments that locate the mystique of male individuality in materializing practices of gender domination that seek to erase the woman as a subject, see Jessica Benjamin, "A Desire of One's Own: Psychoanalytic Feminism and Intersubjective Space," in *Feminist Studies/Critical Studies*, ed. Teresa de Lauretis (Bloomington: Indiana University Press, 1986), 78–101.

6. Peter M. Sacks, *The English Elegy: Studies in the Genre from Spenser to Yeats* (Baltimore: Johns Hopkins University Press, 1985), 8–17.

7. For Lacan's description of the mirror stage, see "The Mirror Stage as Formative of the Function of the I as Revealed in Psychoanalytic Experience," in *Écrits: A Selection*, trans. Alan Sheridan (New York: Norton, 1977), 1–7; and for Freud's account of the *fort-da* game, see his *Beyond the Pleasure Principle*, trans. James Strachey (London: Hogarth Press, 1950). Sacks summarizes these arguments in the context of mourning (*English Elegy*, 9–12).

8. A theory asserting the phallic construction of the gaze and its relationship with a castration threat posed by an ever recapitulating female body has been applied to visual representation, for instance, by Laura Mulvey, "Visual Pleasure and Narrative Cinema," *Screen* 16, no. 3 (Autumn 1975): 6–18; Mary Ann Doane, *The Desire to Desire: The Woman's Film of the 1940s* (Bloomington: Indiana University Press, 1987), 15–22; Griselda Pollock, *Vision and Difference; Femininity, Feminism, and the Histories of Art* (New York: Routledge, 1988), 138–40; and E. Ann Kaplan, "Is the Gaze Male?" in *Powers of Desire: The Politics of Sexuality*, ed. Ann Snitow, Christine Stansell, and Sharon Thompson (New York: Monthly Review Press, 1983), 309–27.

9. Mulvey, "Visual Pleasure," 13.

10. Louise O. Fradenburg, "'Voice Memorial': Loss and Reparation in Chaucer's Poetry," *Exemplaria* 2, no. 1 (Spring 1990): 169–202, esp. 184–86; Gayle Margherita, "Originary Fantasies and Chaucer's *Book of the Duchess*."

11. Readers of *Pearl* have commented on its singular visual focusing; see, for instance, the chapter "Gazing Toward Jerusalem: Space and Perception in *Pearl*" in my book, *Seeing the Gawain-Poet: Description and the Act of Perception* (Philadelphia: University of Pennsylvania Press, 1991), and my essay "Visions of Space: Acts of Perception in *Pearl* and in Some Late Medieval Illustrated Apocalypses," *Mediaevalia* 10 (1984): 133–58; John Finlayson, "*Pearl*: Landscape and Vision," *Studies in Philology* 17 (1974): 314–43; and Barbara Nolan's chapter, "*Pearl*: A Fourteenth-Century Vision in August," in her *Gothic Visionary Perspective* (Princeton: Princeton University Press, 1977), 156–204. These studies explore the tensions between ocular vision and spiritual change in *Pearl*; the relationship between vision and the psychoanalytic or cultural matrices of lines of sight have not, to my knowledge, been addressed in relation to this dream vision.

12. All citations from *Pearl* are taken from the edition by E. V. Gordon (Oxford: Clarendon Press, 1953).

13. In his final visual apotheosis, the vision of the New Jerusalem, words for sight recur every few lines: "As John þe apostel hit syȝ wyth syȝt,/ I syȝe þat cyty of gret renoun" (985–86); "As John deuysed ȝet saȝ I þare" (1021). For references to the Dreamer's gaze, see lines 979, 1021, 1031, 1033, 1035, 1049, 1083, 1143, 1145, 1147, 1151.

14. Mulvey, "Visual Pleasure," 13–14.

15. I am indebted for the comparison to Warhol's Marilyn to a suggestion by Sharon Kinoshita, when I gave an early version of this essay at the University of California at Santa Cruz in January 1991.

16. Rosalind Field, "The Heavenly Jerusalem in *Pearl*," *Modern Language Review* 81 (1986): 11–14.

17. Sacks, *English Elegy*, 102.

18. *Dante's Purgatorio*, ed. and trans. John D. Sinclair (New York: Oxford University Press, 1972), 394–95.

19. Boethius, *The Consolation of Philosophy*, book 1, pr. 1, trans. Richard Green (New York: Bobbs-Merrill, 1962), p. 5. For a fuller discussion of the transgressive woman's gaze in medieval narrative, see my articles "The Virgin's Gaze: Spectacle and Transgression in Middle English Lyrics of the Passion," *PMLA* 106 (October 1991): 1083–93, and "The Lover's Gaze in *Troilus and Criseyde*," in *Chaucer's* Troilus and Criseyde: "*Subjit to Alle Poesye*"—*Essays in Criticism*, MRTS, ed. E. A. Shoaf and Catherine S. Cox (Binghamton, N.Y.: State University of New York Press, 1992).

21. Kaja Silverman, *The Acoustic Mirror: The Female Voice in Psychoanalysis and Cinema* (Bloomington: Indiana University Press, 1988), 31.

22. Linda Williams, "When the Woman Looks," in *Re-Vision: Essays in Feminist Film Criticism*, ed. Mary Ann Doane, Patricia Mellencamp, and Linda Williams (Los Angeles: American Film Institute, 1984), 83–89. For an argument that the woman's look is essentially masochistic, see E. Ann Kaplan, *Women and the Film: Both Sides of the Camera* (New York: Methuen, 1983), 25, 28. See also the discussion

of cinematic masochism and voyeurism by William E. Holladay and Stephen Watt, "Viewing the Elephant Man," *PMLA* 104 (1989): esp. 874–75; and by Gaylin Studlar, who argues that masochism originates in a preoedipal desire for union with the mother rather than in the oedipal drama of domination that Freud posits for masochism and sadism ("Masochism and the Perverse Pleasures of the Cinema," in *Movies and Methods*, ed. Bill Nichols [Berkeley: University of California Press, 1985], 2:602–21).

23. For a discussion of the sexual violence of *The Birds*, see Susan Lurie, "The Construction of the 'Castrated Woman' in Psychoanalysis and Cinema," *Discourse* 4 (Winter 1981–82): 52–74.

24. Naomi Scheman, "Missing Mothers/Desiring Daughters: Framing the Sight of Women," *Critical Inquiry* 15 (Autumn 1988): 64.

25. Laura Mulvey, "Afterthoughts on 'Visual Pleasure and Narrative Cinema' inspired by *Duel in the Sun*," *Framework* 6, nos. 15–17 (1982): 15.

26. I take this term from the special issue of *Camera Obscura* 1991, *The Spectatrix*, devoted to the female spectator.

27. Jackie Byars, "Gazes/Voices/Power: Expanding Psychoanalysis for Feminist Film and Television Theory," in *Female Spectators: Looking at Film and Television*, ed. E. Deidre Pribram (New York: Verso, 1988), 111–12.

28. See especially de Lauretis, "Through the Looking-Glass: Women, Cinema, and Language," chap. 1 of *Alice Doesn't: Feminism, Semiotics, Cinema* (Bloomington: Indiana University Press, 1984), 12–36; and Silverman, "Lost Objects and Mistaken Subjects: A Prologue," chap. 1 of *The Acoustic Mirror*, 1–41.

29. For recent critiques of binarist laws through which psychoanalysis and feminism have theorized sexuality and gender, and especially for discussions of Freud's and Lacan's ellipsis of preoedipal attachments, see, for instance, Patricia Waugh's second chapter, "Psychoanalysis, Gender, and Fiction: Alternative Selves," in *Feminine Fictions: Revisiting the Postmodern* (New York: Routledge, 1989), 34–87, and esp. 62–78; and Jane Flax, *Thinking Fragments: Psychoanalysis, Feminism, and Postmodernism in the Contemporary West* (Berkeley: University of California Press, 1990), 107–26. For a critique of binarist divisions that also takes issue with Julia Kristeva's "semiotic," a naturalized maternity, see also Judith Butler, "Subversive Bodily Acts," chap. 3 of *Gender Trouble: Feminism and the Subversion of Identity* (New York: Routledge, 1990), 79–141. For a critique challenging universalizing assumptions of psychoanalysis that interpret the marks of gender difference through an oedipal plot, see Page du Bois, *Sowing the Body: Psychoanalysis and Ancient Representations of Women* (Chicago: University of Chicago Press, 1988), esp. chap. 1, "To Historicize Psychoanalysis," 7–17; see also 24–29. See also my essay, "The Virgin's Gaze."

30. Silverman, *The Acoustic Mirror*, 15.

31. Nancy Chodorow, *The Reproduction of Mothering: Psychoanalysis and the Sociology of Gender* (Berkeley: University of California Press, 1978), 104–8, 144–46. See also the discussions of Chodorow in Waugh, "Psychoanalysis, Gender, and Fiction," 45–48; and in Benjamin, "Desire of One's Own," 80, 82; and see discussion of Dorothy Dinnerstein and Nancy Chodorow in Flax, *Thinking Fragments*, 159–68.

32. In a subtle redirection of the terms of loss, Susan Lurie argues that the real terror the body of woman inspires is not that she lacks a penis (Lurie's *p.c.p.*, "powerful castrated penis"), but that she functions quite well without one ("The Construction of the 'Castrated Woman' in Psychoanalysis and Cinema," *Discourse* 4 [Winter 1981–82]: 52–74).

33. Silverman (*The Acoustic Mirror*, 15) makes this point: "To admit that the loss of the object is also a castration would be to acknowledge that the male subject is already structured by absence prior to the moment at which he registers woman's anatomical difference—to concede that he, like the female subject, has already been deprived of being, and already been marked by the language and desires of the other."

34. See in particular the studies by Caroline Walker Bynum: *Jesus as Mother: Studies in the Spirituality of the High Middle Ages* (Berkeley: University of California Press, 1982), esp. 110–69; *Holy Feast and Holy Fast: The Religious Significance of Food to Medieval Women* (Berkeley: University of California Press, 1987), 269–76; and "The Female Body and Religious Practice in the Later Middle Ages," in her *Fragmentation and Redemption: Essays on Gender and the Human Body in Medieval Religion* (New York: Zone Books, 1991), esp. 205–22. See also Karma Lochrie, "The Language of Transgression: Body, Flesh, and Word in Mystical Discourse," in *Speaking Two Languages: Traditional Disciplines and Contemporary Theory in Medieval Studies*, ed. Allen J. Frantzen (Albany: State University of New York Press, 1991), 118.

35. See, for instance, Muriel Whitaker, "*Pearl* and Some Illustrated Apocalypse Manuscripts," *Viator* 12 (1981): 183–96; Nolan, "*Pearl*"; Field, "Heavenly Jerusalem in *Pearl*"; and Stanbury, "Visions of Space."

36. Peter H. Brieger, ed., *Trinity College Apocalypse* (London: Eugrammia Press, 1967), 52; this exquisite work contains a text, a translation of the commentary, and a facsimile of the Trinity Apocalypse.

37. See Stanbury, *Seeing the Gawain-Poet*, 28–29.

38. In *Death and the Regeneration of Life* (New York: Cambridge University Press, 1982), 4, editors Maurice Bloch and Jonathan Parry cite Robert Hertz, who makes the cross-cultural observation that infants and young children rarely receive complex funeral rites, for they have not yet been fully incorporated into the social order: "The death of a stranger, a slave, or a child will go almost unnoticed; it will arouse no emotion, occasion no ritual" (Hertz, "A Contribution to the Study of the Collective Representation of Death," in *Death and the Right Hand*, trans. R. and C. Needham [London: Cohen and West, 1960], 76). For a discussion of the new interest in the newborn in fifteenth-century Tuscany, see Christiane Klapisch-Zuber, *Women, Family, and Ritual in Renaissance Italy*, trans. Lydia G. Cochrane (Chicago: University of Chicago Press, 1985), 113–16.

39. Robert Pattison, *The Child Figure in English Literature* (Athens: University of Georgia Press, 1978), 21.

40. Klapisch-Zuber, *Women, Family, and Ritual*, 101–2; she also documents the preference for sons in fifteenth-century Italy with data from familial memoirs, 101–2. A preference for sons seems to be suggested by statistics assembled by Richard Trexler indicating that 60 percent of children in foundling hospitals in early

fifteenth-century Florence were female ("The Foundlings of Florence, 1395–1455," *The History of Childhood Quarterly* 1 [1973]: 259–84). For references to paternal grief for the death of sons, see Philippe Braunstein, "Toward Intimacy: The Fourteenth and Fifteenth Centuries," in Philippe Ariès and Georges Duby, eds., *A History of Private Life*, vol. 2: *Revelations of the Medieval World*: trans. Arthur Goldhammer (Cambridge: Harvard University Press, 1988), 616.

41. Caroline Walker Bynum, "The Body of Christ in the Later Middle Ages: A Reply to Leo Steinberg," in her *Fragmentation and Redemption*, 102.

42. Julia Kristeva, "The Father, Love, and Banishment," in *Literature and Psychoanalysis*, ed. Edith Kurzweil and William Phillips (New York: Columbia University Press, 1983), 396; and for an argument that a repressed desire for the mother manifests itself in a masochistic representation of Christ's Passion, especially in what he calls "father ineffective" cultures, see Michael Carroll, *The Cult of the Virgin Mary: Psychological Origins* (Princeton: Princeton University Press, 1986), 67.

43. Many readers of *Pearl* have accepted the formal outlines of consolation and argue that the poem moves to a satisfying closure. See especially Lynn Staley Johnson, *The Voice of the Gawain-Poet* (Madison: University of Wisconsin Press, 1984), 162, 177; and A. C. Spearing, "The Gawain-Poet's Sense of an Ending," in his *Readings in Medieval Poetry* (New York: Cambridge University Press, 1987), 213–15. For an opposing argument that the ending reflects human alienation, see Theodore Bogdanos, *Pearl: Image of the Ineffable* (University Park: Pennsylvania State University Press, 1983), 145; and for an argument that the ambiguous closure of the ending of *Pearl* is typical of the dream-vision genre, see Margaret Bridges, "The Sense of an Ending: The Case of the Dream-Vision," *Dutch Quarterly Review* 14, no. 2 (1984): 81–96.

44. I would like to thank Charles Blyth, Lynn Layton, Kathryn Lynch, Nadia Medina, and Elizabeth Scala for their helpful suggestions on this essay.

Gayle Margherita

Originary Fantasies and Chaucer's
Book of the Duchess

Medieval studies shares with psychoanalytic discourse an obsession with the problem of origins, an obsession that in both cases is linked to a traumatic loss. Within Freudian and post-Freudian theory, this trauma is often associated with the maternal body, the original "lost object" whose absence enables the entry into language. Within medieval literary studies, the lost origin is synonymous with the cultural/historical context of medieval texts, the historical "real" which can never be fully recovered by any discursive system.

The epistemological dilemma of historicist thinking, that is, the difficulty and contradiction inherent in conceptualizing what can only be known in terms of absence or lack, is nowhere more evident than in the writings of "first wave" historicist critics like D. W. Robertson, who coupled an insistence on the alterity of the past with a belief in its recoverability.[1] The leap of faith that enables the work of contextualization was in this case a literal leap *into* Faith; for exegetical literary scholars, theological universals merge with historical particulars in classic dialectical resolution.[2] This Hegelian/romanticist strain in historicist writing has exerted—and continues to exert—a powerful influence on the field as a whole. In works as thematically and chronologically distant as Robertson's *Preface to Chaucer* and Caroline Bynum's *Holy Feast and Holy Fast*, theology bridges the gap between "us" and "them" as scholarship alone cannot.[3] Interestingly, both of these texts bring the problem of history and loss back to the question of body, albeit in radically different ways. Bynum's work continues to move the materiality of the body to the forefront, but ultimately backs away from the mutual implication of pathology and epistemology that her study seems to suggest. Robertson's "recovery" of the Middle Ages is in large part dependent on a theologically sanctioned repudiation of the body; as Carolyn Dinshaw points out, "disgust with the modern self is registered most often in Robertson's writings as a disgust with sexuality."[4] Both studies are underwritten by a commitment to a dialectical synthesis of the particular and the universal, both turn to theology as a means of giving closure and meaning to a reading of the past in its local specificity.[5]

The privilege accorded the body in current cultural and historicist criticism speaks to the sense in which the nexus of loss, desire, and specularity continues to structure our relation to both the present and the past.[6] In particular, recent work by Renaissance scholars has focused on the body as the central object around which historical struggles for power and dominance are played out. Influenced to varying degrees by the work of Michel Foucault, these critics seem to read the past as a series of specular moments; their relation to the problematic of historical loss and difference is not unlike that of the fetishist who knows, and yet doesn't want to know, that something is missing.[7] Less bothered by the tension between literature and history than their medievalist colleagues, Renaissance historicists and cultural critics move freely between the fantasmatic and the real, creating an often fascinating dialogue between the two. Within post-Foucauldian historicisms, the body effectively "stands in for" the dilemma of origins and of the real; its very materiality gives it a kind of irreducible quiddity that compensates for the absence/loss at the heart of all historicist writing.

For medievalists, the question of origins is not so easily resolved or dismissed. Burdened by the "stewardship" of (vernacular) literary beginnings, medieval scholars must constantly confront the metaphysical and epistemological problem of the real-as-origin. The often politically motivated desire to acknowledge the real as prior to "the entry into language," combined with an equally strong wish to avoid the charge of positivism and (mere) empiricism, has led many of the most innovative medieval literary critics into a bit of a quandry. In his introduction to *Literary Practice and Social Change in Britain, 1380–1530*, Lee Patterson admits that while "textuality is inescapable," and that "we cannot reproduce the past *wie es eigentlich gewesen* [*ist*]," neither should we fall into the unstable realm of "deconstructive formalism," by which we are to understand a critical practice that "[sequesters] the world of events into a realm of presence closed to the irreparably deficient activity of writing."[8] While the rhetorical or phenomenological critique of metaphysical binarisms would seem to have opened up the possibility for a new dialogue between literature and history in Renaissance studies, historicist medievalists have stepped only gingerly into the poststructuralist arena; this particular "entry into language" seems to carry with it all the anxiety about lost plenitude and immediacy that psychoanalysis claims as a condition of psychic life.[9]

Recently, however, medievalists have begun to explore the relationship between origins, loss, and representation more closely. Allen Frantzen's ground-breaking book *Desire for Origins* offers a long-overdue analysis of the role of originary and nationalist fantasies in the foundation of Anglo-Saxon studies. Louise Fradenburg's excellent article on loss and reparation in Chaucerian poetics addresses the problem of loss—both in the field and in Chaucer's texts—by way of a reading of the psychoanalytic literature on mourning. Her analysis centers on the Chaucerian elegy, with particular emphasis on the relationship between "loss" and "authority" in a genre she sees as fundamentally "coercive" and misogynistic.

Like many psychoanalytically oriented medievalists, she is reluctant to accept the Lacanian/deconstructive reading of Freud's texts and seems to bypass the question of loss as it relates specifically to the situation of the subject-in-language.[10] Not surprisingly, her study circumvents the issue of desire almost entirely; the relationship between loss and lack—or loss and desire—that has preoccupied post-Lacanian feminist theory is itself conspicuously "not there" in her reading of the elegy. Her circumlocution of desire is symptomatic of the reluctance or difficulty with which she admits the question of language into her argument at all. While she admits that "it is still possible to speak . . . of man's 'submission to language,'" she qualifies this possibility by privileging the univocity and rhetorical "presence" of certain kinds of speaking: "The authoritarian rhetoric often used to keep the notion of the 'symbolic order' in place—like the moral rhetoric sometimes used by psychoanalysts to prohibit 'excessive' grief and keep the notion of the 'substitute [object]' in place—is problematic."[11] In questioning the *political* subtext of injunctions against excessive mourning, she ignores an aspect of mourning that Julia Kristeva, Nicolas Abraham and Maria Torok, and Freud himself all emphasize: the sense in which melancholia is itself a problem of language, of "speaking loss."[12] The notion of the substitute object in fact stages a confrontation between language and what Kristeva calls "melancholic asymbolia," a retreat into silence and even death. The stakes in the business of mourning are thus much higher than she acknowledges, and the elegy itself much less monolithic. While it does offer (rhetorical) reparation for the lost (material) object, the elegy also acknowledges the unstable situation of the subject in language, or, more specifically, of the *desiring* subject of elegiac discourse.

Fradenburg is right in seeing the elegy as the site of a certain kind of recuperative impulse within a patriarchal literary tradition. I would suggest, however, that it is also the site of literature's greatest anxiety about the relationship between the imaginary, the symbolic, and the real— between fantasy, authority, and reality—and that this anxiety circulates most frantically around the problem of loss *as a condition* of poetic speaking, and around the difficulty of establishing a tradition when the origin of poetry (experience, or reality) is itself constantly receding, "always already" not there.

The problem of loss in the elegy, as in some historicisms, frequently centers on the question of the (always already absent) body as the material/maternal origin of poetic discourse. More than any other genre, the elegy reveals the connection between loss and sexuality, or disappropriation and desire. As such, it can potentially point the way to a reassessment of the intimate relation between sexual and historical fantasies, a relation whereby sexual difference is installed as a defense against the potentially privative and destabilizing effects of historical difference. As a first step to such a reassessment, I would like to turn to the medieval elegy that deals most precisely with origins, loss, and sexuality: Chaucer's *Book of the Duchess*. Specifically, I would like to see if a psychoanalytic reading of the text in the tradition of Lacanian feminism might reveal a text that is not only "coercive," as Fradenburg claims, but also subversive of its own "authoritarian" assumptions. In short, I would like to ascertain whether or not a reading of the elegiac subject *in* language might uncover a political subtext that is at the very least at odds with itself. If the reparative impulse that grounds elegy is, as Fradenburg suggests, founded upon misogyny, then it depends in large part upon the establishment of stable sexual identities. Given the fact that loss is inseparable from desire, however, "elegiac misogyny" can only be enacted as a futile gesture toward an irreducible sexual difference—a gesture in which the absent body of the lost object has no small role to play.[13]

Several scholars have noted that Chaucer's *Duchess* concerns itself explicitly with the problematics of literary origins. In keeping with the generic preoccupations of elegy, it also deals with the question of literary inheritance: the right to mourn, as Peter Sacks points out, implies the right to inherit.[14] Given these concerns, it is not surprising that the text sets up a confrontation between history and gender: it mourns the lost body of Lady White (identified with Blanche of Lancaster), while simultaneously establishing a filial relationship to the classical past. The poem attempts to assert its hereditary right to a literary tradition by dramatizing the "dis-incorporation" or abjection of the lost object that is part of the "work" performed by the elegiac/melancholic subject.[15] Only by asserting his difference from the abject/object can the masculinist poet recover his losses and affirm the exteriority and authority necessary to the continuity of a paternalist poetics.

In the remainder of this essay, I will be exploring this strategy in the context of a theoretical reading of the *Duchess* itself. I will suggest that, in the Chaucerian elegy as in Freudian theory, the exteriority and paternal authority of both poet and analyst are undermined by the return of what both attempt continually to repress: the materiality of language itself, the ma(t)ter which/who inevitably threatens the stability of the paternal system of discursive production. If the elegy is about inheritance, authority, and patriarchy, it is also about desire—desire that circulates throughout texts, exceeding both narrative control and sexual difference.

Paternal Fantasies, or How To Start a Tradition

Throughout English literary history, sleep has been a productive metaphor for the poetic process.[16] In sleep, consciousness is suspended and dreams are generated; dreams reenact history through condensations and displacements that turn the familiar into the uncanny. Given the poetic nature of dreams, moreover, it is not surprising that poems invoking the figure of sleep seem to concern themselves with issues of transmission and inheritance. For example, John Keats begins his *Sleep and Poetry* with an epigraph from *The Floure and the Lefe,* a medieval verse allegory that was erroneously attributed to Chaucer in Keats's time. Keats ends his poem with a metaphor linking poetic creation to a parturition that separates father and son: the speaking subject of poetry is generated by and alienated from a father/maker through whose name the immortality of the artifact is ensured.[17] The pseudo-Chaucerian epigraph calls this paternal closure—and thus the poem's transcendent value—into question, however. It remains outside the borders of the poem itself, and yet threatens the poet's assertion of primacy, of fatherhood. The poem's "legitimacy" hinges on a resolution of the oedipal conflict, but its last line, which would seem to offer this resolution, takes us back to the epigraph, to the "father" of English poetry, whose presence forces us to acknowledge the legal dilemma of fatherhood, the indeterminacy of poetic origins. The fact that the attribution to Chaucer is erroneous further complicates matters. If poetry is patrilineal, what are the consequences of misremembering one's fathers?

This is a question that seems to have occupied Chaucer throughout his career. In *Anelida and Arcite*, poetic continuity depends upon memory, which is always in danger of disappearing. The tale of Anelida and Arcite is an old story,

> That elde, which that al can frete and bite,
> As hit hath freten mony a noble storie,
> Hath nygh devoured out of oure memorie.
>
> (11–13)

Memory is also perilous to the medieval poet, however. There is always the chance that his poetry may remain, like Anelida herself, "thirled with the poynt of remembraunce," that is, paralyzed by an imaginary relationship to the past. In *Troilus and Criseyde*, the paternal figure of Lollius stands in for the narrator's anxieties about literary history. His name is a morphological paradox that represents the poet's own troubled relation to the literary past: its ending evokes the nobility of a lost classical tradition, while its stem brings to mind a contemporary heterodox movement. As a "front" for the poet himself, Lollius at once commemorates the classical fathers of vernacular poetry and heretically violates their legacy.[18]

In Chaucer's earliest narrative poem, the *Book of the Duchess*, the dilemma of memory and its relation to tradition is played out in a rather different and perhaps less explicit way. Critics have long been aware of the poem's indebtedness to French courtly poetry: the *Duchess* is in fact a mélange of conventional moments borrowed from Machaut, Froissart, and Guillaume de Lorris.[19] Surprisingly, however, nearly all of the poem's readers have overlooked the political implications of this "borrowing." Its appropriation and "Englishing" of these conventional texts certainly represents an ideological intervention on behalf of a national vernacular that was finally gaining ascendency. The poem speaks to and of the need for a specifically English literary tradition that might rival that of the Continent. Given John of Gaunt's probable role in the genesis of the poem, and his well-documented efforts to promote the official use of English, the poem's political investment in "originating a tradition" can hardly be ignored.[20] Within the poem itself, this political imperative takes on an aesthetic urgency. As we shall see, the absence of tradition, of literary fathers, is recast as a drama of loss in which sexual difference plays a determining role.

Before turning to the *Duchess* itself, however, it may be useful to see how yet another "founding father"—the father of psychoanalysis—worked to paternalize the origins of his own theoretical discourse by associating woman with the category of the lost real. Several feminist theorists have noted Freud's refusal to disassociate the maternal seduction scene from the realm of the real: while paternal seduction is said to be a hysterical fantasy, seduction by the mother "touches the ground of reality."[21] In *Beyond the Pleasure Principle*, the "*fort-da* game" becomes a story of loss in which the mother's absence is mastered through representation. Through the child's "artistic play," the pleasure of representation alleviates the unpleasure of the mother's disappearance.[22] Again, the mother remains outside the game itself; she is bound to the realm of reference and thus lost with the entry into language and signification. With the mother exiled to the realm of matter, her body can serve as the "ground" for the metaphors that sustain the myth of paternal productivity. This exclusion of woman from the act of representation is nonetheless a semiotic gesture that—paradoxically— serves to relegate her to the *interior* of the mimetic circuit, while placing the male artist or analyst at the point of textual origin. In short, women can represent loss or lack, but only men can cover over that loss with representation.

In a fascinating recent study, Wayne Koestenbaum shows how Freud metaphorically appropriates the female power of generation in establishing an originary narrative for psychoanalysis.[23] In fact it is Josef Breuer's patient Anna O. who invents the "talking cure," and it is through her hysterical pregnancy that psychoanalytic theory is born.[24] In transforming the hysteric's narrative into "case histories that read like short stories," Freud succeeds in displacing the origins of theory from the body of the mother—Anna O.—to the discursive collaboration between himself and Breuer. Her hysterical pregnancy, which Breuer omits from his own narrative, becomes a gap in the text which Freud fills; the hysteric's material female space (her womb) is translated or metaphorized into the analyst's textual space.[25] The feminine body is written out of the originary drama, only to return in the form of tropes that affirm the generative power of discursive unions between men.[26]

The *Book of the Duchess* is also the story of generative collaborations between men: between Chaucer and Ovid, between Chaucer and the French courtly poets, and between the poem's narrator and the Black

Knight.[27] The poem enacts its own version of "artistic play": here, too, the body of woman is *a priori* a lost object that grounds tropological substitutions, metaphors that work to sustain the illusion of paternal productivity and male discursive mastery. Because the success of this illusion depends upon the author's ability to displace the origins of discourse from ma(t)ter to father, from the world of objects to that of figures, it finds effective expression in both the elegy and its generic sibling, the dream-vision. Both genres assert that loss can be productive: the elegy proclaims language as death's opposite and adversary, thereby endowing poetry with an illusory plenitude, while the dream-vision establishes the foreclosure of the waking or referential world as the price of a transcendent vision. In Lacanian terms, both the elegy and the dream-vision enable the poet to work through the trauma of loss or castration that accompanies the entry into language, and, as in the case of the *Duchess*, to project that lack onto woman by locating her in the realm of the lost real. Once the realm of mother-as-matter has been foreclosed as the site of textual production, origins can be relocated within language itself: the father's "olde stories" supplant the mother's body, and a literary tradition is born.

Following the Freudian model of the *fort-da* game, then, we may be tempted to conclude that Chaucer's *Book of the Duchess* succeeds in mastering loss through representation, in placing unpleasure in the service of the economic demands of the so-called pleasure principle. The anxiety the poem has aroused within the critical community, however, is one indication that the poem is not the "closed system" its readers would like it to be. There has been a marked tendency among the poem's critics to close off the unpleasurable moments within the text, either by proposing allegorical readings that the work itself ultimately resists, or by attempting to "suture" the poem's various disjunctions ideologically. For the allegorists, the Black Knight is the embodiment of *tristitia*,[28] or of melancholic narcissism;[29] the narrator represents "imagination" as against the Black Knight's "intellect";[30] and Lady White—if she is discussed at all—is most often associated with "life itself" or with a Boethian false felicity that must be accepted as such.[31] Recently, critical attention has turned to the meta-poetics of the text; these readings in particular betray an anxiety about closure and unity. Robert Jordan's recent analysis of the poem focuses on its "structural irregularities and violations of tone and scale," but ultimately relies on a conventional panegyric gesture to give the poem an ideologically necessary transcendent value: "If the *Book of the Duchess* lacks the smoothly integrated texture of an organic unity, it amply compensates with its aggressive brilliance, its rhetorical energy, and its rich variety of tone and nuance."[32] Having identified the poem with lack, the critic must find a way to "compensate" for it, lest the paternal origins of English poetry be destabilized and thus called into question. For Robert Hanning, this "undeniably idiosyncratic" poem dramatizes a process of externalization or objectivation of affect that finally leads to an affirmation of male bonding as the basis of artistic productivity:

> The narrator-dreamer and the Black Knight establish a human community of *routh* and mutual involvement which, by overcoming isolation, seems to transform their life-threatening sorrow—both have survived thus far in defiance of "nature" or "kynde"—into states of personal acceptance and renewed creativity.[33]

Male generativity can only take place in the absence or "defiance" of nature, in which category are contained the traditionally feminine subcategories of matter and affect. The externalization or, in Kristevan terms, abjection of femininity is essential to the homosocial interests of the male poetic and critical community, here universalized as "human." Both Jordan's reading and Hanning's say more about the institution of Chaucer studies than about Chaucer's poem: for the former, criticism is a mirroring of critical ego and poetic ego-ideal, while the latter envisions an ideal artistic community where heroic critics join masculinist poets in a productive union.

These readings are particularly interesting to the feminist reader of Chaucer, in that they foreground the issue upon which the poem's masculinist ideology founders: the problematic relation between fantasy, desire, and identification. The critical insistence on mirroring unities, on recuperating the poem's "excesses," partakes of the fantasy of coherence that the *Duchess* both creates and subverts. For both the poem and its critics, femininity—as excess or as "nature"—is the psychic danger that necessitates and undermines this fantasy. The male critic's identification with a masculinist poet, I will argue, is continually threatened by that poet's own deviant identification with feminine desire. In the remainder of this essay, I will not only confront the lack that fuels the fantasy of paternal generativity; I will also explore the poet's own identification with that lack. It is my hope that this analysis may contribute to a rethinking of our relation to the *Book of the Duchess* and, more generally, to a reassessment of some of our assumptions about the patrilineal tradition Chaucer is said to have fathered.

The Poetics of Loss

The *Book of the Duchess* begins by asserting the narrator's melancholic alienation from life. He traces his "defaute of slep" to a "sicknesse" for which
"there is phisicien but oon." But, he says, "that is don." The reference to
a particular physician would seem to indicate that the narrator is suffering
from lovesickness, and that only the return of his lost love can restore him
to health. The efficacy of this conventional sentiment, at least in the lyric
tradition, normally depends upon a maintenance of the fiction that such a
restoration is at least possible. The narrator's abrupt assertion that "that is
don" closes off the possibility of further experience. Life, it would seem,
can offer no more to literature. His condition, moreover, is said to be
"agaynes kynde"; he is cut off from nature, from the world of objects.
These opening lines attempt to evoke a state of absolute negativity, of pure
difference made manifest as in-difference. In this fantasy of absence, the
narrator's pathological isolation is the antithesis of a distanced objectivity,
for it is precisely critical judgment that fails him:

> by my trouthe, I tak no kep
> Of nothyng, how hyt cometh or gooth,
> Ne me nys nothyng leef nor looth.
> Al is ylyche good to me
>
> (6–9)

Needless to say, subjectivity and (thus) poetry are impossible where difference does not exist; the fantasy cannot be sustained. Indeed, indifference
yields to *différance* when the narrator tells us that "sorwful ymagynacioun"
is always "hooly" in his mind: no sooner is imagination linked to lack,
than that lack is recuperated as wholeness and plenitude. Like the figure
of sleep itself, these opening lines tread the borderline between presence
and absence, loss and reparation. On the one hand, poetry is said to originate in loss of the real: experience is foreclosed as the source of mimesis.
On the other hand, that absence is said to constitute a different sort of
wholeness or presence, as "sorwful ymagynacioun" and "fantasies" take
the place of pure negativity and absolute alienation from the signifying
process.

As in the Freudian paradigm, the unpleasurable tension between presence and absence is here mitigated through representation, which is seen
as "play." The narrator's sleeplessness or lack of poetic inspiration leads

him back to "olde stories," in this case Ovid's tale of Ceyx and Alcyone. The Ovidian text is itself endowed with an originary plenitude that compensates for the narrator's own unnatural state; it is found among a book of

> fables
> That clerkes had in olde tyme,
> And other poets, put in rime
> To rede, and for to be in minde,
> While men loved the lawe of kynde.
>
> (52–56)

The classical text possesses the connection to nature that the narrator lacks, for it is said to derive from an age of prelapsarian textual innocence, before the "lawe of kynde" was occluded by the laws of signification.[34] The narrator's pathological state of alienation from nature or experience, which initially subverts his desire to generate poetry, is mitigated when the paternal text becomes naturalized as the true origin of poetic inspiration. The realm of matter or experience, foreclosed with the narrator's assertion that "that is don," is supplanted as the source of poetic speaking. In effect, the Ovidian text fetishistically compensates for the lost real, and sleep—or poetry—follows soon after.

Clearly the matter is not closed, however. Chaucer's Ovidian tale, unlike the original, is everywhere obsessed with the gap between what seems to be and what is, or, more specifically, between representation and reality. In Chaucer's tale of Ceyx and Alcyone, much is made of the fact that Morpheus appears Alcyone's dream in the body of Ceyx. In the poetic world of dreams, we witness the appearance of life, not life itself. Juno's instructions to Morpheus are explicit:

> Bid hym crepe into the body,
> And do hit goon to Alcione
> The quene, ther as she lyeth allone,
> And shewe hir shortly, hit ys no nay,
> How hit was dreynt thys other day;
> And do the body speke ryght soo,
> Ryght as hyt was woned to doo
> The whiles that hit was alyve.
>
> (144–51)

Like poetry, dreams can only re-present reality; they have no immediate relation to experience. In this respect, Alcyone's dream calls the narrator's own "sweven" into question: if animation is not life, and sleep, however "dedly," is not death, then perhaps the Black Knight's codified sentiments are not genuine passion. The Black Knight's elegiac narrative—certainly the segment of the poem that carries the most ideological weight—is thus also the site of its deepest anxiety and doubt. The relation of conventional poetry to reality becomes an ethical issue when placed in the context of grief and mourning: if elegiac poetry is cut off from genuine affect, then what possible social function can it serve? More important, what social role—if any—can a poet have?

This question is less answered than displaced in the poem. The systematic installation of sexual difference as the overriding opposition in the text works to shift the burden of discursive impotence from male to female figures. Before the Black Knight even appears in the poem, we learn that elegiac narrative is sexually specific. While he will lament the loss of his lady at length, replacing her lost body with language, Alcyone is incapable of generating a narrative that will similarly stand in for her lost husband.[35] In Chaucer's version of the tale, she is denied both speech and vision:

> With that hir eyen up she casteth
> And saw noght. "Allas!" quod she for sorwe,
> And deyede within the thridde morwe.
> But what she sayede more in that swow
> I may not telle yow as now;
> Hyt were to longe for to dwelle.
>
> (213–17)

The Knight's extended conventional lament must be set against Alcyone's failure to elegize Ceyx. Here, as in the Freudian game of loss, women are called upon to represent lack so that men may cover over that lack with language. In this way, sexual difference is set in place as a defense against the trauma of loss/castration. Just as Alcyone is denied speech, so Lady White remains a pure negativity—the only word she speaks is "nay"—so as to obscure the sense in which the poem itself is merely negation, or "not-life."

Founded in absence or loss of reference, the text must nonetheless affirm its own plenitude and unity by reconstituting the presence/absence dyad within the diegesis proper. The text's authority thus comes to depend on an affirmation of the boundaries separating inside and outside, that is, on its ability to relegate woman, and thus lack, to the interior of narrative space.[36] It must affirm its positive value as against the negativity inscribed as woman. At the same time, however, it must maintain the fiction that representation bears some positive relation to reality, that what seems to be (fiction, or the dream-world) and what is (life) are not forever alienated from one another. The two imperatives constitute an unresolvable paradox for the poet, in that one necessitates an affirmation of boundaries, the other a negation of them. Given this dilemma, literature can do little more than reenact the foreclosure of the real from representation, placing woman at the vortex, the vanishing point of narrative: the place where speaking and reading are alike impossible. This strategy is not without danger, however. Lady White is the "chef myrour of al the feste," reflecting the male subject's castration, specularity, and narcissism, as well as the site of hermeneutic "implosion," if you will. "Hir lokyng" is a barrier, through and beyond which reading is impossible:

> Hir eyen semed anoon she wolde
> Have mercy; fooles wenden soo;
> But hyt was never the rather doo.
> Hyt nas no countrefeted thyng;
> Hyt was hir owne pure lokyng
> That the goddesse, dame Nature,
> Had mad hem opene by mesure,
> And close; for, were she never so glad,
> Hyr lokynge was not foly sprad,
> Ne wildely, thogh that she pleyde;
> But ever, me thoght, hir eyen seyde,
> "Be God, my wrathe ys al foryive!"
>
> (866–77)

The Knight's inability to read Lady White's look allies her with Fortune, who "baggeth foule and loketh faire," while the destructive power of her gaze ("many oon with hire lok she herte") evokes the Medusa, the "monstres hed" concealed behind Fortune's fair face. Like Lady White's look, however, femininity continually threatens to exceed the limits defined for it within the text. Refusing to remain unproblematic, femininity becomes the site of a radical instability in the poem, an instability that works to subvert the male subject's attempt to distance himself from the spectre of loss and lack.

The reenactment of the trauma of loss, the foreclosure of the real, is made explicit in the dream. The narrator describes his dream-chamber as a kind of poetic "cathedral"; the walls are painted with the text of the *Romance of the Rose*, while the stained-glass windows tell the story of Troy. The Trojan story does not prevent the dreamer from seeing outside, however:

> My wyndowes were shette echon,
> And throgh the glas the sonne shon
> Upon my bed with bryghte bemes,
> With many glade gilde stremes;
> And eke the welken was so fair,
> Blew, bryght, clere was the ayr,
> And ful attempre for sothe hyt was;
> For nother to cold nor hoot yt nas,
> Ne in al the welken was no clowde.
>
> (335–43)

The story of Troy is transparent. Beyond it we may see what lies outside: the "real" world of nature, of objects. The world beyond the chamber is no more real than the chamber itself, however. The outside world is a cross between a courtly *locus amoenus* and a *forêt d'aventure*: a place where difference seems not to exist ("nother to cold nor hoot yt nas"), where "hert-huntynge" has meaning only as a pun. It is, in short, the realm of conventional poetry, a fact the narrator further attempts to disavow by negating the split between the body and the word, between sincere emotion and formalized sentiment.[37] When we first see the Black Knight, he is uttering a "lay," a conventional lament for his lost love (475–86). Immediately after his song, we are asked to look inside his body, as the narrator affirms the correspondence between conventional expression and clinical fact:

> Hys sorwful hert gan faste faynte,
> And his spirites wexen dede;
> The blood was fled for pure drede
> Doun to hys herte, to make hym warm—

> For wel hyt feled the herte had harm—
> To wite eke why hyt was adrad
> By kynde, and for to make hyt glad;
> For hyt ys membre principal
> Of the body; and that made al
> Hys hewe chaunge and wexe grene
> And pale, for ther noo blood ys sene
> In no maner lym of hys.
>
> (488–99)

The integrity of the body and the word, inside and outside, is further problematized by the text's obsession with the word "hool" (lines 15, 115, 326, 553, 554, 746, 751, 756, 766, 991, 1224, 1269). The phallic ideal of wholeness foregrounds the dreamer's own discursive insufficiency, just as, on a larger scale, his initial disavowal of the boundary between the interior and the exterior, clinical fact and codified convention, represents an attempt to compensate for the originary loss of the world of objects that literature must continually reenact.

It is only through the phallic character of the Black Knight that the male subject/dreamer is able to protect himself effectively from the spectre of lack, from knowledge of his own discursive inadequacy. The Knight's mastery of literary conventions allows him to move between inside and outside with ease, to place his other/opposite, Lady White, at the text's vanishing point, thereby securing the illusory wholeness of the poem. In his description of Lady White, the Knight continually crosses the boundary between exterior and interior. He moves from the realm of thought (885) to a description of the Lady's face (895ff.), from her voice (919) to her neck (939). Moreover, he equates artificers and physicians (the word and the body) in his assertion that he can be neither healed nor distracted from his "sorwes" (567–71). The dreamer's imaginary transference onto the idealized male figure of the Black Knight constitutes a denial of the originary loss of objects, of history, of the phallus itself. The Knight's fetishization of literary convention effectively permits male desire to masquerade as presence rather than absence.

As Freud pointed out, however, a fetish is always a sign of a split subjectivity. In the *Duchess*, this split manifests itself along the lines of sexual difference: the homosocial identifications in the poem coexist alongside heterosocial and heterosexual identifications that are perilous to the poem's masculinist recuperative agenda. If there is a "feminist Chaucer," as has been suggested recently,[38] he can perhaps be found on the borderline where desire slips into identification, where desire for the object becomes identification with the object's desire. One way of approaching this perilous borderline, I would argue, is through the disturbing and fascinating phenomenon of fetishism itself.[39]

The Desire to Desire

In his essay on fetishism, Freud relates the case of a young man who "had exalted a certain sort of 'shine on the nose' into a fetishistic precondition." We learn very little of the etiology of this particular fetish, except that it had to do with the loss of the mother-tongue (*Muttersprache*):

> The patient had been brought up in an English nursery, but had later come to Germany, where he forgot his mother-tongue almost completely. The fetish, which originated from his earliest childhood, had to be understood in English, not German. The "shine on the nose" [in German, *Glanz auf der Nase*]—was in reality a "*glance* at the nose." The nose was thus the fetish, which, incidentally, he endowed at will with the luminous shine which was not perceptible to others.[40]

Freud goes on to say that "the fetish is a substitute for the woman's (the mother's) penis that the little boy once believed in and—for reasons familiar to us—does not want to give up."[41] Fetishism is thus presented as added evidence for Freud's theory of the castration complex: it is a symptom of the disavowal (*Verleugnung*) with which the child greets the sight of the female genitalia and thus his own fear of loss. The fetish, in this case the nose, stands in for the lost object, which Freud identifies with the mother's penis. His narrative reveals something else, however: the fetish is linked to the mother-tongue, the *Sprache* of the mother, as well. What the child disavows through the fetish is not (merely) the mother's lack of a penis, but rather her lack of *Sprache*, of discursive potency. In her perceived inability to generate authoritative narrative, he sees the possibility of his own failure to do so. Speaking becomes linked to looking (the glance); the continuity of narrative is made to depend in large part on the "glance at the nose," that is, the gaze at the fetish.

While fetishism installs sexual difference as a defense against loss, it is perhaps first and foremost an identification with the position of lack: if mother lacks, then so must I. Moreover, the position is a pleasurable one for the fetishist; Freud points out that fetishism provides sexual gratification in a simple and "convenient" way. The externalization of the fetishized object, necessary to the specular disavowal of loss, is thus also the point at which desire for the lost object slips into identification with the lost object, or with the position of lack.

This fetishistic dilemma plays a significant role in the *Book of the Duchess*. As we discussed earlier, the loss of the real, the realm of ma(t)ter, is partially mitigated when the origins of poetic speaking are relocated in the paternal classical text. As in the oedipal myth, the "normative value" of this move depends on the narrator's identification with the paternal figure. Instead of identifying with Ovid as the maker of the tale, however, the narrator responds empathically to the tale's feminine victim, Alcyone herself:

> Such sorwe this lady to her tok
> That trewly I, which made this book,
> Had such pittee and such rowthe
> To rede hir sorwe, that, by my trowthe,
> I ferde the worse al the morwe
> Aftir, to thenken on hir sorwe.
>
> (95–100)

The narrator here claims the authorial role, while simultaneously affirming his identification with a woman who will come to represent discursive inadequacy in the poem.

Within the dream-vision itself, the narrator's homosocial identification with the Black Knight seems to compensate for his previous deviant identification with Alcyone. Indeed, the dream landscape is presented as a place of natural plenitude, in contrast to the landscape of Alcyone's dream, which is barren and empty. When the narrator first comes upon the Knight in the forest, the Knight is heard lamenting the death of his lady. The narrator is so impressed with the Knight's demeanor and speech, however, that he disavows what he has heard, thereby enabling the Knight to replace his lost lady with a lengthy elegiac narrative. The fetishistic game goes awry when the Knight himself begins to identify with Lady White, the "blank place" upon which the entire reparative system depends. The Knight claims the lady's blankness for himself when he tells the story of his amatory education, assuming an explicitly feminine position:

> I was thereto most able,
> As a whit wal or a table,
> For hit ys redy to cacche and take
> Al that men wil theryn make,
> Whethir so men wil portreye or peynte
> Be the werkes never so queynte.
>
> (779–84)

In this fantasmatic moment, the Knight himself moves to the interior of the mimetic or representational space, thereby destabilizing the narrator's own homosocial and compensatory identification, and thus the poem's larger strategy of recuperation. This perilous inversion is explicitly linked to language when the Knight relives his lady's initial rejection of his "tale" of love. His sorrow was so great, we are told,

> That trewly Cassandra, that soo
> Bewayled the destruccioun
> Of Troye and of Ilyoun,
> Had never swich sorwe as I thoo.
>
> (1246–49)

By identifying himself with Cassandra, perhaps the most renowned exemplar of feminine discursive impotence, the Knight proclaims the genuineness of his sentiments—the truth of his "tale"—but also the impossibility of ever transcending a state of rhetorical insufficiency.

Perhaps the most dangerous moment in the text, the point at which identification is most unstable, is in the specular description of the lady herself. Here, as in later Chaucerian works such as *Troilus and Criseyde* and the *Knight's Tale*, specular pleasures become perilous precisely because of the potential slippage of desire into identification. After describing the lady's demeanor and appearance, the Knight moves from her eyes to her look:

> And whiche eyen my lady hadde!
> Debonaire, goode, glade and sadde,
> Symple, of good mochel, noght to wyde.
> Thereto hir look nas not asyde,
> Ne overthwert, but beset so wel
> Hyt drew and took up, everydel,
> Al that on hir gan beholde.
>
> (859–65)

The parallel between the lady's look, that "drew and took up" everyone who gazed upon her, and the Knight in his youth, ready to "cacche and take" every impression, is striking. The scopophilic moment is also the moment when desire for the object becomes a mirroring identification with the object's own desire. It is the moment when desire becomes "the desire to desire": the desire to be in a position of lack. Lady White's look, associated with a feminine desiring excess, is also a dangerous gap that threatens to overturn the fragile homosocial substructure of the poem itself. There is always the danger that the poet will become trapped by "the myrrour perillous" of Narcissus, as Chaucer calls it in his translation of the *Romance of the Rose.* "Drawn in and taken up" by a fantasy of deviant identification, the poet will be unable to reassert the exteriority necessary to the more normative fantasy of male discursive mastery.

The paradoxical and unstable position of the fetishist is that of a subject compelled by the illusion of plenitude and caught up in the pleasurable drama of lack. Within the *Book of the Duchess,* both the narrator and the Black Knight are constructed by this play of presence and absence, normative and deviant identifications. Although the poem works to contain the trauma of loss by placing the feminine body at the innermost point of narrative space, it ultimately refuses to sustain the illusion of masculine authorial exteriority by failing to "draw the line" between object cathexis and the narcissistic mirroring that structures desire. Moreover, the poem establishes its divisions and losses prior to its "discovery" of sexual difference: the narrator's alienation precedes Alcyone's rhetorical failure, and Lady White's fixed absence in the text is only installed after the dream itself unfolds as a foreclosure of reference. The projection of lack onto woman thus constitutes a defensive response to what Lacan has identified as symbolic castration: the loss of the real necessitated by the entry into signification.

The poem disavows this originary loss, but can only defer the acknowledgment of the division that underpins its own illusory wholeness. Between the narrator's "that is don" and the Black Knight's "she is ded," the "artistic play" of *différance* unfolds. On the other side of these statements is the body of the mother, exiled to the lost realm of matter and reference. Ideologically committed to the assertion of the paternal origins of poetic speaking, the poem must repress the maternal desire that both sustains and subverts its patriarchal agenda. Through these fantasmatic moments of deviant identification, however, ma(t)ter returns as something uncanny, something familiar and strange, pleasurable and threatening.

The *Book of the Duchess*, like much of Chaucer's later poetry, reveals the instability at the heart of a paternalist poetics, and thus the fragility of any historicist or nationalist ideology based on a patrilineal system of inheritance. The poet's speaking subjectivity continually proclaims its sexual undecidability, even as the conventions it enlists persist in installing sexual difference as a defense against the loss wherein they originate. The *Duchess* initiates Chaucer's exploration of what I have called the fetishistic dilemma: the tension between an ideologically necessary recuperative impulse and a fantasmatic identification with the position of lack. This dilemma, and its relation to the construction of a historically specific subjectivity, is explored most fully in *Troilus and Criseyde*. The *Duchess* can—and perhaps should—be read as a preface to Chaucer's great romance, in which Criseyde inherits the dangerous position of Lady White, becoming the focus of the narrator's—and the poet's—desire to desire.

Notes

Quotations from the *Book of the Duchess* are taken from F. N. Robinson, ed., *The Works of Geoffrey Chaucer*, 2d ed. (Boston: Houghton Mifflin, 1957).

1. In *A Preface to Chaucer*, Robertson asserts that "there are profound differences between the Arts of the Middle Ages and those of modern times. . . . To attempt to explain these differences away so as to make what is medieval seem modern is only to prepare false expectations, and we must guard against the very natural tendency of critics to project modern 'truths' concerning the nature of beauty and of art on a past which was entirely innocent of those 'truths.'" This desire to keep the past "innocent" implies, on the one hand, that we can forget or disavow our own knowledge/cultural context while seeking the "truth" of the Middle Ages and, on the other, that the medieval period itself partakes of the prelapsarian innocence associated with all "golden age" mythologies. Robertson's metaphysical presuppositions veil the epistemological contradictions of his position, that is, the sense in which he uses the trope of "difference" to affirm the identity of critical subject and textual object. See D. W. Robertson, *A Preface to Chaucer: Studies in Medieval Perspectives* (Princeton: Princeton University Press, 1962), 3.

2. Robertson in fact explicitly denies the dialectical assumptions that subtend his own insistence on "hierarchical" as opposed to "synthetic" modes of thought. Conspicuously absent from his argument is a recognition of the sense in which hierarchies are themselves sustained dialectically or oppositionally. This recognition, it seems to me, informs the very structure of the *Canterbury Tales*. See his *Preface to Chaucer*, 3–51.

3. In the concluding segment of her work on feminine piety and food practices, Bynum attempts to contain the disturbing phenomena she has unveiled within theological and thus institutional boundaries: "The notion of substituting

one's own suffering through illness and starvation for the guilt and destitution of others is not 'symptom'—it is theology." The question of pathology, implicit throughout her fascinating study, is finally foreclosed in the interest of accurate contextualization. For Bynum as for Robertson, however, contextual accuracy becomes paradoxically synonymous with allegorization: the epistemologically "bounded" or limited frame of Christian theology forces a kind of moral closure upon a plethora of archival details that fit only with difficulty into that frame. See Caroline Walker Bynum, *Holy Feast and Holy Fast: The Religious Significance of Food to Medieval Women* (Berkeley: University of California Press, 1987), 206.

4. Dinshaw offers a very insightful and interesting "reading of Robertson reading" Chaucer. See Carolyn Dinshaw, *Chaucer's Sexual Poetics* (Madison: University of Wisconsin Press, 1989), 31–35. See also Louise O. Fradenburg's analysis of Robertsonianism in particular, and medievalism in general, in her "'Voice Memorial': Loss and Reparation in Chaucer's Poetry," *Exemplaria* 2, no. 1 (Spring 1990): 169–202. Fradenburg also notes the difficulty of "theorizing the recovery of the irrecoverable" and asserts that "though the difference . . . or alterity of the Middle Ages is . . . urged upon us, the interpretive ideal is one in which hermeneutic otherness, difference, or disagreement, is in fact purged" (173). Fradenburg's study is discussed in more detail below.

5. One of the most revealing articles to emerge from the current movement on behalf of particularity or "detailism" is Alan Liu's "Local Transcendence: Cultural Criticism, Postmodernism, and the Romanticism of Detail," *Representations* 32 (Fall 1990): 75–113. Liu points out the allegorical and romanticist strain in current historicisms and cultural criticisms. There is, according to Liu, a kind of transcendence or sublimation inherent in the "immanent detail" that has so fascinated scholars of late. This paradox of "local transcendence" helps to make sense of the epistemological contradictions that characterize works such as Bynum's.

6. Some examples of this "corporealization" of knowledge are Stephen Greenblatt's much-discussed essay "Fiction and Friction," in his *Shakespearean Negotiations: The Circulation of Social Energy in Renaissance England* (Berkeley: University of California Press, 1988), 66–93. As Joel Fineman points out, Greenblatt is "concerned to establish a specific relation between a field of medical discourse, on the one hand, and Shakespeare's literary representations of human relations, on the other." See Fineman's "History of the Anecdote: Fiction and Friction," in *The New Historicism*, ed. H. Aram Veeser (New York: Routledge, 1989). Other notable examples of this body- and/or detail-centered approach to the human sciences are Naomi Schor's *Reading in Detail: Aesthetics and the Feminine* (New York: Methuen, 1987); Caroline Bynum's latest book, *Fragmentation and Redemption: Essays on Gender and the Human Body in Medieval Religion* (New York: Zone Books, 1991); and Mary Jacobus, Evelyn Fox Keller, and Sally Shuttleworth, eds. *Body/Politics: Women and the Discourses of Science* (New York: Routledge, 1990). I could, of course, go on almost indefinitely. What emerges most clearly here is that aesthetic, political, and epistemological concerns have come to circulate around the image of the body; clearer still, I would argue, is that this "specular criticism" points toward a larger question of origins, a question that links historical/cultural and sexual fantasies in new and fascinating ways.

7. The relationship between "specular critics" and the gaze is somewhat paradoxical, I think. On the one hand, this critical emphasis on the body and the look derives from the Foucauldian and Lacanian critique of ocularcentrism, and should be understood as a political unveiling of the scopic regime within representation. On the other hand, there is no disguising the pleasure that such specular moments bring with them, particularly in a profession that has been, until very recently, informed and even sustained by a paternal(ist) interdict that denied the symbiotic relation between sexual and textual desire. See Martin Jay, "In the Empire of the Gaze: Foucault and the Denigration of Vision in Twentieth-Century French Thought," in *Foucault: A Critical Reader*, ed. David Couzens Hoy (Oxford: Basil Blackwell, 1986), 175–204.

8. Patterson's assessment of deconstructive theory is, of course, somewhat disingenuous here. His reading in fact attributes to deconstruction an assumption that, according to Jacques Derrida, is central to the Western metaphysical tradition. It is precisely the privilege accorded the pre- or- extralinguistic realm of the real that deconstruction calls into question. Deconstruction does not prescribe, but rather describes, the "sequestering" Patterson disparages. "Within this epoch," Derrida writes, "reading and writing, the production or interpretation of signs, allow themselves to be confined within secondariness. They are preceded by a truth, or a meaning already constituted by and within the element of the *logos*" (Jacques Derrida, *Of Grammatology*, trans. Gayatri Chakravorty Spivak [Baltimore: Johns Hopkins Univ. Press, 1976], 14). In revealing the source to be an effect of the supplement, deconstruction works to overturn, *not* to affirm, the binary opposition of speech and writing. Nevertheless, Patterson's concern here is a legitimate one, particularly in the context of medieval studies; the relationship between the real and the origin is not so easily dismissed within a field not only informed, but also (as both Patterson and Allen Frantzen point out) historically constituted, by nationalist and originary fantasies. See Lee Patterson, *Literary Practice and Social Change in Britain, 1380–1530* (Berkeley: University of California Press, 1990), 7, 8; and Allen Frantzen, *Desire for Origins: New Language, Old English, and Teaching the Tradition* (Brunswick: Rutgers University Press, 1990).

9. I do not mean to suggest that this phenomenon is *merely* pathological, that is, to assert that historicist thinking can or should take place without invoking the concept of the real. I would like rather to propose that we preface our gestures toward the real with some exploration of the epistemological limits of the category itself. It is here, it seems to me, that psychoanalytic theory has much to offer; the Lacanian idea of the real as that which "resists symbolization absolutely" has been appropriated by Louis Althusser in his theorization of the "absent cause," and by Frederic Jameson in his effort to articulate a theory of narrative and dialectics that might "[designate] the Real without claiming to coincide with it." See Jameson, "Imaginary and Symbolic in Lacan: Marxism, Psychoanalytic Theory, and the Problem of the Subject," *Yale French Studies* 55–56 (1977): 338–95.

10. Fradenburg's assertion that Freud draws no clear distinction between mourning and melancholia is symptomatic of her reluctance to deal with the issue of loss as it relates to language. In fact, Freud is fairly clear on the difference between the two:

> In one set of cases it is evident that melancholia [like mourning] may be the reaction to the loss of a loved object. Where the exciting causes are different one can recognize that there is a loss of a more ideal kind. The object has not perhaps actually died, but has been lost as an object of love. In yet other cases one feels justified in maintaining the belief that a loss of this kind has occurred, but one cannot see clearly what has been lost, and it is all the more reasonable to suppose that the patient cannot consciously perceive what he has lost either. This would suggest that melancholia is in some way related to an unconscious object-loss, in contradistinction to mourning, in which there is nothing about the loss that is unconscious. ("Mourning and Melancholia," in *The Standard Edition of the Complete Psychological Works of Sigmund Freud*, ed. James Strachey and trans. James Strachey et al., 24 vols. [London: Hogarth, 1953–74], 14: 245; translation modified)

In focusing exclusively on elegy as a form of mourning, Fradenburg ignores the role of the unconscious and thus of tropological substitution, of representation as a system. It seems to me that there is more that is melancholic about the *Book of the Duchess*, for example, than mournful. That Chaucer has combined elegy and dream-vision here makes it clear that the relation between representation and loss is precisely what is at issue. Julia Kristeva's analysis of melancholia (in *Black Sun*) seems more to the point. For Kristeva, melancholia is characterized by "intolerance for object loss and the signifier's failure to insure a compensating way out." In short, the Black Knight's loss of Lady White is inseparable from the narrator's melancholic loss of sleep, and therefore of dreaming or poetry. See *Black Sun: Depression and Melancholia*, trans. Leon Roudiez (New York: Columbia University Press, 1989), 10.

11. Fradenburg, "'Voice Memorial,'" 183–84.

12. See Nicolas Abraham and Maria Torok, "A Poetics of Psychoanalysis: The Lost Object—Me," *SubStance* 43 (1984): 3–18.

13. The theoretical significance of Blanche's absence has been noted by Maud Ellmann in her extremely suggestive but somewhat undeveloped essay "Blanche," in *Criticism and Critical Theory*, ed. Jeremy Hawthorn (London: Arnold, 1984): 99–110. Ellmann also notes the sense in which "Chaucer's poem intimates that mourning is native to narrative itself, which arises in and through the loss of origin" (104). She does not pursue this provocative comment, however; given that the *Duchess* is thought to be Chaucer's "originary" work, and that Chaucer himself is said to have metaphorically "originated" English poetry, the concept of the origin is a good deal more problematic for medievalists than her rather decontextualized reading allows. I am grateful to the anonymous reader for the University of Pennsylvania Press who brought this decidedly underacknowledged essay to my attention.

14. Peter M. Sacks, *The English Elegy: Studies in the Genre from Spenser to Yeats* (Baltimore: Johns Hopkins University Press, 1985).

15. The significance of introjection and incorporation in the constitution of the melancholic subject is discussed by Freud in "Mourning and Melancholia," (*Standard Edition*, vol. 14) as well as by Abraham and Torok in "Poetics of Psychoanalysis."

16. The relation between sleep and poetry is of course the metaphoric foundation for the medieval dream-vision from the Anglo-Saxon period onward. Sleep and/or dreaming is also evoked in this connection in works such as Shakespeare's *Tempest*, Milton's *Paradise Lost*, Spenser's *Daphnaida* (modeled on the *Duchess*), and Keats's *Endymion*, to name but a few.

17. The last lines of Keats's poem in fact echo those of Chaucer's *Duchess*:

> And up I rose refresh'd, and glad, and gay,
> Resolving to begin that very day
> These lines; and howsoever they be done,
> I leave them as a father does his son.
>
> (401–4)

18. Very little has been made of the morphological similarity between "Lollius" and "Lollard." Several readers have suggested that the name Lollius derives from a medieval misreading of Horace's address to Maximus Lollius:

> Troiani belli scriptorem, Maxime Lolli,
> dum tu declamas Romae, Praeneste relegi.
>
> (*Epist.*, 1, 2, 1)

For a compilation of evidence supporting this idea, see R. A. Pratt, "A Note on Chaucer's Lollius," *Modern Language Notes* 65 (1950): 183–87. More recently, the Lollius issue has been reconsidered by Bella Millet, "Chaucer, Lollius, and the Medieval Theory of Authorship," *Studies in the Age of Chaucer*, Proceedings no. 1 (1984), 93–103.

19. See James Wimsatt, *Chaucer and the French Love Poets: The Literary Background of the Book of the Duchess* (Chapel Hill: University of North Carolina Press, 1968), and B. A. Windeatt, ed. and trans., *Chaucer's Dream Poetry: Sources and Analogues* (Towtowa, N.J.: D. S. Brewer-Rowman and Littlefield, 1982).

20. See Donald Howard, *Chaucer: His Life, His Works, His World* (New York: E. P. Dutton, 1987), 86–87.

21. Freud's initial assumption that hysteria resulted from an actual seduction by the father was later revised into a "seduction fantasy"—a move that shifted the "blame" for the illness from the paternal figure to the hysteric herself. Nevertheless, after Dora's case made it clear that attachment to the mother was more to the point, Freud insisted upon the reality of the pathogenic event:

> And now we find the phantasy of seduction once more in the pre-Oedipus
> . . . but the seducer is regularly the mother. Here, however, the seduction
> touches the ground of reality, for it was really the mother who by her activities over the child's bodily hygiene inevitably stimulated, and perhaps even
> roused for the first time, pleasurable sensations in her genitals. (Freud, *Standard Edition* 22:120)

For feminist commentary on this passage and its implications, see Jane Gallop, "Keys to Dora," in *The Daughter's Seduction: Feminism and Psychoanalysis* (Ithaca:

Cornell University Press, 1982), 144; Mary Jacobus, *Reading Woman* (New York: Columbia University Press, 1986) 189; and Kaja Silverman, *The Acoustic Mirror: The Female Voice in Psychoanalysis and Cinema* (Bloomington: Indiana University Press, 1988), 121.

22. In his analysis of the child's "artistic play," Freud explicitly states that the unpleasure of loss may be mitigated by the pleasures of representation:

> We are therefore left in no doubt as to whether the impulse to work over in the mind some overpowering experience so as to make oneself master of it can find expression as a primary event, and independently of the pleasure principle. For, in the case we have been discussing, the child may, after all, only have been able to repeat his unpleasant experience in play because the repetition carried with it a yield of pleasure of another sort. (*Standard Edition* 18:16)

In attempting to foreclose the question of representation, Fradenburg offers what I take to be a somewhat strained reading of the *fort-da* scenario. See "'Voice Memorial,'" 183–84.

23. Wayne Koestenbaum, "Privileging the Anus: Anna O. and the Collaborative Origin of Psychoanalysis," in *Double Talk: The Erotics of Male Literary Collaboration* (New York: Routledge, 1989), 17–42.

24. In *Studies on Hysteria*, Josef Breuer calls Anna O. "the germ-cell of the whole of psychoanalysis." Her role in the genesis of psychoanalytic theory is also discussed by Mary Jacobus in her book *Reading Woman*, 205–28.

25. Koestenbaum, "Privileging the Anus," 30.

26. My argument, like Koestenbaum's, is here indebted to Eve Kosofsky Sedgwick's influential study *Between Men: English Literature and Male Homosocial Desire* (New York: Columbia University Press, 1985).

27. The homosocial aspects of the poem—but not their homoerotic implications—have also been noted by Maud Ellmann, as well as by Elaine Tuttle Hansen in her essay "The Death of Blanche and the Life of the Moral Order," *Thought: A Review of Culture and Ideas*, guest ed. Thelma Fenster (September 1989): 289–97.

28. See Bernard F. Huppé and D. W. Robertson, Jr., *Fruyt and Chaf: Studies in Chaucer's Allegories* (Princeton: Princeton University Press, 1963).

29. This is the position taken by Judith Ferster in her book *Chaucer on Interpretation* (Cambridge: Cambridge University Press, 1985): 69–93.

30. See Robert Edwards, "The *Book of the Duchess* and the Beginnings of Chaucer's Narrative," *New Literary History* (1982): 189–204.

31. A rather strained Boethian reading of the poem is offered by Michael Cherniss in his *Boethian Apocalypse* (Norman, Okla.: Pilgrim Books, 1987), 169–81.

32. Robert Jordan, *Chaucer's Poetics and the Modern Reader* (Berkeley: University of California Press, 1987), 75.

33. Robert Hanning, "Chaucer's First Ovid: Metamorphosis and Poetic Tradition in *The Book of the Duchess* and *The House of Fame*," in *Chaucer and the Craft of Fiction*, ed. Leigh Arrathoon (Rochester, Mich.: Solaris Press, 1986), 125.

34. Cf. John Fyler, *Chaucer and Ovid* (New Haven: Yale University Press, 1979). For Fyler, these lines refer to a golden age of ideal love.

35. Fradenburg points out that "Chaucer's 'good women' are—like Anelida and like Alcyone . . .—usually inconsolable, if not altogether dead; and the capacity of these women to generate narrative from their grief is either problematic or non-existent" (172).

36. Here, as throughout this essay, I draw on Kaja Silverman's brilliant study *The Acoustic Mirror*. For the interiorization of femininity, see pages 42–71.

37. An interesting analysis of the use of conventional language in the *Duchess* is provided by Philip Boardman in his article "Courtly Language and the Strategy of Consolation in the *Book of the Duchess*," *English Literary History* 44 (1977): 567–79.

38. The idea of a feminist Chaucer reflects, on the one hand, recent interest in feminist readings of Chaucer and, on the other, a simultaneous desire to exculpate Chaucer the poet on the charge of phallocentrism. Some of the more politically problematic aspects of this phenomenon are discussed at length by Elaine Tuttle Hansen in her essay "Fearing for Chaucer's Good Name," *Exemplaria* 2, no. 1 (Spring 1990): 23–36. Many of Hansen's points are well taken, particularly her indictment of what she calls the "post-feminist" trend in contemporary medievalism. Her essay is, however, based on some essentializing assumptions about the relationship between "male" versus "female" reading and writing that I find difficult to accept. Hansen defines feminist criticism in terms of "an insistence that the gender of the author and reader/critic matters." This definition carries with it decidedly empiricist assumptions, most notably the idea that writing bears an immediate and unproblematic relation to the experience of gender. If the gender of the *author* is so important, how can feminist criticism address the huge corpus of anonymous works from the Middle Ages? If the gender of the *critic* determines his or her capacity to read politically or not, how can feminism become more than a single-sex discourse? How can it address the equally problematic category of masculinity? Is the gender-category of "man" to remain unproblematic, while that of "woman" remains a site of contention, contradiction, and instability? More to the (political) point, what does Hansen's assumption promise for those of us who are *not* heterosexual, that is, who have only a vexed relationship to our culturally determined gender? These are all difficult questions, questions I will not presume to answer here. I do think, however, that there is more at stake in the idea of a feminist Chaucer than merely "Chaucer's good name." For a provocative analysis of the discursive and cultural implications of gender as an epistemological category, see Nancy Armstrong, "The Gender Bind: Women and the Disciplines," *Genders* 3 (Fall 1988): 1–23.

39. My analysis of fetishism as it relates to the *Duchess* is indebted to the work of feminist film theorists Kaja Silverman and Mary Ann Doane. The subheading of this final section is borrowed from Doane's book *The Desire to Desire: The Woman's Film of the 1940s* (Bloomington: Indiana University Press, 1987).

40. Freud, *Standard Edition* 21:152.

41. Ibid., 152–53.

Elizabeth Robertson

Medieval Medical Views of Women and Female Spirituality in the *Ancrene Wisse* and Julian of Norwich's *Showings*

That women were defined in the Middle Ages by their bodies has become almost a commonplace in studies of medieval concepts of gender. The idea of a woman's essential materiality arises primarily from Hippocratic, Aristotelian, and Galenic medical views of women as they are synthesized with theological commentaries on Genesis. The complexity of medieval notions of the body, particularly in relationship to the experience of women in the religious life, has been explored at length by scholars such as Caroline Bynum and Karma Lochrie.[1] What has perhaps been given less attention is the way specific aspects of medical theory resurface in the imagery used in English medieval mystical writings for and by women to describe female mystical experience. I shall focus here in particular on the medieval belief that women were physiologically cold, wet, and incomplete, and therefore by nature sought heat, purgation of moisture, and union with the male. Within the larger context of the idea that women are by nature rooted in the body, these biological views, I argue, condition the focus on blood, tears, and the concretized erotic vision of union with Christ that predominates in accounts of female spirituality, both by men about women and by women about themselves.

This essay is meant to pose questions about the ways that medical ideology shapes the literary representation of the feminine in mystical works. I begin this essay with a summary of medieval medical beliefs about the nature of the female body. I then explore the ways in which the prescriptive construction of physicality found in medical works informs a male writer's construction of female spirituality in the *Ancrene Wisse*. I question whether or not the male author of the *Ancrene Wisse*, in his use of imagery that has close affinities with imagery found in medical definitions of women, is imposing a "physiologically" driven ideology of female mystical experience upon his female readers. I then turn to the writing of a woman who closely followed the anchoritic life expounded in the *Ancrene Wisse*, Julian of Norwich, and finally, I consider briefly the writing of Margery Kempe. The fact that the same imagery that is supposed to delimit the female mystical experience in the *Ancrene Wisse* also appears even more extensively in women writers' accounts of their own mystical experience raises questions about whether or not women writers internalize or challenge prescriptive medical ideology. This essay assumes that medieval women writers acted responsively to the prescriptions of medieval physiology determined by men. Toward the end of the chapter, I speculate about the nature of those responses: did women writers tend toward submission and accomodation or toward controlling or manipulating the prescription to their own ends?

*   *   *

Medieval medical views of women have a complex history, involving a great number of thinkers whose medical expertise varied widely.[2] The three most influential theorists were Hippocrates, Aristotle, and Galen. Behind all medical theory lies the Hippocratic notion of the four humors, a microcosm that reflected the macrocosm of the four elements. Although Aristotle precedes Galen chronologically, of the two, Galen was initially more influential on medieval thought. Aristotle was not well known until the twelfth century, when he was introduced to the West through Arabic commentators and their translators. In the meantime, Galen's influence was pervasive; as Danielle Jacquart and Claude Thomasset write, the Middle Ages had the deepest confidence in Galen.[3]

Aristotle and Galen ultimately were very similar, however. Galen's major disagreement with Aristotle lies in his belief in the existence of a female seed, though this belief did nothing to shake his fundamental misogyny, one entirely consonant with that of Aristotle. In their discussion of the history of the debate over the existence of the female sperm, Jacquart and Thomasset point out that despite Galen's belief in the female sperm, "for him, male superiority is well established, since the female sperm in no way approaches in quality that of the male."[4] They conclude:

> It seems that the importance of these discussions on the nature of sperm was purely intellectual. All agreed to see in it "man's purest blood," the residue of the last coction; that is, all the theories were so slanted as to prove the preeminence of the product formed by the male. But female seed was at the

centre of a much more bitter quarrel, for the role ascribed to woman in reproduction was part of the setting-up of a hierarchy which, mediated by scientific and theological thought, was not without its effects on society.[5]

Repeatedly medical theory reinforced a hierarchy that placed women at the bottom of the scale.

Despite the span of centuries represented by medical writers as various as Galen, Isidore of Seville, Constantine the African, Vincent of Beauvais, and Thomas Aquinas, and even despite the shift to Christian thought, medical theory remained more or less consistent until the late Middle Ages, when dissection became more common and rigorous. Medical theory and practice were, of course, profoundly shaped by morality and later by theology. While medical practice, though not theory, sometimes diverged from theology, as, for example, in the case of contraceptive advice, which alternately banned contraceptives and provided detailed recipes for them, more often than not they reinforced one another. It is perhaps surprising that the medical theory of the classical age should prove so readily adaptable to Christian purposes, but despite the differences in cultural context, classical medical theory permeates medieval religious commentary, especially on Genesis. In order to provide a background for the mystical works under consideration here, I shall present a condensed summary of the prevailing medieval medical views about the nature of women.

Aristotle's views of women and his definition of gender sprang from his consideration of the nature of reproduction: "The female always provides the material, the male that which fashions it, for this is the power we say they each possess, and this is what is meant by calling them male and female."[6] He also argues for the existence of the male seed alone: "If, then, the male stands for the effective and active, and the female, considered as female, for the passive, it follows that what the female would contribute to the semen of the male would not be semen but material for the semen to work upon."[7] Furthermore, a woman is defined by her incompleteness. A female child was seen as simply an incomplete male. Ian Maclean summarizes Aristotle: "Nature would always wish to create the most perfect thing, which is the most completely formed, the best endowed with powers of procreation, and the hottest. Such a creature is the male, who implants his semen in the female to the end of procreating males. If however, there is some lack of generative heat, or if climatic conditions are adverse, then creation is not perfected and a female results."[8] In both Aristotelian and Galenic terms, "woman is less fully developed than man. Because of lack of heat in generation, her sexual organs have remained internal, she is incomplete, colder and moister in dominant humours."[9]

Because of lack of heat, the female genitalia, including the two female counterparts of the testicles, the ovaries, were believed never to have descended. The female anatomy was viewed, perhaps surprisingly, simply as an inversion of the male. While this similarity in physiology might have led to more egalitarian views of women, Jacquart and Thomasset conclude that it did not, for "although a close relation was established between man and woman, the fact remains that woman was described with reference to man. The model, the positive pole of comparison, was taken as the norm, and the other pole, which was given a negative value, was considered imperfect. In reality, there was in this analogy a correct observation which the strategy of discourse was to transform into an idea that was ultimately dangerous for women."[10] The medieval notion of inversion does suggest that "difference" is less significant when considering medieval views of the nature of the feminine than is the idea of incompleteness.

Fundamental to the idea of the female, according to both Galen and Aristotle, was the belief that women were excessively moist. Menstruation was believed to be a cleansing operation necessary to reduce excess feminine moisture, "a simple phenomenon of purification, meant to expel the residues that cannot be transferred by coction because of the woman's lack of heat."[11] In addition, different kinds of moisture were interchangeable. The Middle Ages adopted the Galenic theory of dealbation, in which blood is transformed into milk, and both these substances, as Jacquart and Thomasset point out were related to semen: "Whereas the blood that had reached a definite stage in its purification became semen, milk was formed from the menstrual blood."[12] Thomas Laqueur summarizes:

> Ancient medicine bequeathed to the Renaissance [and the Middle Ages] a physiology of flux and corporeal openness, one in which blood, mother's milk and semen were fungible fluids, products of the body's power to concoct its nutriment. Thus, . . . as writers from Pliny to Montaigne testified . . . bodily fluids could turn easily into one another. . . . Menstrual blood and menstrual bleeding were, moreover, regarded as no different than blood and bleeding generally. . . . Bleeding in men and in women is regarded as physiologically equivalent.[13]

Bleeding was but one way the body rid itself of excess fluids. As Laqueur writes, "The higher concoction of male semen with respect to that of the female and the fact that males generally rid themselves of nutritional excesses without frequent bleeding bore witness both to the essential homology between the economies of nutrition, blood, and semen in men and women, and to the superior heat and greater perfection of the male."[14] Perhaps most prominent in medieval thought was the belief that blood and milk were homologous. For according to Jacquart and Thomasset, "the affinity between milk and menstrual blood, asserted by Hippocrates, and repeated in greater detail by Galen, was an idea which the Middle Ages referred to again and again."[15] This intimate connection between food, blood (considered to be a product of food), and milk lies behind the array of images examined by Caroline Bynum in *Holy Feast and Holy Fast*.

One might expect a theory of homology, in which male and female fluids are viewed as essentially the same, to lead to a theory of equality between men and women. Bynum argues that while such potential did indeed exist in the later Middle Ages, as seen in its celebration of images of the lactating Mary and Jesus, that potential, at odds with a more dominant theory of the subordination of women, was nonetheless never fully realized. Yet in religious texts the interchangeability of blood, milk, tears, and semen is often stressed, and it is perhaps possible that writers of different genders, or even of different attitudes toward the genders, might seize upon the egalitarian possibilities inherent in the theory. In other words, the images themselves provided the opportunity for writers of either gender to see the egalitarian potential in them and to build upon them. We shall return later to the different ways in which men and women might interpret and use the medieval theory of fluids.

Women were believed to be not only fundamentally moist, but also fundamentally cold and therefore in need of heat. As Laqueur explains, heat was viewed as essential for conception:

> Heat is of critical importance in the Galenic account . . . sexual excitement and the "very great pleasure" of climax in both men and women are understood as signs of a heat sufficient to concoct and comingle the seed, the animate matter, and create new life. . . . Sexual heat was but an instance of the heat of life itself, and orgasm in both sexes the sign of warmth sufficient to transform one kind of bodily fluid into its reproductively potent forms and to assure a receptive place for the product of their union.[16]

Sexual pleasure and fertility were thus linked through the concept of heat.

Although Laqueur's generalizations suggest that the medieval concept of sexual pleasure was egalitarian, in practice it was not. For example, the idea that women who conceived only did so by achieving orgasm could lead to disastrous consequences in rape cases, since the rape victim who conceived was deemed to have given the consent necessary to achieve conception. As in other areas of medieval physiology, ideas about orgasm in relationship to the need for heat led to conclusions in which women were subordinated to men. Jacquart and Thomasset stress the importance of the notion of heat in the development of gender roles: "Heat is an attribute that can easily find its place in the interplay of qualities that contrast female and male."[17] While heat was desirable for both sexes, because the female had less of it her need for it was perceived to be greater than that of the male.

This insufficiency of heat led commentators to argue that women existed in a condition of perpetual desire. Women were believed to be driven by their craving for the hottest, most complete being, that is, the male. Aristotle emphasized the essential need of the female for the male in a basic precept, "Matter desires form as the female the male." Excess moisture further reinforced a woman's condition of perpetual need, for, to commentators such as Adelard of Bath, humidity in women caused desire. Women, though colder and moister than men, were believed to feel a more burning desire than men; it was in fact thought to be insatiable, in part because, as Jacquart and Thomasset point out, women were thought to experience "a pleasure that was greater in quantity, but lesser in quality and intensity than men's."[18] The insatiability of feminine desire, an idea that has its roots in medical theory, permeated medieval thought and literature and reinforced male fear of female sexuality.[19]

Theologians including Jerome and Augustine adopted and reasserted these medical views. For example, Bonaventure, although adopting the Galenic notion of two seeds, nonetheless argues that "the former [man] acts as 'efficient' cause of conception, the latter [woman] as 'material' cause."[20] Aristotelian and Galenic theory especially pervades biblical commentaries on Genesis, where, for example, Adam was seen as the head, Eve as the body: "Man is the *spiritus*, (masc.), the higher rational soul, woman the *anima*, (fem.), the lower sensible soul."[21] As Vern Bullough points out, "Philo defined the female as inferior to the male since the female represented sense perception, the created world, while the male represented the rational soul."[22] That Aristotelian views were not only adopted by theological commentators, but were considered specifically suitable for female readers is indicated by the opening statement of Sloane 2463, the fifteenth-century English gynecological handbook: "Therefore, you must understand that women have less heat in their bodies than men and have more moisture because of lack of heat that would dry their moisture and their humors, but nevertheless they have bleeding which makes their bodies clean and whole from sickness."[23]

It might be argued, and often was, that spirituality offered women an escape from their female nature and that they could transcend their femininity through virginity. As Marina Warner puts it, "through virginity and self-inflicted hardship the faults of female nature could be corrected."[24] This view is supported by Jerome: "As long as woman is for birth and children, she is different from man as body is from soul. But if she wishes to serve Christ more than the world, then she will cease to be a woman and will be called man."[25] And Bullough summarizes: "Progress [for women] meant giving up the female gender, that is, the passive, corporeal and sense perception, for the male gender, that is, the active, incorporeal and rational thought."[26]

Medieval attitudes toward female spiritual potential are further complicated by views of her soul, however. The Middle Ages inherited two opposing views of a woman's spiritual nature, the Platonic notion of the soul's gender neutrality, and the Aristotelian view of the soul as differentiated by gender. Unlike Plato, who saw the soul as conditioned by the degree of virtue it contained, Aristotle perceived the soul as possessing nutritive, sensitive (or appetitive), and reasonable faculties; women were deficient in all three, but especially in reason.[27] To Aristotle then, a woman's soul was more earthbound than a man's. While Platonic views of the soul's gender neutrality sometimes vied with Aristotelian concepts, Aristotle so pervaded theological commentary on women that his assumption of the limited nature of a woman's soul must, to some degree, have conditioned representations of female spirituality. That is, religious writing both for and by women must have acknowledged a woman's appetitive and nutritive soul. If this is so, it would be impossible for a woman to transcend her femininity, since the limitations of femininity would carry on into death. Given the pervasiveness of Aristotelian ideas of the soul, it is unlikely that medieval men writing for women believed that women could transcend their bodily limitations despite their attempts to do so by leading lives of virginity. It is difficult to determine to what degree a given author subscribed to the theory of a limited female soul, but as we shall see, to some extent the authors we will consider assume it.

In the texts we shall consider here, I propose that the contemplative life, far from offering women an escape from their femininity, actually offered them the opportunity to explore and even celebrate those very traits of femininity that were outlined in the medical texts. Because women were viewed—and perhaps indeed viewed themselves—as trapped inescapably in a body designated and even disparaged as female, sexuality and notions of the female body became the central issues for women in pursuit of the contemplative life. Perceived to be rooted physically and spiritually in an inferior body and soul, the female contemplative was deemed able to perceive God only through that body. In this essay, I shall discuss notions of the sensual, the bodily, and the physical as the basis of the medieval construction of the erotic and the sexual. In other words, a woman's perceived bodily needs as outlined in the medical texts are viewed in the Middle Ages as the driving force of her eroticism. Her experience, as we shall see, was defined by Aristotelian ideas of her need for completion—for heat—and for the purging of excess moisture. In addition, the biological parity between blood, sweat, tears, milk, and urine meant that a woman's contemplation of Christ's blood was contemplation of her own blood, and further that her tears were equivalent to Christ's blood. The suffering body of Christ thus allowed a woman not only to pity Christ but to identify in him her own perceived suffering body; moreover, union with his suffering body would allow her to realize her perceived biological needs.

Such images are of course present in male texts as well, but in female writing, blood and tears and the like are central to the contemplative experience because of their reflection of the perceived nature of women. It is in fact difficult to find extensive images of moisture, especially blood, in mystical works written by men. Richard Rolle's *Incendium amoris* and the anonymous *Cloud of Unknowing*, for example, are virtually devoid of such images. They are more common in meditations on the passion, but we might expect to find such images there since these treatises were often written specifically for women.

Caroline Bynum argues that even though women were not created in God's image, and even though they were conditioned by their sensual, appetitive natures, these facts did not prohibit their approach to God.[28] While I agree that they did not *prohibit* women's access to God, I think these views did *condition* their approach to God; that is to say, female spirituality is expressed not only through the body, as Bynum argues, but also through those parts and activities of the body that are understood as specifically or "essentially" female.[29] Moisture, the physical, the flesh, could be adopted as meditative concerns for men as well, but because the very nature of the male soul was perceived as separate from the body, these meditations were only a part of a progress, an ascent to God that ultimately transcended the flesh. Because women were perceived to be unable to transcend the flesh even after death, both men writing for women and women writers themselves had to contend, in one way or another, with these essentialist views of femininity.

*   *   *

A religious guide written by a man for women, the *Ancrene Wisse*, is illustrative of the ways in which biological views of women shape the author's representation of female spirituality.[30] Indeed, the work as a whole reflects notions of the female body; as the work progresses, the author develops an idea of the anchorhold as a womb, a place that the anchoress must prepare for Christ's entry. Especially prominent in the last three chapters of the work, "Confession," "Penance," and "Love," is an interwoven pattern of imagery that focuses on blood. In "Confession," for example, the anchoress is told that "We ahen him blod for blod. ant ure blod þah aȝein his blod þ he schedde for us. were ful unefne change. . . . ant ure lauerd nimeð ed us ure teares aȝein his blod. ȝ is wilcweme." ("We owe Him [Christ] blood for blood, and even so, our blood for His blood which He shed for us, would be a very unequal exchange. . . . And our Lord accepts our tears from us in exchange for His blood, and is well pleased").[31] As in the medical texts, moistures, here blood and tears, are seen as interchangeable. It is, of course, a Christian commonplace to speak of Christ's blood as redemptive. The emphasis on the inferiority of the blood given in payment, however, is particularly apt for women whose excess blood was seen as especially impure. Furthermore, the *Wisse* author develops the image of blood graphically. The author tells the anchoress to contemplate the cross and see how "swa swiðe fleaw þ ilke blodi swat. of his blisfule bodi. þ te streames urnen dun to þer eorðe. . . . þus lo þe hale half ȝ te cwike dale droh þ uvele blod ut. frommard te unhale. ȝ healde swa þe seke" (60–61) ("the bloody sweat flowed so freely and in such quantity from His blessed body that it ran in streams to the ground. . . . Thus the living, healthy part drew out the bad blood from that which was diseased and so healed that which was sick") (49–50). The association of women with excess moisture purged through menstruation makes these images, resonant though they are for both men and women, especially redemptive for women. Purgation, viewed in medical accounts as necessary for women's physical health, is here presented to female readers as necessary for spiritual health as well.

Redemption, in the *Ancrene Wisse*, is made possible not only through the purgation of excess feminine moisture, but also through heat, the heat brought about through sexual union with Christ. While heat, or the fire of love, the *incendium amoris*, is a motif that pervades twelfth-century affective works, the centrality of a sexual union with Christ in this particular work suggests the male author's concern to address the perceived needs of his female readers, including their biological need for heat met through union with the male. In the next chapter, "Penance," the work paves the way for the anchoress's union with Christ by introducing an image of the fetid, wounded body to be redeemed by Christ. Such a focus is particularly apt for a female audience seen to be trapped in deficient bodies. The chapter then introduces the image of the fiery wheel and the flaming sword, establishing a sexualized and bodily framework for the anchoress's spiritual apotheosis. Elijah's wheel is red: "Fur is hat ᴣ read. I þe heate is understonden euch wa þ eileð flesch. Scheome bi þe reade" (181) ("Fire is hot and red. By the heat is signified every pain that afflicts the body. By the redness dishonour") (157). The wheel is transformed into a flaming sword, which stands for both the sun and the cross: "Ne kimeð nan in to pareis. bute þurh þis leitinde sweord þe wes hat ᴣ read" (181) ("No one enters paradise but by this flaming sword, which was hot and red") (157). God will thus win the anchoress with his implicitly erotic flaming sword.

Cleansed by penance, the anchoress is then ready for contemplation of her union with Christ, presented in this work as a literal marriage to a Christ Knight. Christ is particularly associated with fire, the fire of desire presented in medical texts as necessary for conception. What the anchoress conceives through union with Christ is her spiritual self. That the author intends the anchoress to equate union with Christ with sexual union with an earthly man is made explicit at the end of this section, where he introduces images of heat in the context of a discussion of the inadequacies of earthly sexual intercourse in comparison with union with Christ.

The work then culminates in an unusual catachretic image that has never been adequately accounted for, an image that compares God's love to Greek fire. Bringing together biological ideas of women's innate desire, need for heat, and excess moisture, this graphic, even incendiary image suggests that the anchoress may achieve spiritual fulfillment through the explosive transformations of Christ's blood. After discussing the need to kindle sticks to promote desire, the author directs the anchoress: "Grickisch fur is imaket of reades monnes blod. ᵹ þ ne mei na þing. bute Migge. ant Sond. ᵹ eisil. as me seið acwenchen. þis grickisch fur is þe luve of iesu ure lauerd. ᵹ ᵹe hit schule makien of reade monnes blod. þ is iesu crist ireadet wið his ahne blod o þe deore rod" (205) ("Greek fire is made from the blood of a red man and cannot be quenched, it is said, except with urine, sand and vinegar. This 'Greek fire' is the love of Jesus our Lord, and you shall make it from the blood of a red man, that is, Jesus Christ, reddened with His own blood on the precious cross") (178). The emphasis here on Christ's redness underscores his suitability as an object of female contemplation since, like women who are suffused with blood, Christ was believed to have a sanguine temperament.

In its emphasis on heat and moisture, this unusual image of Greek fire reflects biological views of women. The author as before relies on the medieval belief that bodily moistures are interchangeable: the bad blood of the earlier passage becomes the urine or vinegar that threatens the redemptive blood of Christ. Urine was the focus of diagnosis in medieval medicine; here the ill moisture of the body, urine, is transformed and redeemed by the moisture of Christ. Janet Grayson writes of this passage:

> The uncontrollable wildfire, the bloodied Christ, . . . the specifics of urine and vinegar that threaten to smother the consuming Greek fire—all converge here into the emotional, highly concentrated repetitions and refinements of the power of sacrifice. And the pervasiveness of redness (initially the color of fire) provides a definite focus for the Passion, the *memoria Christi*, the affective influence of Christ crossed that kindles the *incendium amoris* between anchoress and Christ, between lady and Christ-knight.[32]

This image particularly intensifies the image of heat, that quality deemed most needed by women, for as Ian Bishop points out, comparing God's love to an incendiary device used in war would be like comparing God's love to napalm.[33] The explosiveness of the image might even suggest orgasm, which the medical texts considered necessary for women both to conceive and to help purge moisture.

The peculiar aptness of this image for women readers is further underscored by the author's departure from his sources, in which Greek fire is equated with lust; here it is equated with its opposite, Christ's love.[34] Perhaps this change can be attributed to the author's assumption that his female audience cannot escape its essentially lustful female nature. By equating Christ with a substance usually associated with lust, however, the author suggests to the readers that lust itself need not be transcended;

rather, it must be properly directed. The female reader's innate lust is thus potentially redeemable not through its transcendence, but through its redirection to a suitable object, Christ. As the culminating image of the work, Greek fire crystallizes the overall theme: the anchoress's bodily realization of union with Christ.

What I believe is significant about this passage and different from medieval conceptions of male spirituality is that for women, union with Christ occurs not as an allegory of the ascent of the mind to God, but as concretized erotic experience, one that redeems her fleshliness and her excess moisture through orgasm. Erotic imagery does, of course, appear in male mystical works, but eroticism seems to be constructed differently for men and women. While some male writers may graphically describe their physical union with Christ (consider, for example, the Monk of Farne's description of plunging himself into Christ's wounds to achieve orgasm, or Rupert of Deutz's homoerotic description of passionately kissing Christ), such erotic imagery seems less driven by the physiological need for redemption of the flesh than do analogous meditations in female texts.[35] Often in male texts, eroticism is chiefly a tool to enhance the mind's contemplation of God, whereas in female mystical works, erotic union with Christ is itself often the end of the meditation.

Further work needs to be done on the similarities and differences between male and female spiritual desire in relationship to received views about male and female experiences of physical desire. The *incendium amoris*—the fire of love for God—is an erotic image equally available to male and female contemplatives in part because early biological views, as Laqueur has pointed out, stress the importance of simultaneity of orgasm for men and women and the necessity of heat for conception. Nevertheless, women are by nature more conditioned by desire for the incarnate Christ both because their essential material nature denies them any other access to God and because their perceived biological natures place them in a condition of perpetual desire.[36]

*   *   *

In the work of Julian of Norwich there are distinctive features that I believe are influenced by her encounter with the standard medieval medical views outlined above. The sensual and physical permeate her work. In particular, running throughout the text is the idea that her body is redeemed through the body of Christ, who is figured in feminine terms.

Like her, Christ, as God incarnate, is dominated by physicality. Indeed, Julian's meditations are prompted by notions of physicality. She says at the beginning of her work: "I desyrede thre graces be the gyfte of god. The fyrst was to have mynde of Cryste es passionn. The seconnde was bodelye sycknes, and the thryd was to have of goddys gyfte thre wonndys" ("I desired three graces by the gift of God. The first was to have recollection of Christ's Passion. The second was a bodily sickness, and the third was to have, of God's gift, three wounds") (125).[37] Julian's revelations thus spring from experiences of the body. She identifies with Christ as someone who, like herself, is wounded. While her stated desires are also common in works of male mystics, the fact that they are central in Julian's work not only reflects her sense of herself as rooted in the body but accentuates her work as distinctively feminine.

Furthermore her revelations are permeated with images of blood. She writes, "with him I desyred to suffer, livyng in my deadly bodie, as god would give me grace. . . . And in this sodenly I saw the reed bloud rynnyng downe from under the garlande, hote and freyshely, /plentuously and lively, right as it was in the tyme that the garland of thornes was pressed on his blessed head" (long text, chap. 3, 293, and chap. 4, 294) ("I desired to suffer with him, living in my mortal body, as God would give me grace. . . . And at this, suddenly I saw the red blood running down from under the crown, hot and flowing freely and copiously, a living stream, just as it was at the time when the crown of thorns was pressed on his blessed head" [181]). Here Christ's blood, like menstrual blood, is purged, matching her own natural purgation of excess. Elsewhere Julian expands this image so that the blood is even more evocative of menstrual blood. Contemplating the crown of thorns, she says, "And in the comyng ouȝte they were browne rede, for the blode was full thycke; and in the spredyng abrode they were bryght rede" (long text, chap. 7, 311) ("as they [the drops] issued they were a brownish red, for the blood was very thick, and as they spread they turned bright red" [187]). Like menstrual blood, "The bledyng contynued" (long text, chap. 7, 311) ("the bleeding continued" [188]) and, as she explains of this vision in the short text, "this ranne so plenteuouslye to my syght that me thought, ȝyf itt hadde bene so in kynde, for þat tyme itt schulde hafe made the bedde alle on blode and hafe passede onn abowte" (short text, chap. 8, 227) ("I saw this blood run so plentifully that it seemed to me that if it had in fact been happening there, the bed and everything all around it would have been soaked in blood" [137]).

Julian's image of blood, evocative of menstrual flow, also suggests blood lost in losing virginity; the blood of Christ is even explicitly connected with her own bed. Furthermore, the fact that the age viewed menstrual blood and semen as homologous underscores the erotic implications of the image. Christ's blood is linked with all kinds of moisture, all redemptive of feminine excess: "God has made waterse plentuouse in erthe to oure servyce and to owre bodylye ese, for tendyr love that he has to us. Botte ȝit lykes hym bettyr that we take fullye his blessede blode to wasche us with of synne; for thare ys no lykoure that es made that hym lykes so welle to gyffe us. For it is plenteuouse and of oure kynde" (short text, chap. 8, 227) ("God has created bountiful waters on the earth for our use and our bodily comfort, out of the tender love he has for us. But it is more pleasing to him that we accept freely his blessed blood to wash us of our sins, for there is no drink that is made which pleases him so well to give to us; for it is so plentiful, and it is of our own nature" [137]). Excess moisture is thus redemptive, and thereby so is femininity itself.

In order to highlight Julian's extraordinary and idiosyncratically female uses of blood imagery, let me digress for a moment to consider a contemplation of Christ's blood by her male contemporary, Richard Rolle. In comparing the two works, we should not overemphasize their differences since it is unclear for whom Rolle wrote his meditations. Indeed, Wolfgang Riehle speculates that many of the Middle English writings of the late medieval English mystics were intended for female readers. Furthermore, meditations on the passion are generically different from mystical revelations. Nonetheless, as we shall see, Rolle's meditation on blood differs quite markedly from that of a woman writer.

> A, Lord, þe pite þat I now se: þi woundys in þi streynynge reche so wyde, þi lymes and þi nayles are so tendre, þou lyst rowyd and reed streyned on þe cros, þe kene crowne on þin hed, þat sytteth þe so sore; þi face is so bolnyd, þat fyrst was so faire; þi synwes and þi bonys styrten owte starke, þat þi bonys may be nowmbryd; þe stremys of þi reede blood rennyn as þe flood; þi woundys are for-bled and grysly on to se; þe sorewe þat þi modur makyth encresuth þi woo.[38]

(Ah, Lord, the pity that I see now: your wounds in your stretching-out stretch so wide, your limbs and the places where the nails pierced you are so tender, you lie, made raw and red, stretched on the cross, the sharp crown on your head sits on you so painfully, your face is so swollen, that once was so fair; your sinews and your bones stick out so starkly that your bones could be numbered; the streams of your red blood run as the flood; your wounds are covered with blood and are grisly to see. The sorrow your mother makes increases your woe.)

Whereas Julian's image of blood ultimately becomes confused with her own blood, here the picture of the suffering Christ evokes not so much identification as pity. If the viewer is to identify with anyone, it is with Mary, who is given much attention further on in the meditation. The blood produced by the crown of thorns is not mentioned, and the blood flowing from the wounds of the body is equally considered with the stretched limbs and swollen face, all of which evoke pity. The Rolle passage presents a systematic and inclusive analysis of Christ's suffering, one that details the shocking anatomy of the wounded body. Yet, despite the personal address to "þou," and despite the affective qualities shared by the Rolle and Julian passages, the Rolle passage lacks the immediacy and intimacy of Julian's description. The end of the passage shifts the focus away from the viewer to Mary. It is as if the male viewer cannot enter the body of the suffering Christ in the same way as can Julian, an impression created in the Julian passage by the blurring of boundaries between Christ's blood and her own. Indeed, when male speakers describe entering the wounds of Christ, they recount a desire to possess Christ, whereas the female speakers tend to describe entering the wounds in order to merge with Christ. At the very least, we can say that excess moisture does not predominate in the Rolle passage as it does in that of Julian.

Another important aspect of Julian's work—that is, her emphasis on the sensuality of Christ—can be accounted for by considering it a reflection or even displacement onto Christ of medieval medical arguments about female sensuality. As Bynum points out in her discussion of the feminized Christ, Julian often figures Christ as a mother.[39] Julian further associates Christ's feminized body, "oure moder Cryst," with sensuality: "he is oure moder of mercy in oure sensualyte takyng" (long text, chap. 58, 586) ("he is our Mother of mercy in taking our sensuality" [294]). And of Christ as the second part of the trinity she says "The lower perty, whych is sensualyte, sufferyd for the salvacion of mankynd" (long text, chap. 55, 569) ("The lower part, which is sensuality, suffered for the salvation of mankind" [288]). The feminized body of Christ, rather than leading the contemplative to a transcendence of the sensual, redeems the sensual by uniting the contemplative's "substance" with Christ's: "for in oure moder Cryst we profyt and encrese, and in mercy he reformyth us and restoryth, and by the vertu of his passion, his deth and his uprysyng onyd us to oure substannce" (long text, chap. 58, 586) ("for in our Mother Christ we profit and increase, and in mercy he reforms and restores us, and by the power of his Passion, his death and his Resurrection, he unites us to our substance" [294]).

As far as I know, Julian's emphasis on the sensuality of Christ is distinctive. As Riehle writes, "Julian's understanding of the image of God is that it embraces the whole man, including his bodiliness, a theory which has been put forward in traditional teaching, but not very frequently. . . . It is thus possible to speak of God taking up his dwelling in man's *sensualite*. This is certainly Julian's most interesting contribution to the theme of the image of God."[40] I suggest that Julian is speaking here not simply of a gender-neutral sensuality, but more specifically of woman's sensuality; moreover, the redemption she explores here, while a redemption of all mankind, is especially redemptive for women. Bynum has argued that the twelfth century's interest in the humanity of Christ, because of its celebration of the flesh, ultimately resulted in a reassessment of the value of femininity. In these passages on sensuality, Julian's emphasis is on Christ's redemption, not only of humanity, but also of that aspect of humanity which male writers repeatedly designate and condemn as particularly feminine, sensuality. While a woman author's association of Christ's redemption with her own feminine characteristics might well have resulted in a reassessment of femininity, it is important to recognize that Julian's approach carries with it at least her initial acceptance of the age's misogynistic views of the nature of her body. She celebrates the incarnated Christ because this is the only God that she can, according to the age's view of her limited nature, truly perceive.

The fact that Julian focuses in her writing so insistently on attributes of female physiology might make us wonder if other women mystical writers do the same. It would be useful to compare her writing to English and Continental female mystical writing. For the moment, let me consider briefly a near contemporary, Margery Kempe. Although I cannot here discuss Margery Kempe in detail, I would like simply to state the case that Margery's visions also are conditioned by her absorption of medieval views of the female body. In his analysis of Middle English mystics, Riehle is particularly troubled by Margery, whose habit of hyperbole he finds to be a sign of her "pathologically neurotic traits": "She is no longer capable of separating the sensual and spiritual and the former is indeed more important to her than the latter."[41] For example, she literalizes her marriage to

Christ: and writes that Christ says to her, "þe mayst boldly, whan þu art in þi bed, take me to þe as for þi weddyd husband" ("you may boldly when you are in your bed take me to yourself as your wedded husband.") [42] She wants literally to hold and taste God. She is wounded with longing and, as one could not fail to notice in her account, cries to excess. Margery's behavior has led some critics to view her as exceptional, if not aberrant, in the history of female religious.[43] But far from being an exception to the female spiritual movement, she is rather at its center. For if we consider her writing in the context of the medieval assumptions about women we have been discussing here, we find that she has simply taken these assumptions, presented more covertly in other women's writing, to their logical extreme. Told by theory that she can only experience God through the body, Margery recounts extreme bodily experiences in her quest for union with God. Told that she has too much moisture, Margery cries excessively, which makes those around her, especially those in power who are challenging her authority, uncomfortable. The very excesses of her writing, her extremes of tears and sensual expressiveness, suggest a destabilization of those assumptions.

If we accept that gender is a sociocultural construct, then gendered subjectivity is an "emergent property of a historicized experience."[44] To understand medieval female subjectivity as it is constructed in texts written by and for women, I have argued here both that we must consider the discourses that shaped this subjectivity and that we should understand images of blood, tears, and other moisture—and indeed the general focus on the physical and sensual in female spiritual works—as internalizations of or reactions to prescriptive medical discourse about women's bodies. Furthermore, these medical views help shape the notion of writers that a woman's experience of union with Christ would be literal and concrete. There are many other examples of such literalization in spiritual writing by both men and women in England, and perhaps on the Continent as well; the erotic is stressed in the Monk of Farne's meditations, in Richard Rolle's writing, in Anselm's *Prayers and Meditations*, and in the work of Saint Bernard. A focus on the erotic is an important part of male spirituality. For female spirituality, it is central.[45]

The prevalence of images of blood, heat, and tears in works written for and by women suggests the writers' familiarity with medical ideology about women. We do not know whether or not these authors endorse this ideology, especially since we know very little about them other than what can be gleaned from the texts themselves.[46] What we do know does not provide us with enough information to determine precisely what the valence of certain signs in the text is. We might argue that Julian is an essentialist, that she has internalized misogynist medieval views about the nature of her body, and further, that through the contemplation of Christ's similarity to herself she redeems some attributes of the feminine. We do not know, however, how she responded to Aristotelian notions of femininity, since she does not tell us directly. (Indeed it is even difficult to determine how men reacted to these views. The thirteenth-century *Hali Meiðhad* tells us that some men viewed pregnancy and childbirth with disgust, but we have no analogous medieval text that describes a woman's view of such experiences.) We might go further and argue that Julian, rather than accepting male views of women, ultimately subverts them, and that rather than being an essentialist herself, she takes an "essentialist" stance only as a strategy, in an Irigarayan sense: she mocks male views by mimicking and hyperbolizing them, and undoes them by overdoing them.

How Julian views the age's construct of femininity remains an open question. The fact that many images associated with the feminine are generally hyperbolic in women's texts signals a complex attitude toward those images that is difficult to interpret. We can at the very least argue that the presence of medical attributes associated with women in these texts makes them gendered and that the hyperbolizing of those gendered signs in women's texts at least destabilizes those categories.

Of course, the meaning of such destabilizations will vary from one woman to another and will be dependent on her historical circumstances.[47] We can determine from Julian's work that she, like the anchoresses for whom the *Ancrene Wisse* was written, was a well-educated, probably upper-class woman whose theology was learned and orthodox. The fact that Margery Kempe cites Julian in her quest for legitimacy suggests Julian's establishment in and acceptance by the religious community. We also know that Julian chose to revise her revelations into a longer and more orthodox version twenty years later.

Despite her relatively secure and apparently orthodox position in the religious establishment, Julian's representation of herself in both versions suggests that she felt considerable anxiety about her authority to speak as a woman, an anxiety that is more overtly expressed in the early short text. There, her meditation on the hazelnut, for example, is intricately bound up with her sense of herself as an inferior, small woman. In her contemplation of the littleness and insignificance of a small object like a hazelnut she acknowledges her own inferiority while at the same time allying herself, in her littleness, with Mary. She writes,

> he schewyd me a lytille thynge, the qwantyte of a haselle nutte, lyggande in the palme of my hande, and to my understandynge that, it was rownde as any balle. I loked þer uponn and thoughte: What may this be? And I was annswerde generaly thus: It is alle that ys made. I merveylede howe þat it myght laste, for me thoughte it myght falle sodaynlye to nought for litille. And I was annswerde in myne understandynge: It lastes and ever schalle. for god loves it; . . . In this god brought oure ladye to myne understandynge. . . . In this sight I sawe sothfastlye that scho ys mare than alle þat god made benethe hir in worthynes and in fulheede. . . . This lytille thynge that es made that es benethe oure ladye saynte Marye—god schewyd it unto me als littille as it hadde beene a hasylle notte—me thought it myght fallene for littille. (short text, chap. 4, 212–14)

(he showed me something small, no bigger than a hazelnut, lying in the palm of my hand, and I perceived that it was as round as any ball. I looked at it and thought: What can this be? And I was given this general answer: It is everything which is made. I was amazed that it could last, for I thought that it was so little that it could suddenly fall into nothing. And I was answered in my understanding: It lasts and always will, because God loves it; . . . In this God brought our Lady to my understanding. In this sight I saw truly that she is greater, more worthy and more fulfilled, than everything else which God has created, and which is inferior to her. . . . This little thing which is created and is inferior to our Lady, St. Mary—God showed to it to me as if it had been a hazelnut—seemed to me as if it could have perished because it is so little. (short text, chap. 4, 130–31)

Not unlike Chaucer's Prioress in the prologue to that problematic tale, Julian here establishes her authority and her kinship with Mary's power.[48] The act of writing itself challenges society's expectations of women, and Julian's anxiety about this destabilization is expressed in this passage. A few pages later, Julian asks her audience to "leve the bahaldynge of the wrechid worme, /synfulle creature, that it was schewyd unto" (short text, chap. 6, 219) ("disregard the wretched worm, the sinful creature to whom it [the vision] was shown" [133]) because, she writes, "I am a womann, leved, febille and freylle," (short text chap. 6, 222) ("I am a woman, ignorant, weak and frail" [135]), thus underscoring her apparent acceptance of the age's view of her inadequacy as a speaker.

In the revised version of the short text twenty years later, however, Julian deletes both the analogy between the hazelnut and Mary and all references to her own inadequacy.[49] Why? Did Julian later recognize the hidden arrogance of comparing herself implicitly to Mary? Since the long text does indicate Julian's desire to make her work more orthodox, did she feel such statements might be unorthodox? Or do the changes suggest that after twenty years as an anchoress acknowledged and admired by her community, Julian no longer felt the same degree of authorial anxiety as she did in her youth? While her sense of security in her authorial identity may have increased from the time she wrote the short text to the time she wrote the long text, Julian's continued reference in the long text to other perceived attributes of women, such as to excess blood, suggests that although she suppresses overt consideration of her status as a woman speaker as she becomes more established in the community, she nonetheless continues to meditate on her "female" condition.

I am inclined to believe that Julian of Norwich was a subtle strategist who sought to undo assumptions about women and to provide, in an Irigarayan sense, a new celebration of femininity through contemplation of Christ's "feminine" attributes. I also believe that her challenge to male constructs of the feminine had no revolutionary intent. That is, while I believe she recognized and, perhaps to some extent, internalized the fact that she was seen to be "other" than men, she wished to participate in the religious hegemony and had the same ultimate goals as did her contemporary male mystics. Yet, while this may be so, achievement of these goals must have been conditioned by her consideration of herself as "inferior" to men, an inferiority that she indirectly challenges in her work.[50] That challenge includes a questioning of her status as "other" as defined by men. Julian's point would thus be similar to that of Irigaray, as summarized by Naomi Schor: "Irigaray's wager is that difference can be reinvented, that the bogus difference of misogyny can be reclaimed to become a radical new difference that would present the first serious historical threat to the hegemony of the male sex . . . mimesis comes to signify difference as positivity, a joyful reappropriation of the attributes of the other that is not in any way to be confused with a mere reversal of the existing phallocentric distribution of power."[51] Thus, rather than calling Julian's use of blood, water, or her own littleness, subversive, it would be more accurate to call such uses celebratory.

Finally, given the pervasiveness of images of moisture in medieval women's texts, the subject of the relationship of fluidity and femininity deserves further consideration. Irigaray has recently become intrigued with the properties of fluids. As she wrote in *This Sex Which Is Not One*, "historically the properties of fluids have been abandoned to the feminine."[52] This statement ushers in for Irigaray an analysis of the fluidity of women's writing. Perhaps Julian's style might also be termed fluid in her refusal to honor time sequences or teleology, and in her repetitiousness.[53] But whatever conclusion we might come to concerning the relationship between her stylistic strategies and her position in society as a woman, we can at least agree that thematically her images have much to do with that aspect of woman considered to be her essence by Aristotle: her moisture. Perhaps that property abandoned to women was adopted to good purpose by Julian. Even though modern science no longer equates the feminine with excess moisture, the fluidity of female style is still very much an issue in contemporary criticism. The relationship of fluidity of style to female "essence" is, however, the subject of another essay.

Notes

In addition to the editors and readers, I would like to thank Gerda Norvig, Sarah Beckwith, and Jeffrey Robinson for their perspicacious editorial advice for the revision of this essay. I would also like to thank Karma Lochrie, whose astute reading of this essay at a late stage helped sharpen my thinking about the subject even though I was not able to respond fully to her comments.

1. Caroline Walker Bynum has written about female mystical experience and notions of the female body in her book *Holy Feast and Holy Fast: The Religious Significance of Food to Medieval Women* (Berkeley: University of California Press, 1987), in her essay "The Female Body and Religious Practice in the Later Middle Ages" (in *Fragments for a History of the Human Body, Part 1*, ed. Michel Feher with Ramona Naddaff and Nadia Tazi [New York: Zone Books, 1989], 160–219), and in her collection of essays, *Fragmentation and Redemption: Essays on Gender and the Human Body in Medieval Religion* (New York: Zone Books, 1991). In these works, Bynum warns readers that medieval notions of the body are considerably more complex than they are usually thought to be and that readers should beware of taking an oversimplified and unhistoricized view of the body in the Middle Ages, a view I also hold. Karma Lochrie has added to our understanding of medieval beliefs about the body in her essay, "The Language of Transgression: Body, Flesh, and Word in Mystical Discourse" (in *Speaking Two Languages: Traditional Disciplines and Contemporary Theory in Medieval Studies*, ed. Allen J. Frantzen [Binghamton: State University of New York Press, 1991], 115–40) and in her book, *Margery Kempe and Translations of the Flesh* (Philadelphia: University of Pennsylvania Press, 1991). In those works, Lochrie makes the important argument that, while

it may be true that in the Middle Ages the body was not always denigrated, the flesh often was, and more often than not, women are particularly associated with the flesh. Because this essay is a revision of a paper I gave at the annual meeting of the Medieval Institute at Kalamazoo, Mich. in 1988, before many of these works appeared, I do not engage the work of either of these important scholars directly in this essay. I shall only say here that Bynum and I differ in general in that she seems to wish to soften the misogyny that informs medieval female mystical experience whereas I wish to explore it, and that Bynum seems more comfortable with essentialist views of women than am I. Lochrie draws out the feminist implications of this subject in her studies of Angela Foligno and Margery Kempe in ways that I think would be fruitful in future studies of Julian of Norwich.

2. The summary of medieval medical views of women to follow is based on chapter 3, "Medieval Views of Female Spirituality," of my *Early English Devotional Prose and the Female Audience* (Knoxville: University of Tennessee Press, 1990), 32–43.

3. Danielle Jacquart and Claude Thomasset, *Sexuality and Medicine in the Middle Ages*, trans. Matthew Adamson (Princeton: Princeton University Press, 1988), 12–80.

4. Ibid., 62.

5. Ibid., 60.

6. Quoted by Christine Garside Allen in her essay on Aristotle, "Can a Woman Be Good in the Same Way as a Man?" in *Woman in Western Thought*, ed. Martha Lee Osborne (New York: Random House, 1979), 46.

7. Vern L. Bullough, "Medieval Medical and Scientific Views of Women," in *Marriage in the Middle Ages, Viator* 4 (1973): 487.

8. Ian Maclean, *The Renaissance Notion of Woman: A Study in the Fortunes of Scholasticism and Medical Science in European Intellectual Life* (Cambridge: Cambridge University Press, 1982), 8.

9. Ibid., 31.

10. Jacquart and Thomasset, *Sexuality and Medicine*, 36.

11. Ibid., 72.

12. Ibid., 52.

13. Thomas Laqueur, "Orgasm, Generation and the Politics of Reproductive Biology," *Representations* 14 (Spring 1986): 8.

14. Ibid., 9. Laqueur's generalizations might require some modification given the variety of elaborations on this theme. Saint Thomas, for example, argued that the blood forming the embryo differs from the blood surrounding it, a theory he produced in order to free the fetal Jesus from contamination by the impurities of menstrual blood. See Jacquart and Thomasset, *Sexuality and Medicine*, 77.

15. Jacquart and Thomasset, *Sexuality and Medicine*, 52.

16. Laqueur, "Politics of Reproductive Biology," 4–5, 9.

17. Jacquart and Thomasset, *Sexuality and Medicine*, 59.

18. Ibid., 81.

19. Isidore of Seville, for example, lamented women's excessive sensuality. See Jacquart and Thomasset, *Sexuality and Medicine*, 14.

20. Quoted in George Tavard, *Woman in Christian Tradition* (Notre Dame, Ind.: University of Notre Dame Press, 1973), 132.

21. Joan M. Ferrante, *Woman as Image in Medieval Literature: From the Twelfth Century to Dante* (New York: Columbia University Press, 1975), 17.

22. Bullough, "Medieval Medical Views," 497.

23. Beryl Rowland, ed., *Medieval Woman's Guide to Health: The First English Gynecological Handbook* (Kent, Ohio: Kent State University Press, 1981), 59.

24. Marina Warner, *Alone of All Her Sex: The Myth and Cult of the Virgin Mary* (New York: Knopf, 1976), 69.

25. Quoted in Bullough, "Medieval Medical Views," 499.

26. Ibid., 497.

27. See Osborne's summary of both Plato's and Aristotle's views of the soul in *Woman in Western Thought*, 15–16.

28. See Bynum, *Holy Feast*, 261.

29. See, for example, Bynum, *Holy Feast*, 263.

30. For a full discussion of the ways in which the *Ancrene Wisse* represents a male construction of female spirituality, see chapter 4, "The Rule of the Body: The Female Spirituality of the *Ancrene Wisse*," of my *English Devotional Prose*, 44–76.

31. J. R. R. Tolkien, *Ancrene Wisse: The English Text of the Ancrene Riwle* (*Corpus Christi College Cambridge 402*), EETS, o.s. 249 (London: Oxford University Press, 1962), 161. All further quotations are from this edition; page numbers are cited in parentheses in the body of my text. Following Tolkien, I have rendered the tironian ampersand as a "z" with a hyphen through it. The translation is taken from the excellent work of M. D. Salu, *The Ancrene Riwle* (London, 1955; rpt., Notre Dame: University of Notre Dame Press, 1956), 139. All further translations will be taken from her work, and page numbers will be given in parentheses in my text.

32. Janet Grayson, *Structure and Imagery in the Ancrene Wisse* (Hanover, N.H.: University Press of New England, 1974), 205.

33. Ian Bishop, "'Greek Fire' in *Ancrene Wisse* and Contemporary Texts," *Notes and Queries* 224 (1979): 170–99.

34. Bishop explains that the author, in his elaboration of the image of Greek fire, departs from his sources, which include the *Moralia super evangelia*, a work closely associated with the *Ancrene Wisse*.

35. According to Mary Wack, "Rupert of Deutz (d. 1129) reports a dream in which he worshiped the Cross. The crucified Christ seemed to return his gaze and accept his salutation. Yet he wanted closer union with his Savior. Rushing to the altar, he embraced and kissed the image. 'I held him, I embraced him, I kissed him for a long time. I sensed how seriously he accepted this gesture of love when, while kissing, he himself opened his mouth that I might kiss more deeply.'" See Wack, *Lovesickness in the Middle Ages: The* Viaticum *and Its Commentaries* (Philadelphia: University of Pennsylvania Press, 1990), 24. I am grateful to Karma Lochrie for drawing my attention to this passage. The Monk of Farne passage is described in Wolfgang Riehle, *The Middle English Mystics* (London: Routledge and Kegan Paul, 1981), 46–47. Bynum discusses some of the problems we face in interpreting male uses of imagery associated with the female in "Women's Symbols" (in *Holy Feast*,

chapter 10), and in *Jesus as Mother: Studies in the Spirituality of the High Middle Ages* (Berkeley: University of California Press, 1982).

36. Given the fact that heat is more important physiologically to men than moisture, it is not surprising that the work of Richard Rolle's that is probably most clearly intended for male readers, the *Incendium amoris*, should focus primarily on the heat of desire rather than on moisture. There is barely a reference to moisture in the entire text. While women, too, might share in the praising of the acquisition of heat celebrated in the *Incendium*, the male mystic has an advantage over the female mystic in his quest for heat since he is by nature already in possession of it.

37. Julian of Norwich, *A Book of Showings to the Anchoress Julian of Norwich: Parts One and Two*, ed. with an introduction by Edmund Colledge and James Walsh (Toronto: Pontifical Institute of Medieval Studies, 1978), short text, chap. 1, p. 201. All further quotations will be taken from this edition; text, chapter, and page will be given in parentheses in the body of my text. Translations will follow those of Colledge and Walsh in their *Julian of Norwich: Showings* (N.Y.: Paulist Press, 1978) and page numbers will be given in the body of the text.

38. Hope Emily Allen, ed., *English Writings of Richard Rolle* (Oxford: Clarendon Press, 1931), 24. The translation is my own.

39. See Bynum, *Jesus as Mother*.

40. Riehle, *The Middle English Mystics*, 148.

41. Ibid., 11.

42. *The Book of Margery Kempe*, ed. Sanford Meech and Hope Emily Allen, English Text Society o.s. 212 (Oxford: Oxford University Press, 1990), 90. The translation is taken from Barry Windeatt, ed. and trans., *The Book of Margery Kempe* (Middlesex, Eng.: Penguin Books, 1985), 126.

43. Although Margery is undergoing considerable critical reevaluation at the moment, few critics other than perhaps Karma Lochrie and Sarah Beckwith have argued that her behavior is a response to the ideologies of her age. See Lochrie's *Margery Kempe* and Sarah Beckwith's *Christ's Body: Religious Culture and Late Medieval Piety*, forthcoming from Routledge. See also Sarah Beckwith, "A Very Material Mysticism: The Medieval Mysticism of Margery Kempe," in *Medieval Literature: Criticism, Ideology, and History*, ed. David Aers (Brighton, Sussex: Harvester Press, 1986), 34–57.

44. Linda Alcoff, quoted by Teresa de Lauretis in "The Essence of the Triangle or, Taking the Risk of Essentialism Seriously: Feminist Theory in Italy, the U.S., and Britain," in *The Essential Difference: Another Look at Essentialism*, ed. Naomi Schor and Elizabeth Weed, *Differences* 1, no. 2 (Summer 1989): 12.

45. The fact that the Monk of Farne writes of plunging himself into the wounds of Christ to achieve orgasm suggests that Luce Irigaray's theory that the wounds of Christ are analogous to the female vulva is not simply a postmodern Freudian interpretation of Christ's wounds, but is also one that was prevalent in the Middle Ages. See Riehle, *Middle English Mystics*, 46–47.

46. Colledge and Walsh summarize what we can guess about Julian's biography in their introduction to their edition of Julian. For a historical survey of the religious structure of Norwich in Julian's day, see Norman P. Tanner, *The Church*

in Late Medieval Norwich: 1370–1532 (Toronto: Pontifical Institute of Medieval Studies, 1984). An excellent essay that explores the subversive potential of a woman's use of physiological discourse much more thoroughly than mine is Lochrie's "The Language of Transgression." Without a fuller knowledge of Julian's relationship to the clergy I hesitate to call her use of such imagery subversive except insofar as the fact that her willingness to speak at all subverts medieval notions of the importance of female silence. The subversive potential of such imagery is certainly worthy of fuller consideration.

47. Given the dearth of information about Julian, it is difficult to determine whether she speaks from within or outside the hegemony. As Diana Fuss writes, "I cannot help but think that the determining factor in deciding essentialism's political or strategic value is dependent upon who practices it: in the hands of a hegemonic group, essentialism can be employed as a powerful tool of ideological domination; in the hands of a subaltern, the use of humanism to mime (in an Irigarayan sense of 'to undo by overdoing') humanism can represent a powerful displacing repetition" ("Reading Like a Feminist," in *The Essential Difference*, ed. Schor and Weed, 86). Is Julian more or less likely to acquiesce to male views of the inferior nature of women because she has been well trained in orthodox religion? Margery Kempe's use of medical traits ascribed to women is certainly more hyperbolic than Julian's. Is she being conventional or hyperconventional in adopting prevalent images? Does her membership in a lower class than Julian's make it more or less difficult than Julian for her to claim authority, despite the fact that the male religious establishment would view them both as inferior by nature? Ultimately it is up to the reader to decide from which positions Julian and Margery speak. While both Margery and Julian share in the privileges of money and education, and while they both share the desire to be acknowledged and accepted by the dominant group, as well as the desire to participate in the ideology of the dominant group (in other words, they are not true outsiders, as, for example, a witch might be), nonetheless their relationship to that ideology is so conditioned by their femininity that they can be said to speak from the position of the subaltern. Margery's insistent focus on self-justification may well be a reflection, not of neurosis, but rather of the unusually difficult place she was in, caught between the desires of the bourgeois and those of the clerical communities; because Margery, unlike Julian, chose not to withdraw from the world as an anchoress, she became all the more subject to the world's skeptical scrutiny. For a discussion of Margery's place within the bourgeois and clerical communities, see Sarah Beckwith's forthcoming book, *Christ's Body*.

48. For a discussion of Chaucer's Prioress's anxiety about her voice, see my article "Aspects of Female Piety in the *Prioress's Tale*," in *Chaucer's Religious Tales*, edited by myself and C. David Benson (Cambridge: Boydell and Brewer Press, 1990), 145–60.

49. I am grateful to Sarah Beckwith for pointing out to me the fact that Julian deletes references to her femininity from her long text.

50. Caroline Bynum perhaps assumes too much similarity between male and female mystics in the Middle Ages. There are, of course, dangers in viewing women either as other or as the same as men. As Naomi Schor puts it, "If othering

involves attributing to the objectified other a difference that serves to legitimate her oppression, saming denies the objectified other the right to her difference, submitting the other to the laws of phallic specularity." Bynum, I would argue, runs the risk of "saming" in her analyses. I want to avoid the risk of "othering." See Naomi Schor, "This Essentialism Which is Not One: Coming to Grips with Irigaray," in *The Essential Difference*, ed. Schor and Weed, 45.

51. Schor, "Coming to Grips," 47–48.

52. Quoted in ibid., 49.

53. B. A. Windeatt discusses these features of Julian's style without reference to her gender in "The Art of Mystical Loving: Julian of Norwich," in *The Medieval Mystical Tradition in England*, ed. Marion Glasscoe (Exeter: Exeter Press, 1980), 55–71.

Wendy Harding

Body into Text: *The Book of Margery Kempe*

Since it was first made available to scholars in 1934, *The Book of Margery Kempe* has generally been analyzed and evaluated in terms of the contribution it makes to the corpus of medieval mystical writings. In this context, Margery Kempe's book is agreed to be interesting but finally somewhat derivative. As one of the first works in English by a woman, *The Book of Margery Kempe* has recently assumed greater significance in the literary canon. Yet although contemporary feminism has inspired a number of rereadings of the text, they tend partly to corroborate the findings of earlier studies, for they determine that Margery's spirituality is shaped by masculine definitions of femininity. Caroline Bynum concludes that "for all her fervor, her courage, her piety, her mystical gifts and her brilliant imagination, [Margery] cannot write her own script."[1] Sarah Beckwith similarly demonstrates that Margery's mysticism "cannot break the mold of [feminine] subjection . . . , for it is the very equation of victimization, passivity, subjection with femininity, that allows the Christian inversion its paradoxical triumph."[2] Thus Bynum implicitly and Beckwith explicitly offer a corrective to feminist theories celebrating as subversive the empowerment that the woman mystic's abjection brings. They insist that although Margery produces a text, she echoes a previously written script.

Nonetheless, a number of scholars feel that the manuscript is distinctive in that it echoes Margery's own charismatic narrative style. B. A. Windeatt suggests that we hear much of the accent of an authentic voice, and he argues that the book's frequent representation of direct-speech exchanges may be a feature of an illiterate composer's text.[3] Robert Stone asserts that "no one who reads *The Book of Margery Kempe* can help feeling the impact of the author's individuality on the way in which thoughts are expressed," and Bynum hears Margery's "own vivid prose."[4] In one of the most fully considered appraisals, Karma Lochrie reads *The Book of Margery Kempe* as the story of a woman's successful quest for literary authority. Nonetheless, she feels that Margery's accomplishment entails a loss. Since Margery cannot read her own book, upon its completion she becomes alienated from her own life—she "becomes a cypher to herself."[5]

Inevitably, Margery's illiteracy raises questions as to her authorship. John C. Hirsh insists "that the second scribe, no less than Margery, should be regarded as the author of *The Book of Margery Kempe*."[6] Discerning in the text the indelible imprint of a masculine, clerical hand, Hirsh argues that the scribe selected the episodes of the narrative to impose order and to give Margery's spiritual life a direction. Moreover, he claims that echoes of devotional writers such as Richard Rolle must necessarily have been inserted by the priest. Indeed, the problem of the scribe's role in writing the book needs to be more carefully studied by feminist readers. Margery's book cannot be considered a uniform, monologic work, for it results from the collaboration between an illiterate woman and her male scribes. Neither entirely a clerk's script nor a woman's original composition,[7] *The Book of Margery Kempe* is dialogic in a startlingly literal sense.[8]

Before exploring this multilayered enunciation, we should consider for a moment the changing politics of women's writing in history. A number of feminist investigations rightly insist that questions of voice and literary authority are not simply resolved by determining who wields the pen. Adrienne Rich describes the woman writer's ongoing struggle with a medium that names her even as she tries to use the power of naming. The language she inherits from the fathers determines the woman poet's utterances; thus Rich reflects, "you have to be constantly critiquing even the tools that you use to define what it is to be female."[9] While she is conscious that her language is freighted with patriarchal ideology, the poet has no other medium in which to express herself: "This is the oppressor's language / Yet I need it to talk to you."[10] The illiterate medieval woman confronts a fascinating variation on this problem. Enjoying only marginal access to "the oppressor's language," she communicates in a medium that is positioned at the boundaries of dominant discourse.

To a certain extent Margery Kempe's illiteracy frees her from the internal constraints that Rich describes. In her exclusion from writing she enjoys a certain freedom to communicate in a medium less stringently controlled by patriarchal authorities. On the other hand, the ransom she pays for that negative freedom is that her message is not fully intelligible to the literate, and consequently her chances of ensuring that some written trace of her discourse remains are almost negligible. Rather than borrowing "the oppressor's language," she must rely on his cooperation in order to enter the historical record. Yet while this necessity creates a redoubled form of enslavement to patriarchy, it also produces a certain incompatibility in expression which the scholar can explore. The encounter between the illiterate woman and the scribe, between dominant discourse and uncharted extraliterary expressions, makes the manuscript a kind of border zone where evidences generally excluded from Western history can be found.

Although the dynamics of the exchange are, as I hope to demonstrate, extremely complex, we could begin by considering *The Book of Margery Kempe* as a dialogue between representatives of opposing orders of medieval society. The second scribe, part editor and part writer of the extant manuscript, belongs to a celibate male priesthood whose power derives in large part from its literacy, whereas Margery belongs to a disenfranchised class of illiterate, married women unattached to any religious order.[11] Although for the purposes of analysis I will make some distinctions between the clerical style and the laywoman's oral utterances, such an objective is finally unrealistic, for the book blurs the boundaries between the two. The exchange recorded in *The Book of Margery Kempe* is at times a conjunction, at times a confrontation, between various dichotomous elements in late medieval society: the dominant and the marginalized, masculine and feminine, mind and body, clergy and laity, and written and oral modes of expression. Shaped in part by an unequal struggle for control of channels of communication, the resultant work destabilizes and subverts these historically hierarchical binary oppositions.

In a preface that is part explanation, part justification, the second scribe, a priest, gives an account of the book's making. We learn that the transcription was begun by an Englishman who had lived in Germany, who resided with Margery for a time, and who died before the work was properly finished.[12] The priestly author of the preface describes his promise to complete the work, his difficulties reading his predecessor's handwriting, and his cowardice in the face of slander about Margery's emotional displays of piety. Finally Margery's prayers and appeals give the priest the courage and the grace to embark on the task of creating a legible and coherent book. Miraculously he deciphers the ill-formed letters, copies the first scribe's manuscript, and continues to record the remainder of Margery's memoirs "after hyr owyn tunge" (221). For a number of possible reasons—the marginal professionalism of the first scribe,[13] the sympathy and perhaps the dissent of both writers, and the choice of the vernacular—the manuscript is more evidently heteroglot than other spiritual treatises. As well as familiar pious formulae, the text includes conversations and descriptions that a more conventional treatise would have suppressed.

Evident in the priest's preface is his effort to position Margery's narrative within recognizable and authorized frames and thereby to transfer the laywoman's oral account into a different order of discourse. The account of his difficulties with the manuscript and their miraculous resolution attests the book's legitimacy by framing its production within the hagiographical tradition.[14] Moreover, he encourages readers to interpret the treatise as an illustration of Christ's works: "how mercyfully, how benyngly, and how charytefully he meved and stered a synful caytyf un-to hys love" (1). Margery's story is offered as an illustration of a familiar pattern in which a reversal of fortune brings a sinner closer to God: "a creature sett in grett pompe and pride of the world, whech sythen was drawyn to ower Lord be gret poverte, sekenes, schamis, and gret repreuys" (5–6). In this formulation, Margery serves as an example of the worldly woman redeemed, an association reinforced by the priest's assertion that he began to write "on the day next aftyr Mary Maudelyn" (6). By suggesting in these ways that Margery's story has divine inspiration and approval, he offers a context in which a woman's voice can assume the authority of a written text.

In addition to these reassuringly conventional formulae, there are moments where the translation is not so smooth, where the priest betrays his consternation at the task of rendering an oral account into writing. For example, he apologizes for the organization of the book, which records Margery's experience "not in ordyr as it fellyn but as the creatur cowd han mend of hem whan it wer wretyn, for it was twenty yer and mor fro tym this creatur had forsake the world and besyly clef on-to ower Lord or this boke was wretyn, not-wythstondyng this creatur had greet cownsel for to don wryten hir tribulations and hir felingys" (6). This comment can be read as a trace of the confrontation between the clerk's linear, historical orientation with its insistence on the precise recording of dates,[15] and Margery's oral expression with its reliance on memory and sensuous or affective association.[16]

While the features of clerical writing are familiar to readers of medieval texts, the particular characteristics of an oral account are less evident. Therefore some distinctions between oral and written modes provide a useful point of departure for analyzing *The Book of Margery Kempe*.[17] As we see from the book's preface, one of the primary aims of writing is instruction; hence the writer needs to establish his authority to teach. In the Middle Ages this is usually achieved by establishing continuities between the new text and its canonical predecessors, either scriptural or classical depending on the genre. Thus the written text is conservative and highly normative. Moreover, writing represents the record of analysis and reflection, for its legibility entails conformity to conventions of argumentation and organization that include logical and chronological development. The text is dependent on the sequentiality of the phrase and the chronology of before and after, yet, insofar as it becomes an artifact, it endures in time. Not limited exclusively to one moment and one place, writing can transmit a message from one person to another without the necessity of bodily contact. Oral discourse conforms to rather different conventions. It does not need to justify itself by rationalizing its utility; its purpose can simply be that of initiating an interaction in order to establish a rapport, a supralinguistic understanding. Dependent on performative skills, oral expression is sensory, immediate, and necessarily transient, inscribed in time. At the same time it permits and even encourages innovation, since new expressions aid in cementing new relationships and defining new social subgroups. Argumentation in oral discourse is not linear but interactive and global. Moreover, the range of available expression involves supralinguistic effects such as intonation and bodily movements. Finally, oral communication mediates the world through the body in its entirety, relying on voice, gesture, and face-to-face interaction.

Some of the differences between clerical writing and Margery's oral expression can be appreciated when we compare some characteristic passages from the manuscript. The opening lines exemplify the authoritative voice of the priestly class: "Here begynnyth a schort tretys and a comfortabyl for synful wrecchys, wher-in thei may have gret solas and comfort to hem and undyrstondyn the hy and unspecabyl mercy of ower sovereyn Savyowr Cryst Ihesu, whos name be worschepd and magnyfyed wythowten ende, that now in ower days to us unworthy deyneth to exercysen hys nobeley and hys goodnesse" (1). The speaker adopts the priestly role of mediator between the deity and the people. Although at the end of the sentence he includes himself among the "unworthy" benefactors of Christ's mercy, he does not ally himself any further with his intended audience. Offering the treatise as an aid to *their* understanding, he implies that he already possesses knowledge of God's workings. Thus he distances himself from readers, placing himself above them in his nearer proximity to the divine mind. His style further supports his priestly authority through its echoes of scripture and prayer, for clerical discourse grounds itself in a textual tradition that reaches back ultimately to sacred writ.

By contrast, the expression of the unlettered laywoman is far removed from this authoritative mode of address. As she reportedly explains to the vicar of St. Stephens, her discourse derives its justification from a very different source:

> Sche teld hym how sum-tyme the Fadyr of Hevyn dalyd to hir sowle as pleynly and as veryly as one frend spekyth to a-nother be bodyly spech; sum-tyme the Secunde Persone in Trinyte; sumtyme alle thre Personys in Trinyte and one substawns in Godhede dalyid to hir sowle and informyd hir in hir feyth and in hys lofe how sche shuld lofe hym, worshepyn hym and dredyn hym, so excellently that sche herd nevyr boke, neythyr Hyltons boke, ne Bridis boke, ne Stimulus Amoris, ne Incendium Amoris, ne non other that evyr sche herd redyn that spak so hyly of lofe of God but that sche felt as hyly in werkyng in hir sowle yf sche cowd or ellys mygth a schewyd as sche felt. (39)

Margery communicates with the same God that the learned clerks claim to represent, but she characterizes him as an immediate and familiar interlocutor, closer to a husband, child, or friend than a supreme and awesome power. She describes herself as receiving the word of God directly and bodily, as if through oral dialogue, rather than through the texts and rituals of the learned clergy. Margery's experience is represented as both like and unlike those described in other spiritual treatises. Her intense affective response is reportedly comparable, but she does not express it in the same way. In referring to other treatises, the scribe implies that Margery's illiteracy entails a deficit in her ability to communicate. Despite its avowal of a certain lack, the text nonetheless invokes a form of expression whose range and immediacy is lost in written language. In response to the intensity of her private communion with God, Margery falls writhing to the ground, making "wondyrful cher and contenawns wyth boystows sobbyngs and grete plente of terys, sumtyme seyng 'Ihesu, mercy,' sumtyme 'I dey'" (40). She actualizes the metaphors that describe mystical union by conveying with voice and body the throes of sexual passion. Her tears and sobs represent a response more direct and spontaneous than words. Inasmuch as the written word is privileged, this nonliterary expression is not acknowledged as a discourse. Nonetheless, this very physical reaction suggests not so much Margery's inability to express herself, as her recourse to a different order of communication. Rather than the madness of a woman who cannot write, this can be seen as a woman's attempt to signify a mystical experience whose intensity cannot be written but must be inscribed by living flesh.[18]

In seeking to define the differences between the two modes, I have of course invoked the very polarities that Margery's book questions. Rather than being exclusive categories, oral and written discourses are in fact complementary and continuous. The Bible itself claims to be the subsequent record of oral communication between God and his creatures. Nevertheless, in the later Middle Ages the scriptural canon is fixed and a body of written law established. Continued communication between God and humanity is not denied, but mystical revelations, particularly to women, are treated as potentially diabolic.[19] Clerical and secular powers promote a hierarchical and somewhat exclusive relationship between written and oral expression, between text and body. The written word is seen as primary rather than as a part or an extension of a dialogic process. In official circles the oral word occupied a secondary role, serving either to gloss or to popularize the canonical text. Moreover, literacy is a privilege enjoyed and protected by the dominant; subaltern members of society are excluded from this prestigious form of discourse. While the elite can communicate on both sides of the split, workers and most women are confined to oral expression.

Since binary oppositions are fundamental to medieval ideology and to patriarchy in general, they clarify certain features of Margery's text. Moreover, they help account for her relationship to her scribes as well as her interactions with the authorities. As a married laywoman, Margery can only express herself orally and carnally through the marginalized medium of her female body. Repressed on account of this body, she communicates from the site of her subjection. Using a discourse refused by the clerical elite, Margery argues for more inclusive forms of worship and schemes of salvation. Her carnal and affective form of devotion denounces restrictive concepts of Christianity that serve to consolidate the power of the male clergy. Her piety and her mode of expression represent a departure from and an alternative to the hierarchical, ordered, masculine spirituality of the pulpit.

The episode that best illustrates the contrast between the discourse of the literate authorities and Margery's alternative mode of communication takes place in the chapel of the archbishop of York, where Margery is brought to answer charges of heresy. Her transgression lies less in the matter of her speech than in the manner of its expression. The accusation of heresy is a pretext to challenge Margery's right to be seen and heard in public: "The clerkys seyden, 'We knowyn wel that sche can the Articles of the Feith, but we wil not suffyr hir to dwellyn a-mong us, for the pepil hath gret feyth in hir dalyawnce, and peraventur sche myth pervertyn summe of hem'" (125). This paradoxical insistence on both the orthodoxy and the subversiveness of Margery's message bears further analysis. In describing her speech with the word *dalyawnce*, the clerks suggest the troubling ambiguity of women who speak in public. *Dalyawns* here denotes spiritual conversation, but in other contexts it means flirtatious behavior or sexual intercourse, an association that is reinforced in the accusation that Margery might pervert her audience.[20] Elsewhere Margery's speech is described as *comownycacyon*, another word that conveys erotic harmonics. Although the term refers to the exchange of words about holy matters, it reverberates with an additional connotation, for in Margery's book the verb *comown* sometimes appears in its alternate sense to refer to copulation. These linguistic co-incidences suggest that Margery's oral, feminine ministry represents a return of much that is repressed in orthodox and authoritarian clerical practices.

In this confrontation the clerks are fighting to keep cultural oppositions in their customary hierarchical order. Though perfectly orthodox in its content, in its adherence to the Articles of Faith, Margery's "dalyawnce" is taken as a challenge to priestly authority. Thus the archbishop asks Margery to swear that she will neither teach nor admonish the people of his diocese. Margery's response to this attempt to protect clerical prerogative is audacious:

> "Nay, syr, I shal not sweryn," sche seyde, "for I shal spekyn of God and undirnemyn hem that sweryn gret othys whersoevyr I go unto the tyme that the Pope and Holy Chirche hath ordeynde that no man schal be so hardy to spekyn of God, for God almythy forbedith not, ser, that we shal speke of hym. And also the Gospel makyth mencyon that, whan the woman had herd owr Lord preychd, sche cam beforn hym wyth a lowde voys and seyd, 'Blessed be the wombe that thee bar and the tetys that gaf thee sowkyn.' Than owr Lord seyd agen to hir, 'Forsothe so ar thei blissed that heryn the word of God and kepyn it.'" (126)

Margery insists that the Church judge her according to law and scripture, and she refuses to be silent until an official decree demands it. Arguing that such an ordinance does not exist, she recalls an instance where a pious woman responds to Christ's words by blessing the womb and breasts of his mother. Citing this exchange that directs attention to Mary's maternal body, Margery justifies her own lay ministry.

In reply to this incursion on what the clerks see as their domain, a priest produces the very book that legitimates hieratic power. To convince Margery of her transgression, he reads her a scriptural injunction: "a gret clerke browt forth a boke and leyd Seynt Powyl for his party a-geyns hir that no woman shulde prechyn" (126). As a member of the learned, literate, masculine elite, the clerk is Paul's heir. He might have read from the Epistle to the Corinthians: "Let your women keep silence in the churches: for it is not permitted unto them to speak; but they are commanded to be under obedience. . . . And if they will learn anything, let them ask their husbands at home: for it is a shame for a woman to speak in the church" (I Corinthians 14:34–35). Alternatively, he may have selected verses from the Epistle to Timothy: "I suffer not a woman to teach, nor to usurp authority over the man, but to be in silence. For Adam was first formed, then Eve. And Adam was not deceived, but the woman being deceived was in the transgression. Notwithstanding she shall be saved in childbearing, if they continue in faith and charity and holiness with sobriety" (I Timothy 2:12–15). Insisting on male superiority, these texts seek to enforce patriarchal law on the female body. The message they convey is that woman must be silenced, confined to the home and the husband's rule.

In replying to the clerk who reads from Paul's Epistle, Margery shifts the grounds of her argument, representing her speech as a language that belongs to another order than that of the clerks. She claims not to usurp masculine prerogative: "I preche not, ser, I come in no pulpytt. I use but comownycacyon and good wordys, and that wil I do whil I leve" (126). Margery insists here on her right to an extraliterary discourse, characterized as an exchange between human beings made up of spirit and flesh. She concedes to the priests the space of the pulpit, which, elevated above the people, equipped with a lectern, and concealing the body of the speaker, would symbolize the connection between language (particularly as writing or as the recitation of sacred writ) and clerical authority. Yet, while granting this vertical, hierarchized dispensation of discourse, she insists on her right to engage in dialogue on a horizontal, egalitarian level. She proclaims the moral and spiritual value of oral communication—her good words—and in so doing she opposes the clerical conception of language as monologic and disembodied.

In the late Middle Ages, sacerdotal authority depended not only on the priest's ability to read and write but also on the subordination of his own corporeality. From the desk and the pulpit, an avowedly celibate clergy denounced the female body as the emblem of sinful humanity, thereby distancing themselves from the fallen souls to whom they ministered. To the degree that it effaces distinctions between soul and body, textuality and orality, masculine and feminine, Margery's discourse undermines this justification for clerical power. This implicit challenge to priestly authority would account for the vehemence with which the clergy sometimes persecuted her.

During a period described by the scribe as a "vexacyon" and by an angel as a "chastisyng" (146), Margery's communication with God ceases and is replaced by a kind of *dalyawns* that indicates the subversive potential of Margery's discourse: "Sche sey as hir thowt veryly dyvers men of religyon, preystys, and many other, bothyn hethyn and Cristen comyn befor hir syght that sche myth not enchewyn hem ne puttyn hem owt of hir syght, schewyng her bar membrys unto hir. And therwyth the Deuyl bad hir in hir mende chesyn whom sche wolde han fyrst of hem alle and sche must be comown to hem alle" (145). Although Margery takes these temptations to be a divine reproof, her recounting of them exposes the deceptiveness of medieval dualities. While Sarah Beckwith rightly argues that this hallucination is represented as "more the sign of her shame than her subversion,"[21] the public retelling of it in her book undermines patriarchal authority in that it reminds readers that both heathens and Christians share the same sexual characteristics and that under their clothing men remain as carnal as women. In a reversal of misogynistic accounts of seductive feminine wiles, Margery draws attention to "mennys membrys and swech other abhominacyons" (145). Men—even priests—take the role of tempters here, threatening to turn Margery's attention from spiritual *comownycacyon* to carnal *comownyng*. In speaking of that which is usually repressed, the narrative undoes some of the hierarchical dualities invoked to maintain masculine authority.

At this point we might ask why the priest risks compromising his authority in order to produce the manuscript. Since the text bears no trace of his identity, he is apparently not interested in augmenting his reputation through an alliance with Margery. Indeed the book's account of her public life suggests she was more notorious than celebrated. Nonetheless, the priest is apparently not Margery's sole supporter. Although she remains a very marginal religious figure in her time, she has a number of sympathizers, some of whom call her Mother, as if to recognize the validity of an alternative form of devotion. Margery's supporters register their dissent from more conservative, hierarchical forms of religiosity advocated in the fifteenth-century Church.

Margery's use of marginalized channels of communication to express divine truth is the difference that polarizes those who encounter her. She is seen not just as an aberration from canonical forms but also as an alternative to them. While Beckwith and Bynum insist on the way in which Margery reproduces conventional medieval dualities, we should not overlook the way in which her book bridges cultural dichotomies. In certain ways Margery and the scribe repair the rift between masculine and feminine, text and body, restoring to writing some of its continuity and complementarity with oral communication.

In the clerical ordering of discourses, Scripture and written gloss precede oral word. *The Book of Margery Kempe* modifies this established ranking of modes of address. Primary, immediate, and most powerful is the direct mystical inspiration Margery receives from God, where soul and body are infused by "wonderful spechys and dalyawns" (2). Her characteristic reply to God is violently physical and affective: "And often-tymes, whel sche was kept wyth swech holy spechys and dalyawns, sche shuld so wepyn and sobbyn that many men wer gretly a wondyr, for thei wysten ful lytyl how homly ower Lord was in hyr sowle" (2–3). Although at times this demonstrative response produces incomprehension among Margery's associates and consequently a certain amount of shame for Margery, it is one she values highly. When she loses for a time the ability to weep and sob, becoming, in the words of the book, "bareyn fro teerys" (199), she feels quite desolate. Second in the order of communication is holy conversation about God and the revelations he grants her. Here again Margery more often meets with scorn than with comprehension and approval. Nonetheless, she insists on her right to speak and hear of God (27), accepting public humiliation as an imitation of Christ's suffering (29). Writing is the third form of address in this sequence of discourses.

The scribe's preface reports that earlier in Margery's life clerks had offered to make a book of her feelings and revelations, but that "sche wold not consentyn in no wey, for sche was comawndyd in hir sowle that sche schuld not wrytyn so soone" (3). The adverbial modifier "so soone" may simply represent either the clerk's linear, historical orientation or his prudent avowal of Margery's humility. From Margery's point of view, however, the refusal of writing implies a reluctance to terminate the exchange between herself and Christ. The making of the book implies an end to private communication and to the special relationship this entails. It takes Christ's assurance to convince Margery to persevere with the book. He insists that writing pleases him as much as tears, since it reaches a wider audience: "For, thow ye wer in the chirche and wept bothyn to-gedyr as sore as evyr thu dedist, yet shulde ye not plesyn me mor than ye don wyth yowr writyng, for dowtyr, be this boke many a man shal be turnyd to me and belevyn therin" (216). Writing is here represented not as so much a contrast to other forms of discourse but as an extension of them, not as an end to an intimate relationship but as another way of pleasing.

The scribe describes how Margery brings to the process of writing all of the forms of communication mentioned above. While he transcribes the woman's sensations into writing, the clerk is overcome by feeling: "whil the forseyd creatur was ocupijd a-bowte the writyng of this tretys, sche had many holy teerys and wepingys, and oftyn-tymys ther cam a flawme of fyer a-bowte hir brest ful hoot and delectabyl, and also he that was hir writer cowde not sumtyme kepyn hym-self from wepyng" (219). Here the scribe reports giving up his position of authority and sharing Margery's affective physical response. The collaboration between illiterate woman mystic and literate male clerk attenuates the boundaries between conventional cultural polarities such as laity and priesthood, feminine and masculine, passion and reflection, body and text.

For the same reasons Margery finds supporters, she also meets detractors. For many she represents a challenge to the social and moral order. First, she breaks strictures against woman's production of public discourse; second, she dares to express the highest truths of the Catholic faith through the inferior medium of the female body. Because it involves this secondary, repressed medium, Margery's means of communication is problematic. It challenges those authorities (secular as well as clerical) whose power depends on the control of texts, and who dominate and define women through Scripture, law, and other authoritative modes of discourse.

As we saw in the passages from Paul's Epistles, the hierarchical opposition between soul and body, man and woman, that Margery's detractors want to enforce enjoys a long history in Christian theology; nonetheless, its motivation and effects alter over time. A somewhat later example comes from the writings of Jerome: "As long as a woman is for birth and children, she is different from man as body is from soul. But when she wishes to serve Christ more than the world, then she will cease to be a woman, and will be called a man." [22] In this opposition female sexuality is incompatible with Christian spirituality; only by renouncing the former can a woman access the latter. In its original context, Jerome's argument may have been liberating for women, justifying their release from the social imperative of reproduction and allowing them the right to devote themselves to God.[23] By the fifteenth century, celibacy is less of a radical departure from social norms. Nevertheless, since Margery chose marriage well before she decided to devote her life to God, this binary opposition justifies her exclusion from the privileges accorded to celibate women. If this mother of fourteen children is to be redeemed, spiritual renewal must come through the medium of her female body rather than through its renunciation.

Thus Margery's text lacks the disembodied quality characteristic of much medieval religious writing. Readers are continually reminded of Margery's corporeality, not only by representations of her spiritual longings and trials in carnal metaphors, but also by the detailed evocation of her involvement with quotidian necessities. In offering descriptions of Margery's bodily sensations, her gestures, journeys, and conversations, the book represents a kind of discourse normally marginalized and hence contained. In this respect we can contrast Margery's book to that of her very different contemporary, the anchoress Julian of Norwich. *The Book of Showings to the Anchoress Julian of Norwich* contains very few references to the writer's material existence; it focuses instead on the visions of infinity granted to Julian in the space of a single night. Her visions are linked with a bodily sickness that immobilizes her in bed and renders her "bodie dead from the miedes downward, as to my feeling."[24] This illness unsexes Julian by paralysing her genitals and her womb. As she receives the last rites, her field of view narrows: "It waxit as darke about me in the chamber as if it had been nyght, save in the image o the crosse, wher in held a comon light."[25] The physical dimensions seem to disappear in Julian's book, while a visionary topography opens. In moving the narrative focus from the woman's body to the body of Christ, from the present to infinity, Julian's text is legitimized in a way that Margery's is not.[26]

While Margery takes a vow of chastity, wearing at times a white robe, she does not abandon the female carnality whose sensuous responsiveness represents her conduit to the divine. Consequently, her signifying presence disturbs or mystifies many of the people who encounter her. When they try to place her embodied discourse in familiar contexts, they meet with her resistance, for she insists that her language describes the very God of whom they claim to speak.

One such conflict takes place when a renowned friar comes to preach at Lynn. When Margery behaves in her characteristically ecstatic devotional manner, writhing, weeping, and rolling on the ground, the friar refuses to allow her to attend his sermons. But his objection is not to the disruption that her presence would cause; rather he resents her claim that these fits are a gift from God. The friar will tolerate Margery's behavior if she concedes that its cause is "a kendly seknes" (151), in other words a bodily rather than spiritual affliction: "he levyd it was a cardiakyl er sum other sekenesse, and yf sche wolde be so a-knowyn, he seyd, he would have compassyon of hir" (151). The friar will not recognize the validity of either Margery's experience or its means of expression. He attempts to represent it as a defect worthy only of condescension. Stubbornly, Margery refuses to deny her revelations and to speak the words that the friar wants to hear: "sche wolde not for al this worlde sey otherwyse than sche felt" (151). Because she claims to know "be revelacyon" (151) that her crying is divinely sent, Margery represents a challenge to the authority claimed by the learned friar. Rather than receiving the Word mediated through his sermons, she embodies it, signifying God's presence through gesture and inarticulate sound.

On a number of occasions narrated in her book, we find men attempting to discipline Margery's body, using threats, insults, or sexual harassment in order to assert masculine power and remind her of her secondary status. On her return from Rome, an anchorite with whom she was formerly on friendly terms falsely accuses her and attempts to shame her by demanding what she has done with the child she begot and bore while overseas. The mayor of Leicester calls her "a fals strumpet" (112), and his steward intimidates Margery with lewd gestures and suggestive speech, making her fearful of rape. Men from diverse social estates attempt to curtail her physical movements, to force her home to Lynn and to her husband's governance. As the duke of Bedford's men lead Margery to prison, the people they meet voice the anxieties that her behavior arouses: "Damsel, forsake this life that thu hast, and go spynne and carde as other women don, and suffyr not so meche schame and so meche wo" (129). In support of this sentiment, women run out of their houses carrying their distaffs, crying out "Brennyth this fals heretyk" (129). The distaffs demonstrate the women's conformity to expected standards of female decorum. Unlike Margery they remain occupied inside their houses with the gender-appropriate work of spinning. We should not be surprised that they fail to show solidarity with Margery. In distancing themselves from their troublesome sister, the women protect the security they enjoy as a result of their obedience.

With women's support, a number of men seek to control Margery's female body by maligning it, confining it, or subjecting it to the orderly repetitions of domestic work. The least oppressive of these confrontations seek to define her, to use the power of naming as a means of control. Behind the persuasive force of nomination, however, lie more brutal threats of rape, imprisonment, and burning. Margery defies these attempts at containment and control, refusing to remain in the private space of the home and insisting on expressing herself in ways other than childbearing or domestic work.

Margery can continue this controversial existence because the kind of religious inspiration she experiences has a legitimate place in the late medieval Church. Particularly on the Continent, affective, ecstatic "feminine" devotional forms are part of the range of available religious expression. This popular affective movement addresses a need that had evidently been unfulfilled by the institutionalized Church. While dominant forms and practices have the advantage of legitimacy, they also run the risk of becoming moribund. Thus the authorities borrow from the marginalized in order to infuse vitality into ossified forms. Rather than an unchanging, monolithic position unrelentingly enforced by the suppression of dissidence, medieval history reveals a rather more dynamic process wherein dissenting groups (one thinks, for example, of the Franciscans) were assimilated into the body of the Church. The strength of the Church came as much from its ability to translate, modify, adapt, and incorporate as from its power to repress.

Although Margery is frequently persecuted by her own countrymen and women, she finds more acceptance among foreigners. Her frequent travels abroad are perhaps motivated not only by the pilgrim's pious intentions, but by the recognition that her form of spirituality finds abroad. In Rome and Jerusalem, for example, her bodily discourse crosses the barriers imposed by language, and her tears, cries, and writhings meet with acceptance and sympathy. In Danzig, where Dorothea of Prussia had earlier practiced a violently ecstatic mysticism,[27] Margery reports that she "had ryth good cher of meche pepil for owr Lordys lofe" (231). The priestly scribe places Margery in the current of popular affective piety, connecting her with Mary of Oignies, Elizabeth of Hungary, Richard Rolle, and the pseudo-Bonaventuran compilation, *Stimulus amoris* (152–54).

As Allen suggests in her prefatory note to *The Book of Margery Kempe*, Margery also has much in common with the fourteenth-century German Dominican women mystics.[28] In a recent comparison of the mysticism of the Beguines of Belgium, the Dominican nuns of Germany, and Margery Kempe, Ute Stargardt characterizes these women's expressions of piety as "serious perversions of mystical concepts."[29] She describes how they appropriate the speculative systems of such mystics as Eckhart, Tauler, and Suso, and transform "spiritual concepts into purely physical sensations and experiences."[30] For example, the *Schwesternbucher*, thirteenth- and fourteenth-century collections of Dominican women's lives, report how in imitating Mary many of the nuns experienced "all the joys, pains, and physical associations associated with an actual pregnancy."[31] The writings of these women merit reconsideration from a feminist perspective.[32] Rather than interpreting the sisters' physical responses as evidence of their failure to comprehend the male clerics, we could understand them as either a protest against the cleft between masculine and feminine, spirit and body, or as an attempt to reconcile the split.[33] Rather than receiving the truth through the mediation of male clerical authorities, the nuns make the Word flesh in a woman's ritual of birthing.

To differing degrees, the literature of the affective movement contains traces of a dialogue between positions that were in other contexts antagonistic in that era. Future investigations could analyze not only texts produced by women but also more canonical works such as the *Meditationes vitae Christi* (addressed, incidentally, to women readers) in order to understand the complex dynamics in exchanges between men and women, body and text, canonical and popular forms.

Interestingly, the history of the reception of *The Book of Margery Kempe* records the extension in time of Margery's search for recognition and of the dialogue reproduced in the text. In the margins of the only extant manuscript we find recorded the endorsement of the monastic readers of Mount Grace Priory, men who must be credited in part with the preservation of the book. The red-ink marginalia comment approvingly on Margery's words and actions. For example, at the point in the manuscript where Margery defends her wearing of white clothes to a priest, who tells her "Now wote I wel that thu hast a devyl wyth-inne the, for I her hym spekyn in the to me" (85), the marginal commentator sides with Margery against the representative of clerical authority by writing "A proud Prist" (85 n. 1), and approves Margery's response with the words "A meke hanswer" (85 n. 3). Elsewhere, the monastic annotator compares one of Margery's bouts of crying to the emotional religiosity of his peers: "so father RM and father Norton and of Wakenes of the passyon" (68 n. 7). Next to the account of an even more violent emotional outburst, where Margery falls down in a field weeping, crying, and roaring, we read the note: "father M was wont so to doo" (174 n. 5). The men referred to here have been identified as Methley, a Carthusian of Mount Grace Priory, and John Norton, the prior himself. Apparently, Margery's piety finds confirmation in that of the writer's fellow monks. Perhaps for the annotator the fathers' authority sanctions the woman's expression. In any case, Margery's carnal and affective alternative to the ordered hierarchical spirituality represented by the pulpit reflects the impulses of the Mount Grace community, and the terse notes in the margin of her book preserve the traces of their own bodily discourse.

At the beginning of this century, the only known version of Margery Kempe's book was the highly selective recension contained in a pamphlet entitled "a shorte treatyse of contemplacyon taught by our lorde Ihesu cryste, or taken out of the boke of Margerie kempe of Lynn." In this pamphlet (c. 1501), Wynkyn de Worde piously remakes the original text by offering almost exclusively the passages where Christ speaks words of guidance and instruction to Margery. In expunging the records of Margery's discourse from the text, the editor has produced an entirely different and much more orthodox kind of work. For example, one of the first passages selected contains the advice, "Doughter yf thou were the haberyon or the here, fastynge brede and water, and yf thou saydeste euery day a thousande pater noster, thou sholde not please me so well as thou dost whan thou art in scylence, and suffrest me to speke in thy soule" (*Kempe* 353). We have seen that unmediated inner communication with Christ is the discourse that Margery values most. Nevertheless, taken out of the context of the book, this avowal has an altered meaning. While Christ's words dismiss the most orthodox form of lay worship in devaluing rote prayer, the divine preference for a silent, receptive woman confirms prevailing prejudices against women's speech. Through his selectivity, de Worde projects such a conventional image of Margery that in his 1521 reprinting of the pamphlet, Henry Pepwell describes her as "a devoute ancres" (357).

Because it records the dialogue between orthodox pronouncements on piety and femininity and Margery's alternative discourse, the complete manuscript is far more controversial. In fact, the history of the book's reception could be read as a testimony to the subversive force of Margery's implicit critique of dominant ideology. Until quite recently, the critical corpus generally evaluated Margery according to patriarchal ideology, a tendency that paradoxically denies the voice that the scribes seem anxious to preserve. Wolfgang Riehle, for example, condemns Margery for being incapable "of separating the sensual from the spiritual,"[34] a charge with which the fifteenth-century friar who preached at Lynn would readily have agreed. Like that medieval friar, twentieth-century scholars have tried to represent Margery as a case for clinical diagnosis.[35] Nevertheless, determinations of hysteria or postpartum psychosis are bizarrely anachronistic ways of accounting for a fifteenth-century lay mystic's religious experiences. If, as I have suggested, Margery calls into question the oppositions that have historically justified patriarchal power, we can understand why her book continues to provide a forum for similar debates. The arguments may be reformulated in new ways, but assumptions about dualistic hierarchies such as text and body, spirit and flesh, man and woman still continue to influence Western thought.

Notes

1. Caroline Bynum, "Women's Stories, Women's Symbols: A Critique of Victor Turner's Theory of Liminality," in *Anthropology and the Study of Religion*, ed. Robert L. Moore and Frank E. Reynolds (Chicago: Center for the Scientific Study of Religion, 1984), 113.

2. Sarah Beckwith, "A Very Material Mysticism: The Medieval Mysticism of Margery Kempe," in *Medieval Literature: Criticism, Ideology and History*, ed. David Aers (New York: St. Martin's Press, 1986), 54.

3. B. A. Windeatt, "Introduction," *The Book of Margery Kempe*, trans. B. A. Windeatt (London: Penguin, 1985), 10, 30.

4. Robert Karl Stone, *Middle English Prose Style: Margery Kempe and Julian of Norwich* (The Hague: Mouton, 1970), 30; Bynum, "Women's Stories," 113.

5. Karma Lochrie, "*The Book of Margery Kempe*: The Marginal Woman's Quest for Literary Authority," *The Journal of Medieval and Renaissance Studies* 16 (Spring 1986): 55.

6. John C. Hirsh, "Author and Scribe in *The Book of Margery Kempe*," *Medium Aevum* 44 (1975): 150.

7. *The Norton Anthology of Literature by Women* makes this claim in introducing the book as "the first extant autobiography in the vernacular" ("Margery Kempe: Introduction," in *The Norton Anthology of Literature by Women*, ed. Sandra M. Gilbert and Susan Gubar [New York: Norton, 1985], 21).

8. My discussion of dialogue in *The Book of Margery Kempe* is partly informed by my reading of Mikhail Bakhtin's theories of dialogics, although his investigations focus on the postmedieval period, specifically on the novel. See *The Dialogic Imagination: Four Essays by M. M. Bakhtin*, ed. Michael Holquist (Austin: University of Texas Press, 1981).

9. Adrienne Rich, Barbara Charlesworth Gelpi, and Albert Gelpi, "Three Conversations," in *Adrienne Rich's Poetry*, ed. Barbara Charlesworth Gelpi and Albert Gelpi (New York: Norton 1975), 115.

10. Adrienne Rich, "The Burning of Paper Instead of Children," *Adrienne Rich's Poetry*, ed. Gelpi and Gelpi, 48.

11. Although in secular circles Margery would have enjoyed some of her bourgeois father's prestige, just as she benefited from his money, in spiritual matters her social position represents more of a stigma.

12. *The Book of Margery Kempe*, ed. Sanford Meech and Hope Emily Allen, EETS., o.s. 212 (London: Oxford University Press, 1940), 4. All subsequent references to this work will be included within the text. I have attempted to normalize somewhat the orthography of the EETS. edition. (Permission to quote from this text was granted by the EETS.)

13. The first scribe has been conjecturally identified as the son whose visit to Margery from "Dewchelonde" and subsequent death are described in Liber 2. (See Hope Emily Allen's "Introduction," vii–viii.)

14. Mary G. Mason, "The Other Voice: Autobiographies of Women Writers," in *Autobiography: Essays Theoretical and Critical*, ed. James Olney (Princeton: Princeton University Press, 1980), 221.

15. The year when the preface was written, 1436, is recorded twice on pages 5 and 6.

16. Sue Ellen Holbrook characterizes the book as organized by association and memory. She finds first that events and images are organized into a cyclic pattern by "the thematic clusters of sex, words, food, and tears," and second "that references to liturgical time provide congruence to events" (Holbrook, "Order and Coherence in *The Book of Margery Kempe*," in *The Worlds of Medieval Women: Creativity, Influence, Imagination*, ed. Constance Berman, Charles Connell, and Judith Rice Rothschild [West Virginia: West Virginia University Press, 1985], 105).

17. For some discussions of oral forms, see P. P. Gigioli, ed., *Language and Social Context* (London: Penguin 1972); Jean Peytard, *Syntagmes*, Annales littéraires de l'Université de Besançon (Paris: Les Belles lettres, 1971); Albert Lord, *The Singer of Tales* (Cambridge: Harvard University Press, 1960); and R. Hoggart, *The Uses of Literacy* (London: Chatto and Windus, 1957). My comparison of oral and written communication is also indebted to conversations about the subject with Jacky Martin. More generally too, this essay has profited from his criticism.

18. In her discussion of Margery Kempe and other women mystics, Danielle Régnier-Bohler investigates their "langage du corps." Although my approach is very different, our conclusions agree on one point, that the mystics' physical responses redress a deficiency in clerical discourse: "La langue des clercs ne peut suffire, le mot est défaillant. Sous la tension, la parole alors devient fleuve, et le cri, langage originel, régressif d'apparence, vient suppléer à la pauvreté du mot, à la prétention d'un pouvoir des mots" (479) ("The discourse of the clerks is not enough, the word is insufficient. Under this tension, words become a river, and the cry, the original language, apparently regressive, comes to make up for the word's poverty, the word's pretention to power"). Danielle Régnier-Bohler, "Voix littéraires, voix mystiques," *Histoire des femmes en occident: Le Moyen Age*, ed. Christiane Klapisch-Zuber, vol. 2 (Paris: Plon, 1991), 443–500 (my translation).

19. Jean Gerson, among others, advocates skepticism in regard to female visionaries. He writes, for example: "All women's teaching is to be held suspect unless it has been examined diligently and much more fully than men's. The reason is clear, common law—and not any kind of common law—but that which comes

from on high forbids them. And why? Because they are easily seduced and deter-mined seducers, and because it is not proved that they are witnesses to divine grace." Quoted by Edmund Colledge and James Walsh, "Introduction," *A Book of Showings to the Anchoress Julian of Norwich*, Studies and Texts of the Pontifical In-stitute of Medieval Studies, 35 (Wetteren, Belgium: Universa, 1978), 151.

20. See the *Medieval English Dictionary*.

21. Beckwith, "Material Mysticism," 53.

22. Quoted in Marina Warner, *Alone of All Her Sex: The Myth and Cult of the Virgin Mary* (New York: Knopf, 1976), 73.

23. See Peter Brown's subtle investigation of the body in early Christian his-tory, *The Body and Society: Men, Women, and Sexual Renunciation in Early Chris-tianity* (New York: Columbia University Press, 1988).

24. Julian of Norwich, *Book of Showings*, 290.

25. Ibid., 291.

26. Modern readers who base their judgment of the two works on orthodox principles find Julian a true mystic and Margery an impostor. For example, Col-ledge and Walsh speak disparagingly of Margery as illiterate, enthusiastic, morbidly self-engrossed, and babbling ("Introduction," 169), while Julian is learned, humble, and restrained.

27. See Allen's Introduction to *The Book of Margery Kempe*, lix.

28. Ibid., lix–lx; Allen includes a bibliography of these writers in appendix 4 to the EETS. edition (376–78).

29. Ute Stargardt, "The Beguines of Belgium, the Dominican Nuns of Ger-many, and Margery Kempe," in *The Popular Literature of Medieval England*, ed. Thomas J. Heffernan, Tennessee Studies in Literature, vol. 28 (Knoxville: Univer-sity of Tennessee Press, 1985), 300.

30. Ibid., 293.

31. Ibid., 300.

32. I am suggesting here the need for detailed analysis of the dialogue be-tween masculine and feminine, body and text, in these works. In her comprehen-sive and convincing study of gender-specific spiritual imagery among male and female religious in the Middle Ages, Bynum has examined the symbolic function of the nuns' mystical pregnancies and lactations. See in particular chapters 3 and 8 of Caroline Walker Bynum's *Holy Feast and Holy Fast: The Religious Significance of Food to Medieval Women* (Berkeley: University of California Press, 1987).

33. Bynum finds in the works of a number of male mystics, including those who advised the Dominican sisters, "the very set of dichotomous symbols that clustered around male/female in the Western tradition" (*Holy Feast*, 287). Suso, for example, writes in the following way to the nuns in his charge: "my dear children, we must all become men and use our strength to turn to God, if we are to be of any use" (quoted in *Holy Feast*, 106).

34. Wolfgang Riehle, *The Middle English Mystics* (London: Routledge and Kegan Paul, 1981), 11.

35. Clarissa W. Atkinson, *Mystic and Pilgrim: The Book and the World of Mar-gery Kempe* (Ithaca: Cornell University Press, 1983), 209–10.

E. Jane Burns

This Prick Which Is Not One: How Women Talk Back in Old French Fabliaux

Among the genres of Old French literature, the fabliau holds the distinction of focusing repeatedly, even obsessively, on the body. In stark contrast to Arthurian love stories, which so often conceal the sexual act behind the inexpressibility topos, claiming that what couples do in the bedchamber is too wonderful to be narrated, fabliau tales of conjugal unrest speak openly, often crudely, about human genitalia and their various functions in the sex act. Racy descriptions of body parts creep in and out of narratives centered on wifely disobedience, *gourmandise*, materialism, and hedonism in various guises. Although most of the 150 fabliaux, composed in the thirteenth and fourteenth centuries in France, are not essentially about women, the genre as a whole bears the marks of misogynous comedy.[1] Women in these tales are featured typically as lascivious, demanding, verbose, irrational, and not very smart. Yet of the entire corpus only a dozen or so fabliaux focus explicitly on female sexuality, giving us a view of the female body as it is defined and constructed by anonymous narrators who purport to "know" what women are like.[2]

What these narrators know, and what their comic tales teach through the moralizing statements often appended to them, is that female identity resides in one key body part: that stereotypically female orifice, the vagina. An especially well known fabliau, "Les Quatre Souhais Saint Martin" ("The Four Wishes of Saint Martin"), makes especially clear the link between what was perceived to be medieval female nature and the woman's genital orifice by exploiting the linguistic homophony between the Old French verb to know (*conoistre*) and the noun meaning vagina (*con*). When the browbeaten husband of this tale attempts to punish his shrewish and lascivious wife by wishing that her body be covered with "cunts," the transformation occurs instantly and the narrator explains tellingly, "Adonc fut-elle bien connue."[3] The literal meaning of the sentence, "thus was she covered completely with cunts," contains a second sense emphasized in the husband's subsequent justification for having caused this anatomical change in his wife:

> Bele suer, ne vous esmaiez
> Que jamès ne vendroiz par rue
> Que vous ne soiez bien *connue*.
>   (MR 5:206; N 4:215)

(Honey, don't worry, because now you will never walk down the street without being well known [i.e., recognized for what you really are].)

Men "know" women in these bawdy tales, not as lovers or mothers or workers or wives, but stereotypically as a single sexual orifice. And that orifice appears more specifically as a vaginal mouth, a mouth without teeth or tongue, a mouth devoid of speech. Rather than a defining feature of female anatomy per se, the vagina is "known," by the male observers who have mythologized it, as a mindless and silent hole begging to be filled. The anonymous narrator of "Le Dit des cons" exhorts his male audience to indulge in sex because that is what "cunts" are known (here expressed by the verb *savoir*) to want:

> Seignor, qui les bons *cons savez*,
> Qui *savez* que li *cons* est tels
> Que il demande sa droiture,
> Foutez assez tant comme il dure.
>   (MR 2:137)

(Noble men, who know cunts, who know that the cunt demands its due, fuck as much as you can.)

Such ribald tales that reduce medieval woman to pure body are of interest to the contemporary feminist reader because they play out, before our eyes, the problematic implications of their own limiting definition of female sexuality. However much the fabliaux reiterate their portrait of woman as a welcoming sexual orifice without thought or speech, they also show us female protagonists, the ones bearing the enviable *con*, who talk and think and know. It is this paradox of the speaking and thinking female body, a contradiction in terms according to the fabliau's standard definition of the wholly corporeal and mindless "cunted woman" that interests me here. What happens when the very tales that purport to know women as *con* also reveal how the *cons conoist*, how the cunt knows, knows enough to speak, and explains, in different ways, what it knows.[4]

Who Is Wearing the Pants and What Do they Cover Up?

"The Four Wishes of Saint Martin" provides a particularly apt point of departure for this discussion because it shows, in a most graphic way, the dangers of allowing women's sexualized bodies to speak. The tale describes the activity of a woman who wears the pants in the family, a wife "qui chauce les braies" (MR 5:201) in a way that conforms to the stereotype of the domineering nag still current today. The implication is that this nameless wife has obtained her power without merit; she does not know what she is doing. Her incompetence is registered through various demeaning characterizations of her speech. Issuing constant threats to her henpecked spouse, this wife complains especially of her mate's laziness, excoriating his inability to earn money or provide for his family. "You've never liked to work," she says. "You love to party. May bad luck befall you since you're not doing your job" ("Vous fetes molt volentiers feste! / A mal eür aiez vous beste, / Quant vous n'en fetes vostre esploit!") (MR 5:202; N 4:212). We hear in these words the standard voice of the medieval scold. Annoying and valueless, it harasses and harps to no avail.

But as the tale unfolds we learn that the wife's dissatisfaction with her husband's meager economic production veils a more specific and devastating complaint. Just before the couple's spat, Saint Martin had arrived fortuitously to grant the husband four wishes. When the hopeful man finally recounts this good fortune to his money-conscious wife, her speech turns immediately humble and honeyed as if she had exchanged her domineering pants for a more conventionally feminine dress. The wife now coyly persuades her pliable spouse to give one of the wishes to her: "When she heard this (news) she hugged him and spoke with humble words . . . 'Sweet one,' she said 'I have always loved you and served you with all my heart. Now you should repay me. I ask you to please give me one wish'" ("Quant cele l'oï, si l'acole, / si s'umelie de parole: 'Ahi,'—fet ele, 'douz amis, / ja ai je en vous tout mon cuer mis / de vous amer, de vous servir. /

or le me devez bien merir: / Je vous demant, se il vous plaist, / que vous me donez .I. souhait'") (MR 5:203; N 4:212).[5] This female voice, no less stereotypical than the first, cajoles and seduces. It is the sweet-talking voice that speaks of deference, subservience, and pleasing men.

When the husband reluctantly gives in to his wife's insistent pleas and grants her one of his precious wishes, she asks not for money, as her first harshly critical voice might have led us to expect, nor for an opportunity to please her husband sexually as her second honeyed voice might imply. The unnamed wife here speaks in a third register lying somewhere between the standard stereotypes of demanding nag and caressing beguiler. She now speaks authoritatively and erotically at the same time, alluding to what is figured here as her pleasure, not his. Drawing out the sexual implications already latent in the scold's denunciation of her husband's failure to "do his job"—*esploit* in Old French can mean both work and performance—[6] the wife now explains that her husband's failure to perform fully as a laborer parallels his failure to satisfy her in bed. And in typical fabliau fashion, the terms that this woman uses to express her putative desire are utterly unladylike. She asks that her husband's body be covered with "pricks" (*vits*), that they appear on his eyes, face, head, arms, feet, and sides. That they be planted everywhere and that all of them be erect and hard. "'Je demant,' dist ele, 'en non Dieu, / Que vous soiez chargiez de vis, / Ne vous remaingnent oiel ne vis, / Teste, ne braz, ne piez, ne coste / Où partout ne soit vit planté. / Si ne soient ne mol ne doille, / Ainz ait à chascun vit sa coille; / Toz dis soient li vit tendu, / Si samblerez vilain cornu'" ("I ask, she said, in the name of God that you be covered with pricks. Let not your eyes and face, head, arms, feet, and sides be without pricks planted all over them. And let them not be soft or pliable. Rather let each prick have its own [soft] balls. May the pricks always be stiff so you will appear to be a horned / horny guy") (MR 5:204; N 4:213).[7]

When the fabliau wife's wish comes true and her husband's body literally breaks out in penises, the extra members are long, square, fat, short, puffy, curved, and pointed: "Si ot vit lonc et vit quarré, / vit gros, vit cort, vit reboulé, / vit corbe, vit agu, vit gros" (MR 5:204–5; N 4:214).[8] It is at this point that the humiliated husband responds by wishing that the wife's body be covered with cunts (*cons*) in number equal to his pricks. And soon she has vaginas everywhere, making her physical state reflect the exaggerated libido that her body is supposed to have contained and concealed:

Adonc fu ele bien connue
qu'ele ot .II. cons en la veüe,
.IIII. en ot ou front coste à coste,
et con devant et con d'encoste,
Si ot con de mainte maniere
et con devant et con derriere.

(MR 5:206; N 4:215).

(Thus was she well-known, well cunted, such that she had two cunts on her eyes, four on her forehead, next to each other, cunts in front and cunts on her sides. Thus did she have cunts in many places, cunts in front and cunts behind.)

Eventually the couple regret their impulsive choices and decide to request an end to the mad proliferation of genitalia. They plan to use their one remaining wish wisely, asking only for money—the husband's original intent. In a fatal lapse of reasoning, however, these partners forget to stipulate that their original sex organs should remain intact, and with the hasty formulation of the third wish their genitals disappear altogether. They are forced to use their last wish to regain the normal sex organs with which they began.[9] Because of the woman, her unreasonable demands, her cajoling, her wild erotic desires, her uncontrollable speech, we are led to believe, this couple has lost all promise of profit or improvement.

Who Knows What?

In narrating its tale of conjugal unrest and the struggle over mastery in the bourgeois household, this fabliau addresses issues of money and who controls it, male prowess and who evaluates it, and female sexuality and who describes it. When the female protagonist in the "Four Wishes" asks for an abundance of penises to appear on her husband's body, readers familiar with Old French literature will hear in her brash statement a typical medieval characterization of the libidinous woman. Impossible to satisfy, always demanding more sex as she also often seeks more money or more food, this craven woman simply cannot ever get enough of "her man." We find her in such tales as "Du Vallet aus XII fames" (MR 3:186; N 4:146)[10] as the lustful female used to illustrate the standard medieval contention that women are more sexually demanding than men. In this instance a husband, overcome by "too much" of his oversexed wife, gives her to a criminal as a punishment worse than death. Female desire, which is otherwise welcomed as an avenue to male pleasure, is here denounced as excessive. Extending beyond reasonable limits, beyond the limits imposed by his rational head, this female libido, like that of the wife in the "Four Wishes," has surpassed the male's ability to control and dominate it.

And yet it is significant that the competing forces portrayed in the "Four Wishes" are circumscribed in its closing moral statement in terms of a struggle between female pleasure and male knowledge. The moral of the tale warns predictably, "He who listens to his wife instead of himself is not wise [il n'a pas savoir]; shame and trouble often result."[11] The "Four Wishes" here shows us how the standard struggle between the fabliau's male and female protagonists over sexual prowess and erotic desire masks a more crucial dichotomy that erects male knowledge as an authoritative control over what is perceived to be the voicing of female pleasure. Whereas the man in this tale knows and thinks, his wife merely wants. Or at least that is how the husband in the "Four Wishes" sees it and how the narrator tells it.

But what does this husband know? The value of money, and how to choose wisely and make his wishes count. Yet this knowledge proves ineffectual when it comes up against the unpredictability of female desire. That is the very thing that the husband of the "Four Wishes" does not in fact "know." By his own admission he remains thoroughly ignorant of his wife's deepest wishes: "Ne connois pas bien vos amors," he says before she makes her wish, warning that her very words could turn him into a bear, a mare, a goat, or an ass: "Se deïssiez que fusse uns ours, / Ou asnes, ou chievre, ou jument, / Jel seroie tout esraument" (MR 5:204; N 4:213). Would she want to do that, he wonders in an echo of Freud's later query about what women want. She contends not. What then would she want? Sewing supplies of hemp or wool or linen thread he guesses.[12] Like Freud, he does not know, he hasn't a clue. Hence the need for male-defined *savoir* that this fabliau promotes. It will help keep the unknown terrain of female desire in check.

What the husband of the "Four Wishes," along with the anonymous author/narrator of this cautionary tale, purports to know then about female sexuality boils down to an extreme, even parodic, rendition of Luce Irigaray's logic of the same. At first reading at least, the "Four Wishes" seems to illustrate in a most tangible way how the expression of female desire in the western literary tradition often amounts only to a sham, a mimicry, as Irigaray says, of male speech and imagining about women.[13] Indeed, the wife in this tale is shown to want men, and more of them, more pricks, as she herself candidly explains, because "one prick alone was never worth much to me" ("Sire, dist el, je vous di bien / C'un seul vit ne me valoit rien") (MR 5:205; N 4:214). The phallus, ultimate guarantor of meaning in a system that privileges the male head over the female's lack of rational ability (49), is here enshrined as what women really want.

This is what Irigaray calls the view of the penis-eye, whose knowledge of female sexuality and desire derives from a wholly male model. Women, in this scenario, provide the necessary ground on which the male subject constructs itself: "A hinge bending according to their exchanges. A reserve supply of 'negativity' sustaining the articulation of their moves, or refusals to move, in a partly fictional progress toward the mastery of power. Of knowledge. In which she will have no part. Off-stage, off-side, beyond representation, beyond selfhood."[14] As the man's negative counterpart, the mirror image of the male model, woman cannot fully possess the capacity of the speaking subject that the binary logic dividing mind from body reserves for him alone. The issue becomes not what she wants but whether or not she can express desire within the constraints of the dominant patriarchal language. The voicing of female desire becomes an impossibile conundrum; it can only echo what males imagine female sexuality might be like.

As the unnamed wife of this fabliau is essentialized into erotic body parts, reduced to an amorphous heap of cunts crying out for male penetration, she seems to speak more as a body than a mind. Or does she? Who is speaking in the different voices that the wife articulates in this tale? Must we assume that all the voices inscribed in this fabliau represent the authoritative speech of the text's author/narrator, filtered through individual characters but constructed essentially by the logic of the penis-eye? Or can we hear within the woman's voice that asks boldly, brashly, and immodestly for more pricks a more complex dynamic between the subject's speech and its objectified other? Is there a way in which, as the anonymous fabliau narrator makes a female character speak, that character can also be heard to talk back at her author?

This possibility is suggested within Irigaray's critique of Western thought. For while she demonstrates at length how woman's body—figured as absence, silence, and nonrepresentability in the phallocentric discourses of Western metaphysics—provides the groundwork for the construction of male subjectivity, Irigaray also posits that same female body as a locus of possible revision.[15] As Elizabeth Grosz has cogently explained, the female body in Irigaray's analysis is both the direct empirical referent for all that has been theorized about femininity and also a place from which to dismantle the male inaginary and begin constructing a speaking female subject on different terms:

> Irigaray does not aim to create a new women's language. Her project, rather, is to utilize already existing systems of meaning or signification, to exceed or overflow the oppositional structures and hierarchizing procedures of phallo-centric texts. She stresses their possibilities of ambiguity, their material processes of production and renewal. She affirms the plurality and multiplicity dormant in dominant discourses, which cover over and rely on the inclusions and exclusions of femininity and its associated attributes.[16]

What if we, as feminist readers of medieval texts, were to do the same? What if we were to affirm, along with Teresa de Lauretis, the multiple, heteronomous nature of female subjectivity and begin to read "for the female" in the margins and interstices of hegemonic discourses?[17] Our task would then focus less on recovering expressions of female desire hidden within male-authored texts than on actively listening for ways in which female characters might be heard as resisting, speaking against, and dissenting from the very discourses that construct female nature.[18]

I do not mean to argue here for an inherent "female subjectivity" in Old French fabliaux. Such a move would simply replicate, while inverting its terms, the existing ontological, theological model of male subjectivity. Rather, in examining the varied ways in which female protagonists speak "from the body" in Old French fabliaux, I want to record how medieval heroines can speak both within and against the social and rhetorical conventions used to construct them. I am proposing, in short, a reading strategy that takes as a point of departure Teresa de Lauretis's definition of woman as standing both inside and outside gender, at once within and without representation (10, 11). I want to chart this crucial contradiction across a selection of Old French fabliaux, exploring how the female body, while often functioning as the site of partiarchy's construction of femininity, can also open up possibilities for an alternative reading of female subjectivity.

Castration Anxiety?

That the "Four Wishes" records, on some level at least, a fundamental male fear of castration needs no explanation. When the wife articulates her wish, she seems, as we have said, to ask for too much of her man, challenging his manhood by putting his sexual prowess to an embarrassing public test. But what interests me is how male castration anxiety is registered in Old French texts of the thirteenth and fourteenth centuries in terms of strategies to control woman's speech.

In the "Four Wishes," the complementary characterizations of woman's speech—first as nagging babble and then as sweet nothings—work in tandem to reduce her words to mere bodysound. Hélène Cixous has revealed how the tendency to construct woman's voice as innocuous noise depends on a distinction between talking and speaking. Women in this view "do utter a little," she says,

> but they do not speak. Always keep in mind the distinction between speaking and talking. It is said, in philosophical texts, that women's weapon is the word, because they talk, talk endlessly, chatter, overflow with sound, mouthsound: but they don't actually *speak*, they have nothing to say. They always inhabit the place of silence, or at most make it echo with their singing. And neither is to their benefit, for they remain outside knowledge.[19]

The implication played out in both initial depictions of female speech in the "Four Wishes"—that women are babblers and cajolers—is that woman cannot speak properly or effectively because she has nothing significant to say.[20] Standing outside the privileged ranks of male cognition, she does not know enough to accede to the dominant position of speaking subject who, by definition, knows its object.[21] Woman in this fabliau is denied meaningful speech because she lacks the rational male head necessary for thought. As Cixous reminds us further, in "Castration and Decapitation," efforts to decapitate and silence women in Western narratives, especially those that stage a battle between the sexes, represent the castration complex at its most effective: "If man operates under the threat of castration, if masculinity is culturally ordered by the castration complex, it might be said that the backlash, the return, on women of this castration anxiety is its displacement as decapitation, execution, of women, as loss of her head" (43).

Headless Women

Old French fabliaux construct female protagonists as headless and unknowing in very specific, bodily ways. Elaborate strategies of female decapitation focus on one particular aspect of the head, the mouth, which in males serves as the organ that articulates thoughts from the brain. In female protagonists, association with the rational mind is denied as the female mouth is reduced—by association with the eroticized female body—to a wholly sexual orifice. The women of fabliau narrative lose their heads metaphorically to the extent that their mouths are shown to function as vaginas. Instead of bearing two distinctly different mouths— one facial and one vaginal, each with independent functions—the sexualized female is shown to have only one kind of orifice. Whether it appears on her face or between her legs, the female mouth is erotic and wholly corporeal.[22]

The image derives from the sensual similarity between the eroticized lips of the mouth and the genital labia. In "Le Fabliau du moigne," for example, a monk who dreams of purchasing the ideal cunt from a salesman rejects one prospect because it is not sufficiently mouthlike to satisfy his desire. Its *lips*, as he explains, are too thin and blackened to please adequately: "Il avoit les levres ansdeus / Maigres et plus noires que fer" ("Both its lips were thin and blacker than iron").[23]

Such a favorable cunt that talks in silence wins the contest among three sisters vying for the same mate in "Le Jugement des cons" ("Cunt Conundrum"). After testing the women by asking each to answer the question, "Which is older, you or your cunt?" the uncle judging the contest awards the desired knight to the sister who boasts a welcoming orifice that sucks like a mouth: "Mes cons a la goule baée / Jones est, si veut aletier" ("My cunt has an open mouth. It is young and thus wants to suckle") (MR 5:114; N 4:32–33). That the vagina is an orifice to be nourished by male sperm is attested in the tale of "Connebert," where a *con* willingly receives the sexual "food" of a priest: "Qant li orlages fu cheüz / Et Conneberz fu repeüz" ("When the storm/passion had subsided and Conneberz was sated") (MR 5:165). In "De Porcelet," a woman whose vagina is called "piggy" devours all the "food" provided by her husband's "little nothing" until his wheat is completely depleted. This tale links the wife's voracious vagina specifically to her devouring mouth, stating that "the more her cunt eats, the hungrier it is" ("Quant plus manjue, plus fain a") (MR 4:146; N 6:191). An equally rapacious and equally silent set of lips appears in "Le Debat du Cons et du Cus," where the mouthlike *cons* is said to eat a sausage: "Ersoir menjas tu une andoille" ("Last night you ate a sausage") (MR 2:134). The vagina that eats, sucks, swallows, opens and closes its mouth appears routinely as a *goule* (gaping mouth;

"Le Dit des cons," "Du Chevalier qui Fist les Cons Parler"), even in one instance a "goulu Goliath" (a giant gaping mouth; "La Veuve").[24]

But different from the visible, public mouth, the vagina bears no necessary connection to the brain. Rather than emitting words or sound, it takes in the penis in a wholly corporeal gesture that could not be more mindless. "Le Dit des cons" defines the problem most succinctly, stating that "li cons est .I. nice douaire" ("The cunt is an innocent dowry") (MR 2:139). As a dowry, or marriage gift from wife to husband, this female orifice is by definition the husband's rightful property—his to have and to hold as he pleases, when it pleases him. But even more telling is the adjective *nice*, which characterizes the quintessential female orifice as wanting, stupid or without value, and most significantly for our purposes, *niais* or *sot*—naïve in the sense of *unknowing*. Positioned physically as far from the head as possible—one fabliau in particular reiterates the standard Old French portrait of women that proceeds from the head to the mouth, face, breasts, and finally the *con* ("Du Chevalier qui Fist les Cons Parter," MR 6:82; N 3:168)—the female orifice designated to represent woman's identity signals a brainless pleasure-giving body.

The erotic joy of lips that do not speak, lips that please sensually without threatening to displease verbally, appears in "Du Chevalier qui Fist les Cons Parler," where the young knight, about to be seduced by a maiden's sensuously talkative labia, questions her motive. Guarding against the potentially deceitful speech of the woman's mouth, the knight asks specifically that her other lips provide a truthful reply. The sensuous labia explain predictably that the maiden has come to please the knight, to offer "soulaz et joie" (MR 6:82; N 3:168). The Old French homophony between *con* (cunt) and *conter* (to tell a tale) reinforces linguistically the bond between the woman's lips and labia when the maiden later explains to her lady how her vaginal lips had been made literally to speak to the knight: "mes cons li conta" ("my cunt spoke to him/my cunt told him a good story") (MR 4:83; N 3:169).

The flip side of this paradigm make the female mouth itself into a vagina. Sarah White has shown how many of the fabliaux addressing female sexuality link woman's garrulousness to rampant libido, the constant movement of the female mouth signaling the equally intense activity of its companion orifice.[25] The body here speaks in spite of the brain, even without the use of words. One of the few female figures in fabliaux to voluntarily repress her speech, the wife in "Li Sohaiz desvez" forgoes the opportunity to express her dissatisfaction with her husband's sexual performance only to have that desire reemerge in an erotic dream;[26] she shops for penises in a market filled with pricks of all sizes and shapes:

Plaines estoeynt les maisons
Et les chanbres et li solier
Et tot jorz venoient coler
Chargiez de viz de totes parz
Et à charretes et à charz
    (MR 5:187; N 6:269)

(The houses and rooms and attics were full of them. Everyday cartpullers covered with pricks arrived in carts and wagons.)

This fabliau wife's failed remarks give way to the narrator's description of an enormous and enormously desirable penis that underscores by contrast the limits of her less fully endowed mate. In this case the excessive bodily desire that normally conditions the woman's voice in fabliau narrative is displaced temporarily into a visual representation of erotic indulgence. When this wife finally expresses her true feelings, explaining to her husband how she bought the biggest and fullest penis at the market ("lo plus gros et lo plus plenier") (MR 5:189; N 6:271), it is as if her mouth has been conditioned by the uncontrollable urges of her body. The wife here speaks erotically, irrationally, as if talking from the vagina, not the head.

Whether the fabliau woman demands more and better sex or refuses insistently to grant sexual favors, her voice is condemned as suffering from bodily—and specifically vaginal—contamination. In the tale of "Black Balls," female speech figures literally as a guilty partner in woman's refusal of sexual activity.[27] This fabliau recounts the legal trial of a woman who commits two related offenses: refusing to sleep with her husband after discovering that he has "black balls," she dares further to accuse him publicly of this deviation, "oiant toute la cort" (MR 6:93; N 5:188). The trial concludes with an overt denunciation of female genitalia for anatomical reasons. The proximity between anus and urethra is deemed to be unhealthy, as it is in the "Le Debat du Cons et du Cus" where the vagina itself conveys the patriarchal view that "he who put you so near to me did a bad job. . . . If you were a little further away everyone would incline toward me. But in you I have such a disgusting neighbor, something you don't even realize or know. To all those who love you may God give bad luck, because they do so against Nature" ("Mauvesement en esploita / Qui si près moi te herbrega. / Tu ne fleres pas comme uns coins / Se tu fusses .I. poi plus loins, / Toz li mons fust à moi aclin; / Mès j'ai en toi si ort voisin / Que tu ne vaus ne tu ne sez. / A toz cels dont tu es amez / Doinst Dame Diex male aventure, / Quar il le font contre nature") (MR 2:135).

The tale of "Black Balls" links this commonplace denunciation of the dangerously ambiguous female genitalia with a concomitant devaluation of woman's speech. When pleading her case in the courtroom, the wife in this tale is cut short by her husband's protestations; he overrides her explanation with accusations of his own, literally cutting off her voice: "Sa parole li tranche" (MR 6:93; N 5:188). The court then deems the woman insane, dismissing her defense because of the disruptive speech used to articulate it; "And the woman was held to be crazy because of all the noise she made" ("Et la dame se tint por fole / De la clamor qu'ele a fait") (MR 6:94; N 5:188–89). This woman's voice is degraded and dismissed because of a metaphorical association with her unseemly genitalia. In this instance an unclean body is thought to have contaminated the female mouth and head, suggesting that the brain which makes the mouth speak has been replaced by another governing organ less capable of the task. This head talks like a cunt, and like a cunt it should keep quiet.

Such is the case with the wife in "The Little Rag Mouse" whose cunning speech successfully enables escape from her conjugal duty in sex.[28] This wiley and sexually experienced wife convinces her peasant spouse on their wedding night that she has left her genitals in the neighboring town at her mother's house. The unassuming man obtains from his mother-in-law a basket of rags containing a mouse with which he tries unsuccessfully to have intercourse.[29] It is the woman's verbal trickery in this case that enables her to withhold sexual gratification, a move that the legal judgment in the tale of "Black Balls" is designed to curtail.

The problem with the female voices attached to these cunts is that they attack and bite as if armed with teeth.[30] Different from the subdued and properly sensual voice of the vaginal mouth defined by lips alone, these mouths resemble more closely the male speaking mouth equipped with teeth and tongue. The "Jugement des cons" reveals the model for these two types of female speech through contrasting functions of the vagina. The first image, as we have seen before, emerges in the reply of contestant number three, who boasts of an accommodating orifice that provides the pleasure of a mouth. The second sister suggests the potential danger of a vagina that might truly resemble a mouth, possessing menacing teeth as well as inviting lips: "I have large, long teeth, and my cunt has none."[31] The implication here is that some vaginas can literally bite.

This fabliau more than any other draws attention to the rich mythical heritage behind the medieval association of mouth and vagina, alluding most directly to the Indo-European tradition of the *vagina dentata*.[32] A woman whose vagina contains a tooth, a poisonous snake, a penis, is in Indo-European myth always an alluringly erotic woman, but one whose eroticism mimics that of the male. As Wendy O'Flaherty describes her, this mythic woman, luxuriating in her libido, experiences pleasure in sex in a way that usurps a long-standing male prerogative. When the male mythmaker identifies these women as evil and dangerous, it is because the woman's sexuality, her desire to have sex on her own terms, makes her a dangerous rival of man.

But if the emphasis in Hindu myth falls most heavily on the sexual aspect of the *vagina dentata*, recording a perceived threat to male sexual hegemony, the medieval fabliaux emphasize men's corollary fear of losing their heads. The desiring male subject in Old French fabliaux, who reluctantly allows himself to be engulfed by the woman's dangerously erotic lips in the sex act, reserves the right to dominate her through the companion orifice, through speech from the mouth. "Du Chevalier qui Fist les Cons Parler" provides a particularly apt case in point (MR 6:68; N 3:158). The chivalric protagonist in this tale succeeds in keeping both his sexual prerogative and his head intact with the aid of several fairies who grant him three boons. The first and most practical gift, that he would never be penniless, is accompanied by two talents of less obvious use: he would have the power to make cunts talk and, failing that, to make assholes speak. The knight puts these skills to use at a nearby castle when a countess dares him to make her cunt talk. Hoping to win the bet, she stuffs her vagina with cotton until its "whole mouth was full" ("la geule tote plaine") (MR 6:87; N 3:172).[33] The trick works, but the knight, drawing on his third boon, makes the woman's asshole speak instead, and because of a confusion between the woman's ass and her vagina that typifies Old French fabliaux, he wins the bet.[34] Having lost in this struggle for power against her male opponent, the female protagonist forfeits the independence of her speech. She is told by witnesses to the contest that her losing means she must now be silent: "Qu'el a perdu; ne parolt mais" ("Once she had lost; she spoke no more") (MR 6:88; N 3:173). If the victorious knight did not successfully appropriate the power of woman's sexual lips to himself, he did gain the power to impose silence on her speaking lips.

Women Talk Back

Despite the fabliau's elaborate efforts to circumscribe its female protagon-ists' voices, the fact remains that these women are not literally headless. They do speak. If as fictive characters fabliau wives remain the literary fabrications of an anonymous author/narrator who constructs their voices along with their bodies, these women's words often reveal at the same time the unresolved paradox of the headless, speaking female. Showing, on the one hand, how to make woman headless despite her ability to speak—how to reduce her speech to inconsequential bodysound—Old French fabliaux also reveal how woman, despite the imposition of her headless status, does "utter a little." Indeed, the voice of the nag, though dismissed, suggests the possible threat of female dominance in speech. The voice of the beguiler, though avowedly subservient, threatens to get what it wants through cajoling.

Whereas these voices do not represent what women might say or how they might express their desire, they do show that women could have a say, could have a head and a mouth and use them. At stake in this narra-tive, then, is not just female desire and how it might be articulated, nor is the central issue castration anxiety. Rather, the fabliau husband's fear of being swallowed up by his wife's desiring and devouring vaginal lips ex-presses a struggle over the status of the gendered subject. In other words, who has access to subjectivity and the authority that accompanies it?[35] Who should speak knowledgeably about money, power, conjugal re-lations, and sexual desire, men or women? The battle is staged in terms of an either/or proposition. If men give up their subjective stronghold, they will fall into the dreaded category of object: object of the cajoler's unpre-dictable desire, of the nag's threatening speech, an object without power or purchase on the world.

Yet it is these very terms of the subject/object dichotomy that the female protagonists' voices in the fabliaux we have been discussing disrupt. As they move from the position of object of desire (or disdain or jest) to that of the desiring subject, these fabliau women begin to erode, through their speech, the mind/body dichotomy that the tales they inhabit work so hard to assert.

The scenario of "Li Sohaiz desvez" presents a female protagonist, not unlike the wife in the "Four Wishes," who wants "viz de totes parz" (pricks everywhere), but this woman's dream is not only about enjoying a larger, stiffer penis. Her dream world allows her to have sex on her own terms, specifically when she wants it, rather than according to her husband's whim, and with a partner of her own choosing. Her imagined wanderings through the prick market constitute a dream of selection, of locating a penis that will, as she explains to the merchant, satisfy her, "Que Deus m'an doint joie certaine" ("Let God grant me certain joy") (MR 5:188; N 6:270). If she wants more pricks, indeed cartloads of them, it is not necessarily because she wants more men, more of man; having more pricks can also mean having more pricks to choose from, having more options.

The countess in "Du Chevalier qui Fist les Cons Parler" responds similarly to the knight's tactic of controlling what vaginal lips say. She proposes her challenge to rectify the experience of the maiden who went to seduce the knight only to have him, as the maiden explains, control her: "Il prist mon con à apeler; / Assez l'a fait à lui paller" ("He called to my cunt and thus made it talk to him") (MR 6:83; N 3:169). The knight's takeover of the maiden's vaginal lips is staged, tellingly, as a conversation between two men; because "Sire cons" addresses the knight as "sire," the woman and her putative voice are completely displaced.[36] This appropriation of female speech and desire is what the countess tries, albeit unsuccessfully, to rectify by stuffing her vagina with cotton. Her challenge indicates that the vagina should speak for women not men: "Jamès cons n'et si fous ne yvres, / Qui por nos parolt un seul mot" ("Never will a cunt be so crazy or drunk as to say, on our behalf, a single word") (MR 6:85; N 3:170). Women's mouths, both private and public, should have a say.

The battle lines are drawn in "Black Balls" more specifically around the issue of knowledge. After five years of marriage, this wife has just learned of her husband's blackened genitals, to which she attributes his abstinence from sexual activity: "Que cinc ans m'a bien meintenue / Mes barons; ains mès nel connui: / Ersoir or primes aperçui / L'ochoison por coi il remaint" ("He persisted for five years [in refraining from sex], my lords. Never before did I know why. Last night for the first time I learned the reason for his abstinence") (MR 6:92; N 5:187). The moral calls women "unwise" who chastize their husbands for having black genitals, "Fame ne fait pas savoir" (MR 6:94; N 5:189). Her professed knowledge of his ailment is thus discredited, as it is earlier in the tale by verbal sparring that suggests the woman knows less than her spouse. He claims she is to blame for their not having sex because she was so busy soliciting sex from others; she denies having engaged in any such activity (MR 6:93; N 5:188). Then the husband triumphantly wins the debate with a comic twist of logic that asserts his superior knowledge: "Jel *savoie* bien: / Por c'est ma coille si noircie" ("I knew it; this is why my balls are so blackened!") (MR 6:93–94; N 5:188). The marital battle has been fought over who knows more and how each player in the marriage duo can assert that superior knowledge through speech.

The wife in the "Rag Mouse," is married to a man who knows nothing about pleasing women, "Qui fame prist, et rien ne sot / De nul deduit q'apartenist / A fame, se il; la tenist" ("He took a wife and knew nothing about women's pleasures and he held her in that way") (MR 4:158; N 6:178). He cannot even find her "cunt": "'Je voil,' fait il, 'vit avant traire / Si vos fotrai se j'onques puis, / Se vostre con delivre truis . . . O est il donc? Nel me celez'" ("I want, he said, to pull my prick out and fuck you if I can, if I find your cunt free. Where is it anyway? Don't hide it from me") (MR 4:159; N 6:179). She offers knowledge of female genitalia: "Sire, qant savoir lo volez / Jel vos dirai o est, par m'ame" ("Sir, since you want to know, I will tell you, by God") (MR 4:159; N 6:179). If her first directives send him on a wild goose chase, subsequent explanation teaches what he does not know: "Sire, il est ja entre mes jambes" ("Sir, it is still between my legs") (MR 4:164; N 6:182). Here the moral, which warns against female deceit through speech—"Qant el viaut ome decevoir / Plus l'an deçoit et plus l'afole / tot solemant par sa parole" ("When she wants to deceive a man, she deceives him most and makes him craziest simply by using her voice")—also attests to women's knowledge: "Enseignier voil por ceste fable / Que fame set plus que deiable" ("I want to teach through this story that woman knows more than the devil") (MR 4:165; N 6:183).

The fabliau women we have been discussing thus redefine, in different ways, the knowledge/pleasure dichotomy used typically in these narratives to structure their identity as gaping, hungry holes. When they ask for more sex, or for more pricks in echo of the wife in the "Four Wishes," their words do not, as it might first appear, simply reenshrine the phallus as ultimate guarantor of meaning in a system that privileges the male head over the female's lack of rational ability. As these unnamed wives speak from the impossible position of the headless woman, their very activity as speaking subjects defies the gendered hierarchies of mind and body, knowledge and pleasure, head and ass that Old French farce and fabliau so often promote. These fabliau women speak rather as both subject and object, knowledgeable and pleasure-seeking, as the active and empowered recipient of sexual relations that they not only want but want also to define. Each of these female protagonists suggests alternatives to the stereotype of the indiscriminately avid female who simply wants men and more of them by arguing instead for having more choices, more of a voice, more say about the roles imputed to them in sex and in marriage. Like the outspoken wife in the "Four Wishes," these protagonists' demands for more sex upset the very hierarchy of the speaking male head and silent female body that their fictive anatomy is designed to underwrite.

The Wife's Wish

If the wife in the "Four Wishes" speaks from the body, it is not a body constructed as the subservient opposite of her husband's dominant head. Rather she occupies a space in between the mind/body extremes as her voice situates itself, uncomfortably, impossibly, at the nexus of male and female positions, playing simultaneously the roles of subject and object. Speaking of sex and female desire, this protagonist says that she wants her male mate, wants to be the object of his desire, wants to receive him, to have more of him. But in demanding more, more than he can give, she puts him in the position of the object, one that must deliver in order to fulfill her demands. When she states that "one prick alone was not enough for me," this woman speaks rationally about an irrational desire. And, as a result, substantial change is inaugurated in the male mode of existence. Not only do the wife's words order a restructuring of her husband's anatomy, calling for a plurality of penises where normally there is only one; they also reshape his voice. Tellingly, in this bawdy contest of one-up-manship, the woman speaks first and the man responds, patterning his speech after hers: "Je n'avoie preu en .I. con," he explains, "Puis que tant vit me doniiez" ("I didn't see any value in one cunt, since you had given me so many pricks") (MR 5:206; N 4:215).[37] This reconstructed male voice issues from a reconstructed male body, which the wife has created through her speech.[38]

Indeed her voice has produced a most graphic depiction of how knowledge and pleasure might merge. When the wife in the "Four Wishes" asks for "more pricks," causing extra sexual members to break out in unexpected places on her husband's body, they appear significantly on his face and head as well as his limbs. The concentration of penises on the man's forehead, eyes, nose, and mouth deftly destroys the pat medieval distinction between the thinking head and the sensual body. This reformulated male anatomy provides a striking visual conflation of the traditional sites of knowledge and pleasure, demonstrating graphically that these functions need not necessarily be held apart. The female speaking "subject" here generates an image that suggests beneath its comic veneer something quite serious: that one can know pleasure, that knowledge can take shape in a way that differs from knowing something in the abstract or with the rational mind.

If woman's speech here proves literally valueless because it dashes the couple's chance to "get rich quick," its greater threat is to question the very logic of a system that reduces women to body parts while granting ultimate authority to the male head. Despite the typically conservative endings of Old French fabliaux which reinstate male wisdom and authority over the wanton chaos of female pleasure, these texts demonstrate vividly how woman can disrupt the standard scenario of male/female relations by the very exercise of those orifices used traditionally to typecast and dismiss her.

If the voices of the outspoken female protagonists in medieval fabliaux do not become the dominant voices in the texts that contain them, their words play a crucial role in that dominant structure, infiltrating it in ways that can reveal to the attentive feminist reader its fundamental weakness and vulnerability. When female protagonists take control verbally and actually "wear the pants" in the family, the very role and function of those pants as a literal covering for the male sex organs and a metaphorical emblem of conjugal authority undergo a radical reformulation. By revealing the inadequate performance of her husband in bed, the disobedient wife of the "Four Wishes" also lays bare the insufficiency of philosophical and rational systems that privilege one true answer over the possibility of competing truths. In insisting that "one prick alone was not enough for me," she rejects not only her husband's meager sexual member but the binary logic that enshrines the male head/phallus duo, a logic that pits men against women and knowledge against pleasure only to privilege the first term of each binary pair.

In asking for "more pricks," the fabliau woman's voice sounds a richly ambivalent note that has been replayed for us much more recently in the purposefully ambiguous title of Luce Irigaray's *This Sex Which Is Not One*.[39] Depending on how one reads it, "this sex which is not one" can appear to echo the rationale of specular logic that grants primacy to the male phallus while relegating female genitalia to the status of an absence or a lack: His is the model sex while hers exists only as an impoverished reflection of the potent phallus. If her vagina is but a hole or envelope for the male organ, cast as the "negative, the underside, the reverse of the only visible and morphologically designatable sex organ" (26), then woman's sex is not number one, not primary, not really even a sex in its own right at all (23). But conversely, "this sex which is not one" can proclaim that, different from the monolithic status of the male phallus, the female sex is not limited by the constraints of a single sexual member or a single erogenous zone. Female sexuality "is not one" because it derives not from the unitary phallus but the two lips of the vagina. And the subject speaking from this anatomical configuration is similarly not monolithic but multiple, for it speaks, as does the wife in the "Four Wishes," as an object of desire and a desiring subject simultaneously in a way that engages Irigaray's now-famous rhetorical question: "But what if the 'object' started to speak? Which also means beginning to 'see,' etc. What disaggregation of the subject would that entail?"[40]

This is precisely the question posed, some five hundred years earlier, by "The Four Wishes of Saint Martin" and related fabliau narratives. What happens when the socially constrained, philosophically silenced, metaphorically decapitated female speaks? What are the consequences of acknowledging that women have two mouths instead of one: a facial mouth complete with the teeth and tongue necessary to emit speech, and a vaginal mouth bearing erotic lips that do not speak? Even in the fabliau, the female mouth reduced to a vagina still speaks, and herein lies the problem. The fabliaux show in essence how this dual construction of femaleness cannot be tolerated by the specular logic that views anatomy in terms of presence or absence of the phallus. From the perspective of the penis-eye there can be only one head as there is (normally) only one penis. Acknowledgment of the female head along with her body threatens the very logic that sets man up as the master in his house, head of the household, wearer of the proverbial pants.

In that fleeting moment of asking for more pricks, the wife in the "Four Wishes" challenges this view by asserting, in the language of Old French fabliaux, that "this sex is not one," not reducible to a body without voice or to a talking cunt. This female sex, represented by the seemingly libidinous body of the fabliau wife, is paradoxically a body endowed with a voice, an object of desire that speaks also as a subject, an erotic sexual mouth and a toothed viril one simultaneously. Standing outside the limits of either/or logic that constructs woman as man's necessary and inferior opposite, this speaking female body can question the hierarchy that privi leges one over two, call for a new understanding of the relation between head and body, ask for new rules of the game, change our view of the world.

In saying "I want more pricks," she says in essence I want more than one prick, more than the monolithic phallus, more than this phallocentric world view.

Notes

1. For a recent assessment of the problem of antifeminism in the fabliau and a recap of previous studies, see Norris J. Lacy, "Fabliau Women," *Romance Notes* 25, no. 3 (1985): 318–27. On the dozen or so fabliaux that treat female sexuality explicitly, see Sarah Melhado White, "Sexual Language and Human Conflict in Old French Fabliaux," *Comparative Studies in Society and History* 24, no. 1 (1982): 185–210. Leslie Johnson has argued convincingly for the ways women come out "on top" in certain fabliaux, thereby mitigating the wholesale antifeminism most often found in the morals to these tales; "Women on Top: Antifeminism in the Fabliaux?" *Modern Language Review* 8, 2 (1983): 298–307.

2. R. Howard Bloch has shown that the fabliaux are more than naturalistic tales about sex and bodies. But his analysis remains remarkably blind to issues of gender. See *The Scandal of the Fabliaux* (Chicago: University of Chicago Press, 1986); and in partial response, E. Jane Burns, "Knowing Women: Female Orifices in the Old French Farce and Fabliau," *Exemplaria* 4, no. 1 (Spring 1992): 81–104.

3. Anatole de Montaiglon and Gaston Raynaud, *Recueil général et complet des fabliaux*, 6 vols. (Paris: Librairie des Bibliophiles, 1872–90), 5:206; and Willem Noomen and Nico Van Den Boogaard, *Nouveau Recueil Complet des Fabliaux* (*NRCF*), 6 vols. (Assen, The Netherlands: Van Gorcum and Co., 1984), 4:215. I will indicate volume and page from Montaiglon's edition (e.g., MR 5:206) and from Noomen's edition where available (e.g., N 4:215). Translations are mine throughout this essay. For an inspired English translation of "Les Quatre Souhais Saint Martin," see *Gallic Salt: Eighteen Fabliaux Translated from the Old French*, trans. Robert Harrison (Berkeley: University of California Press, 1974), 177–89.

4. Problems of origin, audience and reception of works in these reputedly "realist" genres remain unsolved. See especially Joseph Bédier, *Les fabliaux: Etudes de littérature populaire et d'histoire littéraire au Moyen Age* (Geneva: Slatkine, 1982); Jean Rychner, *Contribution à l'étude des fabliaux* (Geneva: Droz, 1960); Per Nykrog, *Les Fabliaux* (Geneva: Droz, 1973). For a thorough discussion of the arguments on both sides regarding the fabliau's provenance and delivery see Charles Muscatine, *The Old French Fabliaux* (New Haven: Yale Univ. Press, 1986), 1–46; and his own argument that the fabliau should be taken seriously as evidence of medieval French cultural history, 152–69.

5. Noomen's text omits the wife's mention of service and merit and supplies instead the following exchange: "Mes amis, me dites vos voir? / —Oil, ma bele suer, por voir!" ("My dear, is that true?—Yes, dear it is") (vv. 59–60).

6. *Esploit* ranges in meaning from action or execution to success, ardor or passion, advantage or profit, gain, and revenue. The wife in the "Four Wishes" is getting none of these.

7. Noomen's text substitutes "nose" for "face" (*nariz* for *viz*): "Que tot soiez chargiez de viz: / Ne remaigne oil ne nariz" (vv. 95–96).

8. In Noomen's version, the pricks are even colored, "Sor lui avoit maint vit carre, / Et grant et grox et rebole; / Maint noir, / maint blanc et maint vermoil" ("On him there were many square pricks, large, thick and puffy ones / Many black, many white, many red") (vv. 115–17).

9. "'Sire,' dist ele, 'souhaidiez / Le quart souhait qu'encore avon, / Qu'aiez .I. vit et je .I. con; / Si ert ausi comme devant, / Et si n'avrons perdu noiant'" ("Sir, she said, use our fourth wish to ask that you have one prick and I one cunt. Then all will be as before and we will have lost nothing") (MR 5:207; N 4:215).

10. In "Du Chevalier confesseur," the wife explains the rarity of women who are content with their husbands alone, and offers infidelity as the obvious solution (Philippe Ménard, *Les Fabliaux: Contes a rire du Moyen Age* [Paris: Presses Universitaires de France, 1983], 178). Other fabliaux that reiterate this image are "De Porcelet" (MR 4:144; N 6:185), "Du Vallet aus XII fames" (MR 3:186; N 4:131), ("De la Morel sa provende avoir" (MR 1:318), "La Veuve" (Charles Livingston, ed., *Le Jongleur Gautier le Leu: Étude sur les fabliaux* [Cambridge: Harvard University Press, 1951], vv. 432–88), "Du Pescheor de Pont seur Saine" (MR 3:68; N 4:107), "De Cele qui se fist foutre sur la fosse de son mari" (MR 3:118), "Du Chevalier qui fist sa Fame confesse" (MR 1:178; N 4:227).

11. In Noomen's edition the word *savoir* appears in the A text only, N 4:208. A similar moral ends "Du Vilain de Bailleul" (MR 4:212; N 5:223), in which the wife deceives her foolish husband to have an affair with a priest. Rather than expressing her sexual desire outright, as does the wife in the "Four Wishes," this woman cajoles and tricks her husband into allowing her to exercise her sexual prerogative. The moral, "C'on doit por fol tenir celui / Qui mieus croit sa fame que lui" ("One should consider a man crazy if he believes his wife rather than himself"), underscores the loss of control in conjugal affairs as a loss of reason, a falling into folly.

12. "Tost demanderiez .III. fusées / De chanvre, de laine ou de lin" ("You will ask for three bobbins of thread: hemp, wool and linen") (MR 5:203).

13. Luce Irigaray, *Speculum of the Other Woman*, trans. Gillian C. Gill (Ithaca: Cornell University Press, 1985), 13–129. In the French edition, *Speculum de l'autre femme* (Paris: Minuit, 1974), 9–162.

14. Ibid., 22. In the French edition: "Charnière se pliant selon leurs echanges. Reserve (de) *négativité* soutenant l'articulation de leurs *pas* dans un progrès, pour une part fictif, vers la maîtrise du pouvoir. Du savoir. Auxquels elle n'aura pas de part. Hors scène, hors représentation, hors jeu, jors je" (21).

15. For a lucid reading of the political implications of Irigaray's thought, see Margaret Whitford, "Rereading Irigaray," in *Between Feminism and Psychoanalysis*, ed. Teresa Brennan (London: Routledge, 1989), 106–26. For other explanations of why Irigaray is not an essentialist, see Naomi Schor, "This Essentialism Which Is Not One," *Differences* 1, no. 2 (Summer 1989): 38–58; Diana Fuss, *Essentially Speak-*

ing: *Feminism, Nature and Difference* (London: Routledge, 1989), 55–72; Jane Gallop, "Lip Service," in her *Thinking Through the Body* (New York: Columbia University Press, 1988), 92–99.

16. *Jacques Lacan: A Feminist Introduction* (London: Routledge, 1990), 176.

17. Teresa de Lauretis, *Technologies of Gender: Essays on Theory, Film, and Fiction* (Bloomington: Indiana University Press, 1987), 26.

18. This approach builds on Nancy Miller's work on female authors where she defines women's writing as a "feminist literature of dissent," *Subject to Change* (New York: Columbia University Press, 1988), 5, 44.

19. Hélène Cixous, "Castration or Decapitation," trans. Annette Kuhn, *Signs* 7, no. 1 (1981): 41–55.

20. See Jane Gallop, "Snatches of Conversation," in *Women and Language in Society and Culture*, ed. Sally McConnell-Ginet et al. (New York: Praeger, 1979); and Catherine Belsey, *The Subject of Tragedy: Identity and Difference in Renaissance Drama* (London: Methuen, 1985), intro. and chap. 6.

21. Belsey, *Subject of Tragedy*, chap. 3.

22. Thomas Laqueur explains how metaphorical connections between the throat and the cervix/vagina/pudenda are common in Antiquity and persist through the nineteenth century. He offers a particularly striking nineteenth-century illustration of a larynx that bears strong resemblance to female genitalia (*Making Sex: Body and Gender from the Greeks to Freud* [Cambridge, Mass.: Harvard University Press, 1990], 37). For a specifically medieval attribution of a vaginal function to the woman's mouth see depictions of the birth of the Antichrist contained in Renate Blumenfeld-Kosinski's *Not of Woman Born: Representations of Caesarean Birth in Medieval and Renaissance Culture* (Ithaca: Cornell University Press, 1990), plates 23, 24.

23. "Le Fabliau du moigne," ed. A. Lanfors, *Romania* 44, no. 3 (1915–17): 562, l. 116–117.

24. For a survey of psychoanalytic commentary linking the female mouth and vagina see Kaja Silverman, *The Acoustic Mirror: The Female Voice in Psychoanalysis and Cinema* (Bloomington: Indiana University Press, 1988), 67. In *Trubert*, a woman's detached genitals are claimed to be the mouth and nose of a man, "la bouche i est / de Goulias et les narilles," *Trubert*, ed. G. Renaud de Lage (Geneva: Droz, 1974), v. 1968, and in "Des Ceux Vilains."

25. White, "Sexual Language," 185–210.

26. She laments only to herself, "Qu'il deüst veillier, et il dort!" ("He should be awake but he sleeps!") (MR 5:186; N 6:286).

27. "De la Coille noire" (MR 6:90; N 5:186).

28. "De la Sorisete des estopes" (MR 4:158; N 6:178). As the moral states, "Qant el viaut ome decevoir / Plus l'an deçoit et plus l'afole / Tot solemant par sa parole" ("When she wants to deceive a man, she [woman] deceives him most and makes him craziest simply by speaking") (MR 4:165; N 6:183). Alexandre Leupin offers a very different reading of this fabliau and the "Four Wishes" itself in his *Barbarolexis: Medieval Writing and Sexuality*, claiming that castration, "symbolized by the whiteness of asexuality, is the irrefutable figure through which the text touches the real, inscribing on it the missing signifier. Castration marks that mo-

ment when the text must begin to speak in infinite metaphor." And woman is erased: "the woman's body is thus the symptom of a lack" (Trans. Kate M. Cooper [Cambridge, Mass.: Harvard University Press, 1989], 100).

29. A similar scenario structures "Du Fol Vilain," ed. Livingston, *Le Jongleur Gautier le Leu.*

30. More often they threaten man's sexual prowess as they critique his ability to perform. The wife in the "Li Sohaiz desvez" says pointedly to her husband that his penis cannot measure up to even the smallest in her dream: "Mes li vit à la povre gent / Estoient tel que uns toz seus / En vaudroit largemant ces deus / Teus con il est" ("But the poorest men's penises were such that one alone was worthy of two of his, such as it was") (MR 5:190; N 6:272). The wife in "Black Balls" avers more aggressively, "Je ne gerra mais delez moi / Li vilains qui tel hernois porte!" ("I will no longer lie with a man who has this equipment!") (MR 6:91). Noomen's text is even more explicit, "Ja ne gerra mais avoc moi / Li vilains qui tes coilles porte" ("I will not have lying next to me a guy with balls like that") (N 5:186).

31. "J'ai les denz et granz et lons, / Et mon cons n'en a encor nus" (MR 5:113; N 4:32).

32. See Wendy O'Flaherty, *Women, Androgynes and Other Mythical Beasts* (Chicago: University of Chicago Press, 1980), 53–57, 81, 90; Wolfgang Lederer, *Fear of Women* (New York: Grune and Stratton, 1968), chap. 1; Karen Horney, "The Dread of Woman" and "The Denial of the Vagina," *Feminine Psychology* (New York: W. W. Norton, 1967), 113–46, 147–61. For a mythic tale that bears striking resemblance to the "Four Wishes," see "Long Tongue the Demoness" in *Tales of Sex and Violence,* trans. Wendy O'Flaherty (Chicago: University of Chicago Press, 1985).

33. That the cotton which the countess stuffs in her mouth to control her speech also marks her resistance to possible vaginal penetration is made clear in other tales like "Du Pescheor de Pont seur Saine," where stuffing of the woman's mouth is paired with sexual stuffing of her vagina: "A well-fed young woman often wants to have sex" (MR 3:69; N 4:124).

34. On the confusion of vagina and anus, see Burns, "Knowing Women."

35. For a critique of Michel Foucault's *History of Sexuality* demonstrating how his reading misses this essential point, see Victor Seidler, "Reason, Desire and Male Sexuality," in *The Cultural Construction of Sexuality,* ed. Pat Caplan (London: Tavistock Publications, 1987), 82–112. Seidler aptly observes how the very thinker who recognized in his *History of Madness* the extent to which rationality served historically as a means of establishing sociopolitical superiority, failed surprisingly to recognize how reason is also inextricably linked to historical definitions of masculinity.

36. That the voice of the fabliau's talking cunt (or later, its anal equivalent) produces not female speech but a conversation between men is reiterated in the concluding scenes of this tale. The knight, stymied by the cotton stuffing, uses his third boon to request that the woman's anus speak since the vagina cannot. After the anus reveals why the cunt is speechless, "Qu'il a la gueule tote plaine" ("Because its mouth was full,") (MR 6:87; N 3:172), the cunt repeats the explanation:

"G'en ne pooie, / Por ce que enconbrez estoie, / Du coton que ma dame i mist" ("I couldn't [speak] because I was impeded by the cotton that my lady put there") (MR 6:88; N 3:173). On hearing this, the countess's husband laughs heartily, "Quand li quens l'ot, forment s'en rist," underwriting the joke between himself and the knight. Subsequently, at the knight's request for just treatment, the count asks the countess to unpack her vagina (MR 6:87–88; N 3:173), thus bringing her lips back under male control.

37. These lines, omitted from Noomen's text (4:215) appear in Manuscript A, which he cites on p. 206.

38. "Si ot vit lonc et vit quarré, / vit gros, vit cort, vit reboulé, / vit corbe, vit agu, vit gros" (MR 5:204–5; N 4:214).

39. Trans. Catherine Porter (Ithaca: Cornell University Press, 1985).

40. Irigaray, *Speculum*, trans. Gill, 135. French edition, 167.

Helen Solterer

At the Bottom of Mirage, a Woman's Body: *Le Roman de la rose* of Jean Renart

> You turn me into a flower. Before knowing you, I was already a flower. Must I forget it in order to become your flower? The one you intend me to be, the one you design in and around me, the one you would make and keep within your purview?
> Luce Irigaray, *Passions élémentaires*

Underlying the fascination with the female body in much of medieval literature is a primordial tension between symbolic and literal orders of representation. On the one hand, there is the system of allegory, which transforms the carnal through various denatured, ornamental figures. It renders the body abstractly, albeit in an alluring manner. Its outstanding metaphors of flora and fauna thus cater to the desire to dwell upon the bodily, all the while that they convert it into something else. On the other hand, there is the model of representing the female body in literal terms. In both romances and fabliaux, the body is figured anatomically as a variable composite of physical fragments. Instead of a rose, versions of a nude are depicted and put on display. Not only does such literal representation identify the feminine principally with the carnal, but it fashions a female body that appears both accessible and easy to possess.

So powerful are these two opposing representational codes that in many instances they have come to dictate the very reception of medieval works. Reading allegory tends to generate a symbolic mode of interpretation, in much the same way that analysis of the *propre* can confirm the habit of considering most every narrative literally. Ironically, despite their fundamental differences, literal and symbolic orders of representation have had the effect of valorizing the corresponding critical optic: it has proved difficult to broach medieval texts otherwise. More than many other figures, the female body has been caught between these two frames of critical vision—the far-reaching scope of allegory and the scrutiny of literalism.

One case that epitomizes this pattern is the *Roman de la rose*, signed "Jean Renart." This thirteenth-century narrative recounts the travails of a Griselda-style heroine, Lienors, whose virginity is falsely maligned.[1] All her trials revolve around the central mark of a rose on her body: a jongleur first embellishes it fancifully and describes it to her future husband, the emperor Conrad. He in turn fantasizes about the rose, a habit observed by a treacherous seneschal who gains from Lienors's family an account of it. This *afaire de la rose* (ll. 3360–61) enables the seneschal to give the false impression that he has deflowered Lienors.[2] Breaking with the model of Griselda's passivity, the text traces the heroine's effort to dispute the charge, reclaim the rose and her name, and thereby redefine it in her own manner.

This *Roman de la rose* was deemed at one time an exemplar of literal representation. Both its meticulous material descriptions and its attention to the human particular contribute to this picture, and to such a degree that several critics even labeled it a realist text.[3] For Rita Lejeune, this so-called medieval realism is manifest in the "desacralization" of women; that is, in the puncturing of a symbolic aesthetic concerning the feminine and in a privileging of the ordinary, the tangible, the carnal.[4] Such assessments assume strikingly that the literal is substantiated by the feminine and the feminine, in turn, by the bodily. The rose is, quite simply, a physical blemish.

Counterbalancing this position is the allegorical reading of the *Rose*. It is a critical stance that derives its force from the preeminent *Rose* of Guillaume de Lorris and Jean de Meun, all the more so given the perennial tendency to conflate these texts. Yet the attempt to interpret Renart's *Rose* in exclusively allegorical terms exploits the symbolic order of representation in Lorris and de Meun even more radically. The rose, which functions first as a decorous figure of the female sexualized body, is transmuted yet again into a purely poetic sign.

Roger Dragonetti typifies this critical vision. Not only does he argue that the character Lienors is not a woman, but he proposes that the rose may not exist at all.[5] By designating the *Rose* a parable of *écriture*, he turns Lienors into an exemplary trope for the game of fiction. The body of Lienors is thereby reduced to a cipher, a tantalizing illusion generated by the text. Because Dragonetti recasts the rose as figure of female sexuality into that of the delusory virginity of any poetic source, its own specificity is glossed over; the woman's body is metaphorized out of existence in a way that surpasses even the allegorical *Rose*.[6]

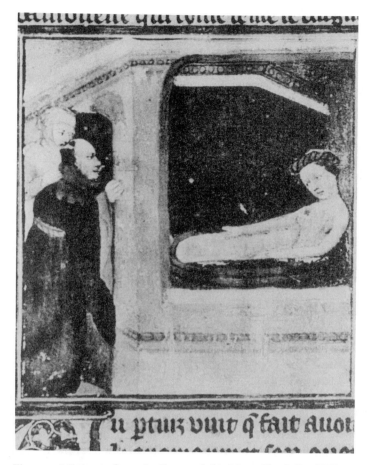

Figure 1. Miniature from the *Roman de la violette*, Ms. fr.Q.v.XIV. 3, fol. 6v. (Courtesy of the Saltykov-Schedrin Library, St. Petersburg.)

Juxtaposing these two rival visions gives rise to a fundamental question: In fixing upon the rose, are we able only to recognize a sexualized body or pure mirage? In other words, are we locked into discerning either an utterly literal or a wholly symbolic feminine?

At the risk of some anachronism, I would suggest that such questions are rendered vividly through the pictorial language of the late medieval period. Witness the miniature from the contemporaneous *Roman de la violette* in figure 1.[7] On the one hand, the representation operates literally: it showcases an odalisque—a woman exposed and reduced to bodily elements. And on the other, it depicts female carnality allegorically through the sign of the rose/violet marking her breast. All this is placed in the framework of a common prurient vision, which invites us to read this woman as erotic flora, that is, in the same reductive way as do the seneschal and his accomplice.

In this essay, I want to pursue these questions somewhat differently, in part because the *Roman de la rose* adduces such a reconsideration. Like the *Violette* miniature, the narrative brings to the fore the tensions and frictions shaping the representation of women. Indeed it externalizes those tensions through the bodily, a point of reference that always remains highly charged.[8] The figure naming the *Rose* is, after all, a birthmark on a woman's thigh. It constitutes a fleshly sign that orients our vision toward the physical. Yet at the same time, the narrative emphasizes how the rose is an entity translated by several representational practices. The rose metamorphoses in such surprising ways that its own status as figure becomes a focal point of the text.

My chief purpose lies in examining the ways allegorical and literal readings of the *Rose* have worked to privilege certain figurative features and, as a consequence, to elide others. Proceeding in this manner, with an eye toward what has fallen out of the picture, means considering the terms of my vision. This essay is a twofold experiment in analyzing critical motivations: the predominant ones together with my own. In what follows, I shall take up those scenes characterizing the *Rose*'s unusual mode of figuration, and my reading will emphasize details missing from the frames of allegorical and literalist vision. For as Naomi Schor has argued persuasively, such blind spots afford us a chance to discern how the equation representation/woman has been construed conventionally.[9] To examine what is not seen is to reckon with the critical predilection for focusing myopically on the female body or looking through it to something else beyond.

i.

We shall begin by considering that habitual representational technique we might call the "assemble-it-yourself" woman. Throughout the *Rose*, as in numerous medieval works, we find characters engaged in piecing together an image of women according to their own designs:

que chascuns i garist et sane
ses oils d'esgarder les mervelles:
tantes faces cleres, vermeilles,
et cez douz viz lons et traitiz,
et cez biaus sorcils porvoutiz,
et cez blons chiez, et cez biaus cors.

(ll. 359–64)

(everyone there [at the festival] soothes and heals his eyes by looking at the marvels, so many radiant and blushing complexions, such refined, well-shaped faces, beautifully arched eyebrows, blond heads, and beautiful bodies.)

In this instance, the narration plots the line of vision of the courtly company. From the moment of apprehending the marvels of women, to the revery on each literal member, it traces the way the gaze assembles their "beautiful bodies." Each element is composed to indulge the spectators' taste. The *Rose*'s audiences are positioned to see as the characters do and to share in their activity because their perspective is aligned with that of the narrator or individual characters. Various audiences are thus encouraged to join fictional characters in inventing the feminine, and in this way, the feminine can be shaped by their common desire.

The *Rose* makes particularly ironic use of this technique in the round of singing, eating, and lovemaking that opens the narrative. Our passage proceeds without a break to serve up other appealing things:

Et quant li quens de Sagremors
Ot chanté une chançonete,
Vïande orent et bone et nete,
Vin cler et froit de la Musele,
Et vaisselemente novele,
Pastez de chevrols et lardez
(De ce i ert granz la plentez)
De chevriex, de cers et de dains,
Et fromages et cras et sains
De la riviere de Clermont

(ll. 365–74)

(And when the count of Sagremors finished his song, they were served good, tasty meat; clear, cool Moselle wine in a new decanter, mutton and lard pasties, and in great quantity, morsels of venison, mutton, as well as creamy and nourishing cheese from the Clermont valley)

The sequence of feminine detail yields imperceptibly to the edible. The phenomenon of assemble-it-yourself women sets up a commingling of various objects of consumption.[10] No distinction is made between women courtiers and foodstuffs. Such a mixture of female bodiliness and diet underscores the avariciousness of the aristocratic society depicted—the same avariciousness informing the assemble-it-yourself woman. Little does it matter what the object of its appetite is, as long as it is appeased. By representing in this exact and literal manner a society that assimilates female bodies as effortlessly as food at a banquet, the *Rose* ironizes the process of converting virtually everything into an object to be expended. It offers a mocking portrayal of conspicuous consumption.

In this setting, the jongleur's ploy of creating the ideal woman to satisfy the emperor's longing is perfectly consistent. From the bits and pieces of the jongleur's grab bag, an individual woman can be tailor-made for his needs. Jouglet devises a female *merveille*, bodying forth Lienors from his repertoire of romance and lyric heroines. As has often been noted, the ingenuity of this particular invention lies in the fact that Jouglet's composition mimics the poet's own. The literal description of Lienors incorporates a thumbnail sketch of Renart's *Lai de l'ombre*.[11] One poet's craft recapitulates another, which resumes another and so on until we are faced with a dizzying *mise en abyme* of the act of poetic composition.

Yet rather than concentrate on this parallel between Jouglet and the *Rose* poet, I want instead to consider the connection established between poetic composition and the "raw materials" of women. This scene of poiesis takes as its object, among all possible choices, a woman—indeed a virgin. The connection is enormously suggestive because of its familiarity. The link between women and rhetorical invention is effective precisely because female experience is invented to a large degree by the prime movers of high medieval society. Such a link makes sense in a signifying world that has always perceived women as plastic entities to be molded like so many Galateas. The scene of Jouglet generating Lienors reveals as much about the deeply rooted convention of shaping exemplary women as it does about any mechanism of writing.

In this respect, Conrad's reaction to Jouglet's ideal woman is telling. However wary he may appear of accepting her, this is clearly his main desire. Each time he deflects the jongleur's seductive account by demand-

ing to know the truth—in effect by introducing the exigency of the
real—he draws closer to embracing Jouglet's assemble-it-yourself woman.

> Fet il: "Nel tenez mie a faule . . ."
> —Ce fust mervelle, ce m'est vis.
> —Ce sachiez vos de verité
> Qu'ele ert tel com ge la devis.
> —"Juglet, fet il, ne me di ja
> Ne plus ne mains que tu en sez."
>   (ll. 657, 690, 721–22, 809–10)

(He said: "don't take it as a mere story . . ."
—This is fantasy, it seems to me.
—You should know this to be true, that she is exactly as I have de-
scribed her.
—"Jouglet," he said, "tell me only what you know, no more no less.")

The banter between emperor and jongleur acts to valorize the ideal
woman over the flesh-and-blood Lienors. Ultimately Conrad is enthralled
by a symbolic form.

   The circumstances surrounding Conrad's seduction reveal the power
of the assemble-it-yourself woman all the more clearly. Jouglet insists on
leading Conrad away from his accustomed route at the moment he begins
to invent Lienors (ll. 649–50). Once he has sparked Conrad's desire, they
regain their path:

> Je lairai nostre conte ici.
> Et vos savez bien ou ge les.
> il est bien tens d'ateindre huimés
> nostre route et noz conpegnons.
>   (ll. 839–42)

(I'll leave off our story here and you'll know well where we are. It is high
time to return to our route and catch up with our companions.)

The process of inventing a woman is situated exactly at that point where
Conrad and Jouglet depart from the conventional route. The narrative sets
up the creation of a female *merveille* as a veritable deviation, that which
takes place off the beaten track.

   This link between the assemble-it-yourself woman and a world apart

is reinforced through the text. For instance, when Lienors's brother Guillaume brings news of her to the emperor, they retreat to their own private
sphere (ll. 1750–59). Such a locus of total detachment suggests that no
contact with women is necessary. If we recognize in it what Eve Sedgwick
calls a spatialization of the male bond, the irrelevance of Lienors is all the
more comprehensible.[12] Guillaume and Conrad are free to devise a female
person on their own terms; in fact, their space realizes this freedom. There,
in a sequestered intimacy, they indulge in a fantasy where Lienors plays
no part. It is important to note that at this juncture the narrative offers no
literal, female portrayal. It does not even represent Lienors; for male imag-
inings, unleashed in a world of their making, can supplant her presence
entirely.

Conrad's first words confirm this state of estrangement:

une amor me desvoie
Et tient esgaré,
Ou j'ai mon pensé,
En quel lieu que onques soie.
(ll. 1773–76)

(a love leads me astray and holds me apart, whatever I am thinking, in
whatever place I find myself.)

Desvoier is the key term here.[13] Traditional conceptions of erotic desire read
women as the source of the lover's disorientation: Conrad is derailed because of Lienors's influence on him. This formulation entails an obvious
case of displacement onto the woman. It is Conrad's attitude toward
women in general that is responsible for his disarray. From the beginning,
he has preferred to remain at a distance from Lienors, imagining her, or-
daining her behavior as he sees fit. He thus finds himself *desvoié*, not because of her, I would argue, but because of his inability to approach the
incalculable of an individual woman. Although Jouglet's invention holds
him in this isolation, his profound ambivalence toward women first
brought him there.

In every aspect of Lienors's engendering, then, the "assemble-it-
yourself" woman supersedes the individual. In the first part of the narrative, the collaborative creation of jongleur and emperor holds sway over
the personage the *Rose* will present. The narrative fosters the expectation
that once Lienors actually does appear, she will conform to the identity

already elaborated for her. Like Chrétien's Enide, the "natural" woman transformed into a courtly spouse, Lienors will realize her preordained role. Or so narrative convention would seem to dictate. Yet, by sharp contrast, the *Roman de la rose* undermines this structure, disabusing the reader of such an assumption. In the scene where Lienors herself comes into view, the very notion of the assemble-it-yourself woman is called into question.

ii.

The first glimpse of Lienors finds her embroidering in the company of her mother. The narrative qualifies this portrait specifically as a *mestier*; that is, sewing is Lienors's appointed social function (ll. 1130–33).[14] This choice of *mestier* is noteworthy given its status during the high Middle Ages. As Rozsicka Parker has demonstrated recently, it is from the twelfth century onward that embroidery becomes allied with a developing notion of femininity.[15] Because it is a time-consuming labor associated increasingly with the domestic sphere, sewing comes to be recognized as women's work. To embroider is to be identified as a discreet woman, occupied without being independently active. This activity is most often placed in a communal setting. Women are depicted sewing together, thereby amplifying the image of serene feminine harmony.[16] Even in the sinister case of the enslaved embroideresses at the Château de Pesme Aventure in Chrétien de Troyes' *Yvain*, the docility of the women is emphasized.[17]

In this manner, the *Rose* sets into play one conventional definition of femininity. The narrative employs the sewing *mestier* as a means of probing various constraints and liabilities of the norm, and it extends its exploration further through the *chansons de toile* Lienors is asked to perform:

> Fille et la mere se sieent a l'orfrois
> A un fil d'or i font orïeuls croiz.
> Parla la mere qui le cuer ot cortois.
> Tant bon'amor fist bele Aude en Doon.
> (ll. 1159–62)

(Daughter and mother were embroidering with golden thread, weaving golden crosses. The mother, with a gentle heart, spoke: with what love beautiful Aude burned for Doon.)

These lyrics portray women who while away the time as they work, plaiting together memories and dreams of love to come. On first sight, they delineate Lienors's position exactly. They identify her with those idealized ladies of the lyric genre—an affinity even her mother notes (ll. 1148–51). So closely matched are their situations that Lienors appears to merge with the lyric heroine: she becomes "bele Aude."[18] Yet couched in this coincidence is one jarring discrepancy. And it is here that the *Rose*'s contrasting of symbolic and literal comes to the fore. Lienors does not realize the symbol of the decorous aristocratic lady who amuses herself with singing and sewing. She is represented, quite literally, as an impoverished young woman for whom sewing is a necessary craft. The irony here is subtle, for it lies less in the fact that the symbolic and the "real" clash than in the fact that the discrepancy is deliberately not recognized. The various personages surrounding Lienors—her mother, her brother, Conrad's envoy—all insist on approaching her as an ideal woman, invented according to the *chansons de toile* model. To do so is to reinforce the symbolic terms of her *mestier*. Were Lienors to be shown acquiescing to them, the narrative would play out unimpededly the ideal plot of femininity.

It is at this point that we must be careful to notice how the narrative suggests the strain in Lienors's compliance to this role. Whereas she concedes to her family's requests and entertains the envoy with *chansons de toile*, at each step of the way she is represented as resisting ever so slightly. After the first song, she voices her discomfort: "Don't ask me anything more" ("Or ne me demandez plus rien") (l. 1194). When her brother persists and she is obliged to play the ideal women again, she invokes the emperor's standard of courtliness: "For he would be discourteous, she said, who would seek anything more of me" ("Or seroit ce sanz courtoisie, fet ele, qui plus me querroit") (ll. 1218–19). Lienors is portrayed as reacting against the strictures of the role. The *Rose* introduces a female protagonist who expresses her aversion to the version of femininity foisted upon her. Through her demuring remarks, the narrative begins to examine the limits, and indeed the arbitrary demands, of this so-called normative female function.

In highlighting this pattern of Lienors's resistance, I do not mean to suggest that Lienors is represented as extricating herself from the filial role, or that she breaks out of the required marital scenario. However iconoclastic this narrative is, it does not in the end elaborate any new plots for its female characters. Nevertheless, what we should detect in this first representation of Lienors is a *mise en question* of the model of *chanson de toile* woman. The narrative creates a persona who, in her first gestures and words, balks at one normative model of femininity. In this limited sense, then, a female persona begins to challenge versions of invented women advanced by the *Rose* thus far.

The scene that poses the question of women's invention most forcefully revolves around "the red rose on her soft white thigh" (ll. 3364–65). This first simple description of the rose begs the question of figuration. To make the symbolic link with virginity is virtually automatic, and the connection is confirmed by many other contexts.[19] And yet we should recognize the rose also as a literal, physical mark. A trace doubling female genitalia but separate from them, a trace emblazoned on Lienors's thigh, this rose delineates the female body in a way the allegorical sign cannot.

This double rose emerges first as the mark of the mother—*Muttermal*—as it is called in German. It belongs to her, for it is the mother who makes the rose known to the inquiring seneschal. Together they set it in motion as a linguistic sign free of any referent. No knowledge on Lienors's part is necessary. She is conspicuously absent at the moment of this revelation, and since the rose is never visible, it is simple to concoct a version that has no link to the physical. What the mother relays, and what the seneschal envisages, exists independently of Lienors's body, indeed in spite of it. Their rose is a construction in language that claims a vital connection to the flesh but in fact possesses none.

The notion that virginity can function primarily as an invention, a sign with no referent, is by no means unique to the *Rose*. Nor is it characteristic of literary texts alone. The domains of canon law, philosophy, and historiography bear this out amply. The twelfth-century medical treatises studied by Danielle Jacquart and Claude Thomasset offer a case in point. They argue convincingly that most anatomical descriptions of the female body in these texts are in no significant way based on observation.[20] Shorn from the body, the scientific representation of virginity exists in isolation. It eschews virtually any contact with women themselves. It gains its legitimacy instead from the Isidorean tradition that establishes a fixed, linguistic relation between men and women. According to Isidore's etymology, virginity is defined as the stamp of softness and weakness (*mulier—mollities*), in opposition to the physical power of men (*vir—vis*).[21] Language dictates the phenomenon, and thus it is irrelevant whether virginity can be ascertained physically or not.

The concept of the hymen reinforces further this schism between the linguistic sign of the female and the state of her body. Although the term itself is not introduced until the late Middle Ages, the idea of an actual tissue ruptured at the moment of defloration is often discussed.[22] In effect, the hymen signals the attempt to designate an actual site of virginity on the woman's body and the impossibility of doing so. For the hymen signifies only insofar as it is destroyed physically.[23] It is, when it is gone. Hence, the majority of medieval commentaries on the hymen concentrate on the occasion of its disappearance, as well as on the desperate stratagems to feign its disappearance.[24] For the mark—the actual site—appears only when the organ has been rent, an enigma that has led Philippe Sollers, among others, to label it "the white space of censure."[25]

In the case of Lienors's rose, it may appear that it too possesses no physical form. Just as in the scientific and philosophical assessments of virginity, in this scene of the *Rose*, it is the linguistic sign that predominates. The dialogue on Lienors's virginity between her mother and the seneschal involves no knowledge of her body at all. The sign of the rose is communicated gratuitously, thus allowing both parties to manipulate it as they so desire. The inevitable result is that a wedge is driven between the linguistic representation of virginity and the physical form it takes. The discourse on the virgin does not correspond to the shape of a woman's body. Indeed, it seems completely detachable from the body. Since the Isidorean discourse commands a monopoly, there is no need to confirm its reliability: a patriarchal invention of virginity prevails.

The crux of inventing Lienors's virginity is further compounded by the malicious intentions of the seneschal. He wields the sign of the rose in order to give the false impression to Conrad that he has deflowered Lienors. The narrative explores here not only the referentless sign, but the lie—the sign with a fraudulent signified. Lack of a referent creates the circumstances whereby the signified can be distorted. Because no one knows the virginity of Lienors, it can easily be defrauded. In fact, since Lienors herself does not control her own carnal knowledge, this fraudulence is unlikely ever to be exposed.

With little chance of investigating the physical referent, and no requirement to verify the meaning imposed by others, lies about the female body pass unremarked. It is utterly conventional for Conrad and Guillaume to accept the description of Lienors's body proffered by another. So it is that the seneschal's report of a defiled rose appears irrefutable. Moreover, the report precipitates the attempt to attack Lienors, to disfigure her physically in a way mendacious language cannot.[26]

This sheer malleability of the sign of the rose becomes clearer once we account for the numerous terms used to designate it. For the mother, the rose is dubbed *une afaire* (l. 3360). It is a harmless expression, yet one that signals the liberties taken in speaking of virginity. By contrast, the treacherous seneschal refers to it as *mehaig* (l. 3552): a wound or injury. Despite the fact that he has never seen Lienors, he considers her rose a material form to be damaged. Worse still, the rose becomes in his language a sign of mutilation that he pretends to inflict on her body. By the time the seneschal recounts his perfidious testimony to Conrad, he uses a legalistic term to denote the fake mutilation, *veraie ensaigne* (l. 3589). The rose is transformed into an article of proof, bearing the full weight of legal evidence. In the final description of the rose, Conrad calls it *une chose aperte* (l. 3724), a turn of phrase that evokes the dialectic of hiding and disclosing, not seeing and seeing, so characteristic of Lorris's *Rose*.

Such permutations of the rose should alert the reader to the dangers of presuming it an infinitely malleable sign. For to do so is to be taken in by the mother and seneschal, to subscribe to their representation, and to regard figures for the female body as variable entities to be manipulated at will. Introducing multiple terms for the rose, this narrative challenges the audience to interrogate the status of the figure of the rose. That is, it focuses our attention specifically on the process of figuration. And on several different processes, for if the *Rose* traces the conventional pattern of inventing a symbolic feminine, then it also portrays a female protagonist who unconventionally contests this symbolic. It introduces a woman who exercises the prerogative of figuring herself. In so doing, the *Rose* pushes us to consider the gendered terms of representation.

iii.

Lienors's efforts in figuration highlight from the outset the relation between the literal and the symbolic. Consider her first contact with the seneschal:

> Vos m'en irez au seneschal,
> Si porterez cest affichal,
> Cest tiessu et ceste aumosniere.
> Tot est brodé d'une maniere
> (ll. 4290–93)

(You will go to the seneschal on my behalf, you will bring this brooch, purse and cloth. Everything is embroidered in some way)

Just as in the *chansons de toile* scene, "tot est brodé." Lienors communicates through her embroidery, whose representational status is very much at issue:

> Si li mande la chastelaine
> Que, s'il ja mes veut q'el le voie,
> Que cest tiessu que li envoie
> Ceigne a sa char soz sa chemise.
>> (ll. 4315–18)

(The châtelaine also orders that if ever he desires that she see him, he must wrap around him the cloth which she is sending. He should wear it under his shirt, next to the skin.)

Lienors's tissue adheres to the flesh. She insists that it be tied tightly around the seneschal's body. This binding, I contend, signals the tension between literal and symbolic representation with which the narrative plays invariably. In one respect, the woman's textile is a material thing. In another, its use has ramifications that show it to be much more than a simple piece of cloth. The narrative proceeds here symbolically in a way that suggests another relation between linguistic signs and the body. The fact that Lienors commands the seneschal to wrap her embroidery around his waist prefigures the carnal force of her language. Whereas the seneschal severs the relation between linguistic signs and the physical, even while he speaks of the female body, Lienors undoes him by constructing exactly the opposite set of relations. His word never touches her; hers, by contrast, will bind and bruise.

The narrative carries this figurative experimentation still further:

> Mout en sot bien venir a chief
> De la mençonge dire et faindre.
> Tant li a dit qu'il li fist çaindre
> Emprés sa char, soz la chemise;
> Si l'i a si destroit mise
> Que la char, tot entor le flanc,
> L'en est avivee de sanc
>> (ll. 4421–27)

(He [Lienors's messenger] knew how to feign and to work the deception so well that he succeeded in getting the seneschal to belt the cloth under the shirt, next to his skin. He convinced him to tighten it so much that the skin all around the waist grew swollen with blood.)

The *Rose* stages a mock defloration, and of a man. In this scene we look at Lienors's embroidered textile and the seneschal's flank, reddened and en-flamed. Unwittingly, in compliance with Lienors's command, the sene-schal girds himself with a feminine article and mimics the sexual act in reverse.[27] X marks the spot: what the seneschal has always claimed to have perpetrated on the body of Lienors is now turned against him and embla-zoned on his skin. This simple line describing the seneschal's flesh en-gorged with blood emblematizes the *Rose*'s deft play with the literal and the symbolic.

Once we apprehend the literal level of this scene, the implications become apparent. Through Lienors's embroidery, the *Rose* is commenting symbolically upon the force of women's representation. Lienors maintains the connection rigorously between her language and its physical referent. Unlike the seneschal, she is mindful of this authenticating bond, particu-larly when it concerns the vexed subject of sexuality. Her word thus retains the power to maim. It can inflict a wound—a *mehaig* of sorts. For the narrative as a whole, then, a different figure of the rose is promulgated, one that countermands and overgoes its male counterpart. Here is a rose stigmatizing the male body in a way that the seneschal's figure did not for female sexuality.

This symbolic representation is introduced in the context of lying. We must remember, as the above citation makes clear, that Lienors's rose brands the seneschal as the result of a certain deception. She convinces the seneschal to wear her embroidery by feigning to be someone else. Yet this feigning is superficial. Lienors undertakes it in order to repudiate a false-hood perpetrated on her. It exists as the necessary means to the end of defending her *propre*. More importantly, her material text is never fraudu-lent. Whereas she may assume a fake name temporarily—the châtelaine of Dijon—her embroidery is of her own making. Lienors never perverts the carnal sign.

The *Rose* pushes the reversals effected by Lienors's figuration to their logical and most ludicrous extreme:

> Uns chevalier li tret et sache
> La robe amont et la chemise,
> Que chascuns vit qu'il l'avoit mise
> Et çainte estroit a sa char nue.
> Si fu la chose coneüe
>
> (ll. 4862–66)

(A knight removed his [the seneschal] tunic and shirt so that everyone could see that he had put it [Lienors' cloth] on and belted it on his bare skin. In this manner it was known.)

Together with Conrad's entire court, we are given the chance to look upon the male body as if it were the usual object of such desirous vision. Toying with readers' expectations to put a woman on display, the *Rose* in fact never shows us Lienors. It is the seneschal who is stripped bare for all to see; it is a gendered rose of another order that is made visible.

With such a moment, the text mounts a delicious parody of the ritualized inspection of the virgin's body. In romance and chronicle literature alike, the scene is ubiquitous. Enide, for example, comes under inspection by the court once Erec announces his intention to marry her.[28] Jean Froissart recounts the case of Isabelle of Bavaria who must be examined by a team of midwives and judges before her future husband Charles VI will allow her to enter Paris.[29] So commonplace are such scenes that it is almost banal to pause and take full account of them. Therein lies the *Rose*'s parody; for by reversing the banality through the substitution of a man for the female object under scrutiny, the text challenges us to look again. By presenting a male nude and, even more comically, an assembly of men busily examining it, the *Rose* mocks the convention of exhibiting the virgin in an especially outrageous way.

Ironically, very few critics have taken notice.[30] Many medieval and modern readers are so invested in the fetishizing of an idealized female body, and in the scrutiny of virginity, that they seem virtually blind to any other representations. But these other anomalous representations—a female tie that binds, flashes of male flesh—are the very features that distinguish the *Rose*. And they are all indicative of a process of women's figuration: its literal results and its symbolic force.

The *Rose*'s play with the implications of women's figuration culminates in a scene of ordeal. Precisely because Lienors's mark has been found on the seneschal's body, he must be examined so as to verify his disclaimer. The requirement to prove virginity shifts to the seneschal; the onus of proof lying, for once, on the male body. This context of ordeal, with all the court standing in judgment, creates the circumstances whereby verbal claims are tested according to the evidence of the body. Initially, the seneschal's possession of the figure of the rose offered sufficient proof of his carnal knowledge. As we have seen, designating the rose *"veraie ensaigne"* (true evidence) bolsters the legalistic pretension of his claim. Toward the end of the text, this claim no longer holds without being corroborated physically through the mechanism of ordeal. However successfully the seneschal works the split between the verbal and the physical, it must be resolved finally through the witness of his body. In spite of himself, it confirms his virginity vis-à-vis Lienors, and thereby uncovers the traces of his deception.

That the male body is forced to discredit lies about the female body reveals the ultimate irony of this narrative. For all the fraudulent accounts elaborated about a woman are turned back against themselves, and by the very person whom they sought to exploit. It is Lienors who effects this reversal: her representation obliges the male body to speak not only itself, but to speak plainly about its female counterpart as well. Conrad's court is brought to recognize the various falsifications perpetrated about a woman through the unimpeachable, physical testimony of one of their own. As a consequence, the principal falsification—"the red rose on her white thigh"—is momentarily released from the stigma of men's inventions. No longer a *veraie ensaigne* in the service of distorted versions of woman, it could become a female property again. "Before knowing you, I was already a flower": as Irigaray puts it, and the *Rose* represents it, the flower is not only the object of patriarchal discourse, but also a figure for women in its own way.

In this context, it is significant that Lienors calls herself rose (ll. 5039–43). Whereas the projection of Lorris's text survives only as *la rose qui doit estre clamée*, Renart's woman is represented as figuring herself. This representation, nevertheless, remains a textual strategy. We cannot ignore the fact that the narrative uses the naming of *la pucele de la rose* (l. 5040) as a way of reaffirming the conventional marital scenario. It would be naïve (and utopian) to think that the *Rose* offers an unmediated and semi-autonomous case of figuration for women. Yet that being said, what remains critical throughout the narrative is the combination of figuring the rose as both flower of rhetoric and physical mark. For by inflecting it doubly, the *Rose* consigns the female body exclusively neither to the impoverished literal register nor to the idealizing symbolic. Experimenting with the two allows instead for a figuration for women that looks to escape their symmetrical, yet distinct, limits.

iv.

What, then, does this *Rose* place before our critical eye? Glimpses of a male nude, a woman's representation scoring the male body. Contrary to most every expectation and assessment, it exhibits a rose for male sexuality of a woman's design. In keeping with such a reversal, the narrative elaborates another rose that conforms strictly to neither literal nor symbolic formulae. It creates a figure for the female body that mixes the two modes together—invisible and physically present, idealized form and carnal mark. Indeed, the text plays one off the other, resisting the valorization of one at the expense of the other.

Once we recognize this pattern of figuration in the *Rose*, the legacy of critical shortsightedness becomes all the more instructive. The fact that the double character of the female rose is rarely perceived reveals the deep ambivalence toward seeing anything other than a sexualized body or pure mirage. That the male nude/rose is never sighted underscores the even more powerful presumption that medieval texts invariably rehearse the same clichés concerning the invention and figuration of women.

This view is, in fact, part of a tradition of misprision that has impinged upon the *Rose* from the moment of its modern reception. The text has been subject to multiple recastings and revisionist gestures, which in the extreme suppressed even its proper name.[31] Further, we can point to the fact that Renart's *Rose* survives in a single copy, a *unicum* that looks all the more the precarious object of censure when placed side by side with the rich manuscript tradition of the other *Roses*. Although the reasons for these various misapprehensions differ, what is striking is the existence of such a pattern. To claim that medieval representation is limited to either reifying the feminine or consecrating it symbolically risks reproducing a long-standing critical perspective that the *Rose*, among other texts, may not always bear out.

Foregrounding the relation between the female body and representation, indeed dramatizing the pressures in representing it at all, the *Rose* prompts all readers to think twice about what they choose to see and do not see. These very lapses may better serve to elucidate the range of representations for women in medieval narrative than the frames of vision prevailing at present.

Notes

1. It is this plot that Gaston Paris typed as a wager romance in "Le Cycle de la gageure," *Romania* 32 (1903): 481–551. For an astute critique of this type, see Roberta L. Krueger, "Double Jeopardy: The Appropriation of Women in Four Old French Romances of the 'Cycle de la gageure,'" in *Seeking the Woman in Late*

Medieval and Renaissance Writings, ed. Sheila Fisher and Janet E. Halley (Knoxville: University of Tennessee Press, 1989), 35–44.

2. All citations are from Félix Lecoy's edition (Paris: Champion, 1962). All translations are mine.

3. The major proponents of this view are Rita Lejeune, "Le Roman réaliste au XIIIe siècle," in *Le Roman jusqu'à la fin du XIIIe siècle*, Grundriss der romanischen literaturen des Mittelalters, vol. 4, ed. Jean Frappier and Reinhold R. Grimm (Heidelberg: Carl Winter Universitätsverlag, 1978), 400–453; and Michel Zink, *Roman rouge et rose rouge: Le Roman de la rose ou de Guillaume de Dole* (Paris: Nizet, 1979), 39–40, 73–74. Anthime Fourrier uses the *Rose* as the point of departure for his study, *Le Courant réaliste dans le roman courtois en France au Moyen Âge* (Paris: A. G. Nizet, 1960), 9.

4. Lejeune, "Le Roman réaliste," 443.

5. Roger Dragonetti, *Mirage des sources: L'art du faux dans le roman médiéval* (Paris: Seuil, 1987), 189. Given Dragonetti's endebtedness to a Mallarméan aesthetic, it is interesting to juxtapose his argument with Barbara Johnson's remarks on the *Rose*—also inspired by Mallarmé's poetry: *The Critical Difference* (Baltimore: Johns Hopkins University Press, 1980), 14–15.

6. In much the same vein as Dragonetti's extreme metaphorization of woman is Henri Rey-Flaud's contention that "la femme n'est jamais là que par métaphore . . . elle n'est jamais présente que dans son absence" (*La Névrose courtoise* [Paris: Navarin, 1983], 78–79). Or, most recently, Jean-Charles Huchet's commentary in *Littérature et psychanalyse: pour une clinique littéraire* (Paris: Presses universitaires de France, 1990), 174.

7. This illumination is one of two known pictorial representations of the floral figure. It appears in a fifteenth-century version of the *Violette*. Despite its much later date, it offers an important example of the conceptualization of the feminine sign. For details of this miniature, consult Alexandre Comte de Laborde, *Les Principaux Manuscrits à peintures conservés dans l'ancienne bibliothèque impériale de Saint-Petersbourg* (Paris: Société française de reproductions de manuscrits à peintures, 1936) 1:53–55. I am endebted to Geneviève Brunel-Lobrichon of the Section Romane, Institut de recheches et d'histoire des textes, for making their microfilm of the manuscript available to me.

8. On this point, see Jane Gallop's suggestive remarks in: *Thinking Through the Body* (New York: Columbia University Press, 1988), 98.

9. Naomi Schor, *Breaking the Chain: Women, Theory and French Realist Fiction* (New York: Columbia University Press, 1985), x.

10. Another rich example of this pattern is found in *Philomela*, discussed by E. Jane Burns in her forthcoming book *Bodytalk: When Women Speak in Old French Literature* (Philadelphia: University of Pennsylvania Press, 1993).

11. See Félix Lecoy, "A propos du *Guillaume de Dole*," *Travaux de linguistique et de littérature* 18, no. 2 (1980): 15; and Norris Lacy, "Amer par oïr dire: *Guillaume de Dole* and the Drama of Language," *French Review* 54, no. 6 (May 1981): 781.

12. Eve Kosofsky Sedgwick, *Between Men: English Literature and Male Homosocial Desire* (New York: Columbia University Press, 1985), 45.

13. *Tobler-Lommatzsch Altfranzösisches Wörterbuch* defines *desvoier* in both a

literal and an extended sense as "aus dem Weg schaffen" and "verwirren, betören" (vol. 2, no. 2, pp. 1819–22). It is precisely this double connotation that the *Rose* explores in relation to Conrad—a lover who is gone off track and is lost unto himself in a dreamlike state. For a discussion of these connotations, see J. Jud, "Rêver et desver," *Romania* 52 (1936): 145–57.

14. This term is used explicitly in the first part of the *Rose* to describe the strict ordering of roles in the emperor's community (l. 99). It is introduced again when referring to Lienors's position.

15. Rozsicka Parker, *The Subversive Stitch: Embroidery and the Making of the Feminine* (London: The Woman's Press, 1986), 10–11. For a teasing out of the Freudian dictum that sewing was women's sole cultural contribution, see Luce Irigaray, *Speculum de l'autre femme* (Paris: Minuit, 1974), 140–43.

16. Georges Duby pushes the connection between these various elements— circles of women, domestic work—still further when he suggests, "aussi l'intérieur de la maison se trouvait-il naturellement en correspondance métaphorique avec le corps féminin." *Mâle Moyen Âge* (Paris: Flammarion, 1988), 119. In this regard, see also the remarks of Danielle Régnier-Bohler on the gynaceum: *Histoire de la vie privée*, ed. Philippe Ariès and Georges Duby (Paris: Seuil, 1985), 2:345–46.

17. *Yvain ou le chevalier au Lion*, ed. Mario Roques (Paris: Champion, 1975), ll. 5188–340.

18. See Zink, *Roman rouge*, 29–30, as well as his *Belle Essai sur les chansons de toile* (Paris: Champion, 1978), 3–12.

19. Brigitte Cazelles surveys this symbolic register in "La Rose et la violette," *Poétique* 68 (November 1986): 405–22.

20. Danielle Jacquart and Claude Thomasset, *Sexualité et savoir médical au Moyen Âge* (Paris: Presses universitaires de France, 1985), 65–66.

21. Ibid., 25.

22. Jacquart and Thomasset give a good overview of scholastic commentaries on the hymen (ibid., 61–63). Giulia Sissa discusses a similar attitude toward the hymen during the classical period. The impetus in Graeco-Roman culture was also to identify the female in purely material terms and, as a result, to posit an actual membrane torn on the occasion of the woman's first intercourse: *Le Corps virginal* (Paris: J. Vrin, 1987), 20–23.

23. Sissa analyzes Peter Damian's commentary on this notion that defloration breaks the *signaculum* of the hymen. See her article "Subtle Bodies," in *Fragments for a History of the Human Body*, ed. Michel Feher, with Ramona Naddaff and Nadia Tazi (New York: Zone Books, 1989), part 2, pp. 144–48. On this paradoxical status of the hymen and virginity in general, see R. Howard Bloch's suggestive remarks in his *Medieval Misogyny and the Invention of Western Romantic Love* (Chicago: University of Chicago Press, 1991), 109–11.

24. The major gynecological text of the high Middle Ages, the *Trotula*, as well as other scientific works dealing with the female body, offers several recipes for feigning virginity. See Joan Cadden's discussion of these accounts in "Medieval Scientific and Medical Views of Sexuality: Questions of Propriety," *Mediaevalia & Humanistica* 14 (1986): 164–70. For a more general review of the literature,

see the issue "Le Souci du corps," *Médiévales* 8 (1985). I am grateful to my colleague Monica Green for discussions on the medical literature of the period.

25. See the full citation as it is quoted by Sissa, *Le Corps virginal*, 131. Derrida also engages in a similar meditation on the paradoxical function of the hymen; see *La Dissémination* (Paris: Seuil, 1972), 235–41.

26. I am referring here to the incident where Conrad's nephew tries to avenge the emperor's shame by breaking into Lienors's private space and assaulting her (ll. 39342–49). If the seneschal's verbal violation did not work, the text hints, then real violence will. The sexual implications of this scene are difficult to ignore.

27. The suggestion of the sexual act is reinforced by the testimony Lienors gives to Conrad's court: "so you will see that he has bound it next to his skin, placing it flesh to flesh. If this is not true, rub a burning coal across my body, and you will see my purse again and, you should know, the missing cloth" ("si verrez qu'il l'a ceinte et mise tot nu a nu, emprés sa char. Se ce n'est voirs, fetes un char tornoier par desus mon cors. Si verrez m'ausmosniere encors, ce sachiez, au tiessu perdue") (ll. 4836–41). The expression "nu a nu" leaves little doubt, being the common phrase used to describe intercourse.

28. *Erec et Enide*, ed. Alexandre Micha (Paris: Champion, 1979), ll. 1532–1668.

29. *Les Chroniques de Jean Froissart*, book 2; see Gaston Paris and Alfred Jean-roy, *Extraits des chroniqueurs* (Paris: Hachette, 1948), 165–73.

30. The one exception may be Rey-Flaud, *La Névrose courtoise*, 104. But his commentary on the "feminized" seneschal demonstrates once again the powerful reflex of regarding the feminine in purely metaphorical terms.

31. In the seventeenth century, Claude Fauchet renamed the *Rose*, the *Roman de Guillaume de Dole*. Every subsequent edition (Langlois, Lecoy), as indeed most every critic, has maintained the misnomer. This episode, I would argue, is symptomatic of a larger obscuring trend; for in an effort to distinguish it from the allegorical *Rose*, the character of the narrative has been consistently distorted. Consider, for example, the license taken by Rita Lejuene when she suggested "ce roman qui ne devrait s'appeler ni *Le Roman de la rose* comme l'a voulu Jean Renart, ni *Le Roman de Guillaume de Dole* comme l'a baptisé Claude Fauchet, mais *Le Roman de Conrad*. Le héros principal est, en effet, le roi Conrad, seul personnage actif d'un bout à l'autre" (*L'oeuvre de Jean Renart: Contribution à l'étude du genre romanesque au Moyen Âge* [Paris: E. Droz, 1935], 36).

The Body, Gender, and Sexuality in History and Theory: A Selective Bibliography

The following citations are drawn from the essays in this collection:

Allen, Christine Garside. "Can a Woman Be Good in the Same Way as a Man?" In *Woman in Western Thought*, ed. Martha Lee Osborne. New York: Random House, 1979.

Amussen, Susan. "Féminin/Masculin: Le Genre dans l'Angleterre de l'époque moderne." *Annales ESC* 40 (1985): 269–87.

———. *An Ordered Society: Gender and Class in Early Modern England*. Oxford: Basil Blackwell, 1988.

Ariès, Philippe, and Georges Duby, eds. *A History of Private Life*, vol. 2: *Revelations of the Medieval World*. Cambridge, Mass.: Belknap Press of Harvard University Press, 1987.

Ashley, Kathleen M., and Pamela Sheingorn, eds. *Interpreting Cultural Symbols: Saint Anne in Late Medieval Society*. Athens, Ga.: University of Georgia Press, 1990.

Bal, Mieke. "Sexuality, Sin and Sorrow: The Emergence of the Female Character (A Reading of Genesis 1–3)." *Poetics Today* 6 (1985): 21–42.

Beckwith, Sarah. *Christ's Body: Religious Culture and Late Medieval Piety*. Forthcoming. New York: Routledge.

———. "A Very Material Mysticism: The Medieval Mysticism of Margery Kempe." In *Medieval Literature: Criticism, Ideology and History*, ed. David Aers. New York: St. Martin's Press, 1986.

Benjamin, Jessica. "A Desire of One's Own: Psychoanalytic Feminism and Intersubjective Space." In *Feminist Studies/Critical Studies*, ed. Teresa de Lauretis. Bloomington: Indiana University Press, 1986.

Bloch, Maurice, and Jonathan Parry. *Death and the Regeneration of Life*. New York: Cambridge University Press, 1982.

Bloch, R. Howard. "Chaucer's Maiden Head: 'The Physician's Tale' and the Poetics of Virginity." *Representations* 28 (1989): 113–34.

———. "The Lay and the Law: Sexual/Textual Transgression in *La Châtelaine de Vergi*, the *Lai D'Ignauré*, and the *Lais* of Marie de France." *Stanford French Review* 14 (1991): 181–210.

———. *The Scandal of the Fabliaux*. Chicago: University of Chicago Press, 1986.

Brown, Peter. *The Body and Society: Men, Women and Sexual Renunciation in Early Christianity*. New York: Columbia University Press, 1988.

Brundage, James. A. *Law, Sex, and Christian Society in Medieval Europe*. Chicago: University of Chicago Press, 1987.

———. "Prostitution in the Medieval Canon Law." In *Sisters and Workers in the Middle Ages*, ed. Judith M. Bennett, Elizabeth A. Clark, Jean F. O'Barr, B. Anne Vilen, and Sarah Westphal-Wihl. Chicago: University of Chicago Press, 1990.

Bugge, John. *Virginitas: An Essay in the History of a Medieval Ideal*. The Hague: Martinus Nijhoff, 1975.

Bullough, Vern L. *The Development of Medicine as a Profession: The Contribution of the Medieval University to Modern Medicine*. Basel: S. Karger, 1966.

———. "Medieval Medical and Scientific Views of Women." In *Marriage in the Middle Ages. Viator* 4 (1973): 485–501.

———. "The Term 'Doctor.'" *Journal of the History of Medicine* 18 (1963): 284–87.

Burns, E. Jane. "Knowing Women: Female Orifices in the Old French Fabliau." *Exemplaria* 4, no. 1 (Spring 1992): 81–104.

Butler, Judith. *Gender Trouble: Feminism and the Subversion of Identity*. New York: Routledge, 1990.

Byars, Jackie. "Gazes/Voices/Power: Expanding Psychoanalysis for Feminist Film and Television Theory." In *Female Spectators: Looking at Film and Television*, ed. E. Deidre Pribram. New York: Verso, 1988.

Bynum, Caroline Walker. *Fragmentation on Redemption: Essays on Gender and the Human Body in Medieval Religion*. New York: Zone, 1991.

———. *Holy Feast and Holy Fast: The Religious Significance of Food to Medieval Women*. Berkeley: University of California Press, 1987.

———. *Jesus as Mother: Studies in the Spirituality of the High Middle Ages*. Berkeley: University of California Press, 1982.

———. "Women's Stories, Women's Symbols: A Critique of Victor Turner's Theory of Liminality." In *Anthropology and the Study of Religion*, ed. Robert L. Moore and Frank E. Reynolds. Chicago: Center for the Scientific Study of Religion, 1984.

Cadden, Joah. "Medieval Scientific and Medical Views of Sexuality: Questions of Propriety." *Mediaevalia & Humanistica* 14 (1986): 164–70.

Carroll, Michael P. *The Cult of the Virgin Mary: Psychological Origins*. Princeton, N.J.: Princeton University Press, 1986.

Casey, Kathleen. "The Cheshire Cat: Reconstructing the Experience of Medieval Women." In *Liberating Women's History*, ed. Berenice A. Carroll. Urbana: University of Illinois Press, 1976.

Cazelles, Brigitte. "La Rose et la violette." *Poétique* 68 (November 1986): 405–22.

Chodorow, Nancy. *The Reproduction of Mothering: Psychoanalysis and the Sociology of Gender*. Berkeley: University of California Press, 1978.

Cixous, Hélène. "Castration or Decapitation." Trans. Annette Kuhn. *Signs* 7, no. 1 (1981): 41–55.

Coletti, Teresa. "A Feminist Approach to the Corpus Christi Cycles." In *Approaches to Teaching Medieval English Drama*, ed. Richard K. Emmerson. New York: Modern Language Association, 1990.

Davis, Natalie Zemon. "The Reasons of Misrule." *Society and Culture in Early Modern France*. Stanford, Calif.: Stanford University Press, 1975.

———. "'Women's History' in Transition: The European Case." *Feminist Studies* 3 (1976): 83–103.

de Lauretis, Teresa. "The Essence of the Triangle or, Taking the Risk of Essentialism Seriously: Feminist Theory in Italy, the U.S., and Britain." *differences* 1, no. 2 (Summer 1989): 3–37.

———. "Feminist Studies/Critical Studies: Issues, Terms, and Contexts." In *Feminist Studies/Critical Studies*, ed. Teresa de Lauretis. Bloomington: Indiana University Press, 1986.

———. *Technologies of Gender: Essays on Theory, Film, and Fiction*. Bloomington: Indiana University Press, 1987.

Dinshaw, Carolyn. *Chaucer's Sexual Poetics*. Madison: University of Wisconsin Press, 1989.

Doane, Mary Ann. *The Desire to Desire: The Woman's Film of the 1940s*. Bloomington: Indiana University Press, 1987.

Douglas, Mary. *Purity and Danger: An Analysis of the Concepts of Pollution and Taboo*. Harmondsworth: Penguin, 1970.

du Bois, Page. *Centaurs and Amazons: Women and the Pre-history of the Great Chain of Being*. Ann Arbor: University of Michigan Press, 1982.

———. *Sowing the Body: Psychoanalysis and Ancient Representation of Women*. Chicago: University of Chicago Press, 1988.

Duby, Georges. *The Knight, the Lady, and the Priest: The Making of Modern Marriage in Medieval France*. Trans. Barbara Bray. New York: Pantheon Books, 1983.

———. *Mâle moyen âge*. Paris: Flammarion, 1988.

———. *Medieval Marriage: Two Models from Twelfth-Century France*. Baltimore: Johns Hopkins University, 1978.

Evans, Ruth. "Feminist Re-enactments: Gender and the Towneley *Uxor Noe*." In *A Wyf Ther Was . . .* , ed. Juliette Dor. Forthcoming.

Ferrante, Joan. *Woman as Image in Medieval Literature: From the Twelfth Century to Dante*. New York: Columbia University Press, 1975.

Fisher, Sheila. "Taken Men and Token Women in *Sir Gawain and the Green Knight*." In *Seeking the Woman in Late Medieval and Renaissance Writings*, ed. Sheila Fisher and Janet E. Halley. Knoxville: University of Tennessee Press, 1989.

Flanigan, Clifford. "Liminality, Carnival and Social Structure: The Case of Late Medieval Biblical Drama." In *Victor Turner and the Construction of Cultural Criticism*, ed. Kathleen M. Ashley. Bloomington: Indiana University Press, 1990.

Flax, Jane. *Thinking Fragments: Psychoanalysis, Feminism, and Postmodernism in the Contemporary West*. Berkeley: University of California Press, 1990.

Freud, Sigmund. "Medusa's Head." In *Sexuality and the Psychology of Love*, ed. Philip Rieff. New York: Macmillan, 1963.

Fuss, Diana. *Essentially Speaking: Feminism, Nature and Difference*. London: Routledge, 1989.

———. "Reading Like a Feminist." *differences* 1, no. 2 (Summer 1989): 77–92.

Gallop, Jane. *The Daughter's Seduction Feminism and Psychoanalysis*. Ithaca, N.Y.: Cornell University Press, 1982.

———. *Thinking Through the Body*. New York: Columbia University Press, 1988.

Gauvard, Claude, and Altan Gokalp. "Les Conduits de bruit et leur signification a la fin du Moyen Age: Le charivari." *Annales E.S.C.* 29 (1974): 693–704.

Gibson, Gail McMurray. "'Porta Haec Clausa Erit': Comedy, Conception, and Ezekiel's Closed Door in the *Ludus Coventriae* Play of 'Joseph's Return.'" *Journal of Medieval and Renaissance Studies* 8 (1978): 137–56.

Given-Wilson, Chris, and Alice Curteis. *Royal Bastards of Late Medieval England.* London: Routledge and Kegan Paul, 1984.

Gold, Penny S. "The Marriage of Mary and Joseph in the Twelfth-Century Ideology of Marriage." In *Sexual Practices and the Medieval Church,* ed. Vern L. Bullough and James Brundage. Buffalo, N.Y.: Prometheus Books, 1982.

Gottlieb, Beatrice. "The Problem of Feminism in the Fifteenth Century." In *Women of the Medieval World,* ed. Julius Kirschner and Suzanne F. Wemple. Oxford: Basil Blackwell, 1985.

Gottfried, Robert S. *The Black Death: Natural and Human Disaster in Medieval Europe.* New York: The Free Press, 1983.

———. *Doctors and Medicine in Medieval England, 1340–1530.* Princeton, N.J.: Princeton University Press, 1986.

Grosz, Elizabeth. *Jacques Lacan: A Feminist Introduction.* London: Routledge, 1990.

Hanawalt, Barbara. *The Ties that Bound: Peasant Families in Medieval England.* New York: Oxford University Press, 1986.

Haraway, Donna. "Situated Knowledges: The Science Question in Feminism and the Privilege of Partial Perspective." *Feminist Studies* 14 (1988): 575–99.

Hastrup, Kirsten. "The Semantics of Biology: Virginity." In *Defining Females: The Nature of Woman in Society,* ed. Shirley Ardener. New York: John Wiley and Sons, 1978.

Heath, Stephen. "Difference." *Screen* 19, no. 3 (1978): 51–112.

Helmholz, R. H. "Bastardy Litigation in Medieval England." *American Journal of Legal History* 13 (1969): 360–83.

———. *Marriage Litigation in Medieval England.* Cambridge: Cambridge University Press, 1974.

Herlihy, David. *Medieval Households.* Cambridge, Mass.: Harvard University Press, 1985.

Hertz, Neil. "Medusa's Head: Male Hysteria under Political Pressure." In *The End of the Line: Essays on Psychoanalysis and the Sublime.* New York: Columbia University Press, 1985.

Hertz, R. "A Contribution to the Study of the Collective Representation of Death." In *Death and the Right Hand,* trans. Rodney and Claudia Needham. London: Cohen and West, 1960.

hooks, bell. "Feminism: A Politics of Transformation." In *Theoretical Perspectives on Sexual Difference,* ed. Deborah H. Rhode. Stanford, Calif.: Stanford University Press, 1991.

Horney, Karen. *Feminine Psychology.* New York: W. W. Norton, 1967.

Howell, Martha C. *Women, Production, and Patriarchy in Late Medieval Cities.* Chicago: University of Chicago Press, 1986.

Huchet, Jean-Charles. *Littérature et psychanalyse.* Paris: Presses universitaires de France, 1990.

Irigaray, Luce. *Speculum of the Other Woman*. Trans. Gillian C. Gill. Ithaca, N.Y.: Cornell University Press, 1985.

———. *This Sex Which Is Not One*. Trans. Catherine Porter. Ithaca, N.Y.: Cornell University Press, 1985.

Jacobus, Mary. *Reading Woman*. New York: Columbia University Press, 1986.

Jacobus, Mary, Evelyn Fox Keller, and Sally Shuttleworth, eds. *Body Politics: Women and the Discourses of Science*. New York: Routledge, 1990.

Jacquart, Danielle, and Claude Thomasset. *Sexuality and Medicine in the Middle Ages*. Trans. Matthew Adamson. Princeton, N.J.: Princeton University Press, 1988.

Jeay, Madeleine. "Sexuality and Family in Fifteenth-Century France: Are Literary Sources a Mask or a Mirror?" *Journal of Family History* 4 (1979): 328–45.

Jed, Stephanie. *Chaste Thinking: The Rape of Lucretis and the Birth of Humanism*. Bloomington and Indianapolis: University of Indiana Press, 1989.

Johnson, Barbara. *The Critical Difference*. Baltimore: Johns Hopkins University Press, 1980.

Jonin, Pierre. *Les Personnages féminins dans les romans français du Tristan au XIIe siècle*. Aix-en-Provence: Ophrys, 1958.

Joplin, Patricia Kleindienst. "The Voice of the Shuttle Is Ours." *Stanford Literature Review* 1 (1984): 25–53.

Kantorowicz, Ernst. *The King's Two Bodies: A Study in Mediaeval Political Theology*. Princeton: Princeton University Press, 1957.

Kaplan, E. Ann. "Is the Gaze Male?" In *Powers of Desire: The Politics of Sexuality*, ed. Ann Snitow, Christine Stansell, and Sharon Thompson. New York: Monthly Review Press, 1983.

———. *Women and the Film: Both Sides of the Camera*. New York: Methuen, 1983.

Kinneavy, Gerald. "Portrayal of Women in the York Plays." *Medieval Feminist Newsletter* 9 (Summer 1990): 10–12.

Klapisch-Zuber, Christiane. *Women, Family, and Ritual in Renaissance Italy*. Trans. Lydia G. Cochrane. Chicago: University of Chicago Press, 1985.

Kofman, Sarah. *The Enigma of Woman: Woman in Freud's Writings*. Trans. Catherine Porter. Ithaca, N.Y.: Cornell University Press, 1985.

Kolodny, Annette. *The Land Before Her: Fantasy and Experience of the American Frontiers, 1630–1860*. Chapel Hill: University of North Carolina Press, 1984.

———. *The Lay of the Land: Metaphor as Experience and History in American Life and Letters*. Chapel Hill: University of North Carolina Press, 1975.

Kristeva, Julia. *Powers of Horror: An Essay on Abjection*. Trans. Leon S. Roudiez. New York: Columbia University Press, 1982.

——— "Stabat mater." In *The Kristeva Reader*, ed. Toril Moi. New York: Columbia University Press, 1986.

Krueger, Roberta L. "Constructing Sexual Identities in the High Middle Ages: The Didactic Poetry of Robert de Blois." *Paragraph* 13 (1990): 105–131.

———. "Love, Honor, and the Exchange of Women in *Yvain*: Some Notes on the Female Reader." *Romance Notes* 25 (1985): 302–17.

———. "Double Jeopardy: The Appropriation of Women in Four Old French Romances of the 'Cycle de la gageure.'" In *Seeking the Woman in Late Medi-*

eval and Renaissance Writings, ed. Sheila Fisher and Janet E. Halley. Knoxville: University of Tennessee Press, 1989.

Laqueur, Thomas. *Making Sex: Body and Gender from the Greeks to Freud*. Cambridge, Mass.: Harvard University Press, 1990.

———. "Orgasm, Generation and the Politics of Reproductive Biology." *Representations* 14 (Spring 1986): 1–41.

Laslett, Peter. *Family Life and Illicit Love in Earlier Generations*. Cambridge: Cambridge University Press, 1977.

———. "Introduction: Comparing Illegitimacy over Time and Between Cultures." In *Bastardy and Its Comparative History*, ed. Peter Laslett, Karla Oostervenn, and Richard M. Smith. Cambridge, Mass.: Harvard University Press, 1980.

Lederer, Wolfgang. *Fear of Women*. New York: Grune and Stratton, 1968.

Le Goff, Jacques. "Head or Heart? The Political Use of Body Metaphors in the Middle Ages." In *Fragments for a History of the Human Body*, vol. 3, ed. Michel Feher, with Ramona Nadaff and Nadia Tazi. New York: Urzone, 1989.

———. *The Medieval Imagination*. Trans. Arthur Goldhammer. Chicago: University of Chicago Press, 1988.

Lejeune, Rita. "La Femme dans les littératures française et occitane du XIe au XIIIe siècle." *Cahiers de Civilisation Médiévale* 20 (1977): 201–17.

Lochrie, Karma. "The Language of Transgression: Body, Flesh, and Word in Mystical Discourse." In *Speaking Two Languages: Traditional Disciplines and Contemporary Theory in Medieval Studies*, ed. Allen J. Frantzen. Albany: State University of New York Press, 1991.

———. *Margery Kempe and Translations of the Flesh*. Philadelphia: University of Pennsylvania Press, 1991.

Luke, Cornelius. *The Role of the Virgin Mary in the Coventry, York, Chester and Towneley Cycles*. Washington, D.C.: Catholic University of America, 1933.

Lurie, Susan. "The Construction of the 'Castrated Woman' in Psychoanalysis and Cinema." *Discourse* 4 (Winter 1981–1982): 52–74.

Macfarlane, Alan. "Illegitimacy and Illegitimates in English History." In *Bastardy and Its Comparative History*, ed. Peter Laslett, Karla Oostervenn, and Richard M. Smith. Cambridge, Mass.: Harvard University Press, 1980.

MacKinnon, Patricia. "The Analogy of the Body Politic in St. Augustine, Dante, Petrarch, and Ariosto." Ph.D. Dissertation, University of California, Santa Cruz, 1988.

Maclean, Ian. *The Renaissance Notion of Woman: A Study in the Fortunes of Scholasticism and Medical Science in European Intellectual Life*. Cambridge: Cambridge University Press, 1982.

McLaughlin, Eleanor Commo. "Equality of Souls, Inequality of Sexes: Women in Medieval Theology." In *Religion and Sexism: Images of Women in the Jewish and Christian Traditions*, ed. Rosemary Radford Reuther. New York: Simon and Schuster, 1974.

McNamara, Jo Ann. "Sexual Equality and the Cult of Virginity in Early Christian Thought." *Feminist Studies* 3 (1976): 145–58.

Miles, Margaret R. *Carnal Knowing: Female Nakedness and Religious Meaning in the Christian West*. Boston: Beacon Press, 1989.

———. "The Virgin's One Bare Breast: Female Nudity and Religious Meaning in Tuscan Early Renaissance Culture." In *The Female Body in Western Culture: Contemporary Perspectives*, ed. Susan Rubin Suleiman. Cambridge, Mass.: Harvard University Press, 1986.

Miller, Nancy. *Subject to Change*. New York: Columbia University Press, 1988.

Mulvey, Laura. "Afterthoughts on 'Visual Pleasure and Narrative Cinema' inspired by *Duel in the Sun*." *Framework* 6, nos. 15–17 (1982): 15.

———. "Visual Pleasure and Narrative Cinema." *Screen* 16, no. 3 (Autumn 1975): 6–18.

Nelson, Janet L. "Queens as Jezebels: The Careers of Brunhild and Bathild in Merovingean History." In *Medieval Women*, ed. Derek Baker. London: Basil Blackwell, 1978.

O'Flaherty, Wendy. *Women, Androgynes and Other Mythical Beasts*. Chicago: University of Chicago Press, 1980.

———. trans. *Tales of Sex and Violence*. Chicago: University of Chicago Press, 1985.

Parker, Patricia. *Literary Fat Ladies*. London and New York: Methuen Press, 1987.

Parker, Rozsicka. *The Subversive Stitch: Embroidery and the Making of the Feminine*. London: The Woman's Press, 1986.

Petroff, Elizabeth Avilda. "Introduction." In *Medieval Women's Visionary Literature*. New York: Oxford University Press, 1985.

Phillips, John A. *Eve: The History of an Idea*. San Francisco: Harper and Row, 1984.

Pitkin, Hannah. *Fortune Is a Woman: Gender and Politics in the Thought of Niccolo Machiavelli*. Berkeley and Los Angeles: University of California Press, 1984.

Pollock, Griselda. *Vision and Difference: Femininity, Feminism, and the Histories of Art*. New York: Routledge, 1988.

Regnier-Bohler, Danielle. "Voix litteraires, voix mystiques." In *Histoire des Femmes en Occident: Le Moyen Age*, ed. Christiane Kalpisch-Zuber. Vol. 2. Paris: Plon, 1991.

Riley, Denise. *"Am I That Name?" Feminism and the Category of Women in History*. Minneapolis: University of Minnesota Press, 1988.

Robertson, Elizabeth. "Aspects of Female Piety in the *Prioresse's Tale*." In *Chaucer's Religious Tales*, ed. Elizabeth Robertson and C. David Benson. Cambridge: Boydell and Brewer, 1990.

Ross, Ellen, and Rayna Rapp. "Sex and Society: A Research Note from Social History and Anthropology." *Comparative Studies in Society and History* 23 (1981): 54–58.

Rowland, Beryl, ed. *Medieval Woman's Guide to Health: The First English Gynecological Handbook*. Kent, Ohio: Kent State University Press, 1981.

Rubin, Gayle. "The Traffic in Women: Notes on the 'Political Economy' of Sex. In *Toward an Anthropology of Women*, ed. Rayna R. Reiter. New York and London: Monthly Review Press, 1975.

Sanday, Peggy Reeves, *Female Power and Male Dominance: On the Origins of Sexual Inequality*. Cambridge: Cambridge University Press, 1981.

Scheman, Naomi. "Missing Mothers/Desiring Daughters: Framing the Sight of Women." *Critical Inquiry* 15 (Autumn 1988): 62–89.

Schor, Naomi. *Breaking the Chain: Women, Theory and French Realist Fiction.* New York: Columbia University Press, 1985.

———. *Reading in Detail: Aesthetics and the Feminine.* New York: Methuen, 1987.

———. "This Essentialism Which Is Not One: Coming to Grips with Irigaray." *differences* 1, no. 2 (Summer 1989): 38–58.

Schulenburg, Jane Tibbetts. "The Heroics of Virginity: Brides of Christ and Sacrificial Mutilation." In *Women in the Middle Ages and the Renaissance: Literary and Historical Perspectives,* ed. Mary Beth Rose. Syracuse, N.Y.: Syracuse University Press, 1986.

Scott, Joan W. *Gender and the Politics of History.* New York: Columbia University Press, 1988.

Sedgwick, Eve Kosofsky. *Between Men: English Literature and Male Homosocial Desire.* New York: Columbia University Press, 1985.

Seidler, Victor. "Reason, Desire and Male Sexuality." In *The Cultural Construction of Sexuality,* ed. Pat Caplan. London: Tavistock Publications, 1987.

Silverman, Kaja. *The Acoustic Mirror: The Female Voice in Psychoanalysis and Cinema.* Bloomington: Indiana University Press, 1988.

Sissa, Giulia. *Le Corps virginal.* Paris: J. Vrin, 1987.

———. "Subtle Bodies." In *Fragments for a History of the Human Body,* ed. Michel Feher, with Ramona Nadaff, Nadia Tazi. Vol. 3. New York: Zone, 1989.

"Le Souci du corps." Special issue of *Médiévales* 8 (1985).

"The Spectatrix." Special issue of *Camera Obscura* (1991).

Spelman, Elizabeth V. *Inessential Woman: Problems of Exclusion in Feminist Thought.* Boston: Beacon Press, 1988.

Stafford, Pauline. *Queens, Concubines, and Dowagers: The King's Wife in the Early Middle Ages.* Athens: University of Georgia Press, 1983.

Stallybrass, Peter. "Patriarchal Territories: The Body Enclosed." In *Rewriting the Renaissance: The Discourses of Sexual Difference in Early Modern Europe,* ed. Margaret W. Ferguson, Maureen Quilligan, and Nancy Vickers. Chicago: University of Chicago Press, 1986.

———. "Reading the Body: *The Revenger's Tragedy* and the Jacobean Theatre of Consumption." *Renaissance Drama* 18 (1987): 121–48.

Stallybrass, Peter, and Allon White. *The Politics and Poetics of Transgression.* Ithaca, N.Y.: Cornell University Press, 1986.

Stanbury, Sarah. "The Lover's Gaze in *Troilus and Criseyde.*" In *Chaucer's* Troilus and Criseyde: *"Subjit to Alle Poesye"—Essays in Criticism,* MRTS, ed. E. A. Shoaf and Catherine S. Cox. Binghamton, N.Y.: State University of New York Press, 1992.

———. "The Virgin's Gaze: Spectacle and Transgression in Middle English Lyrics of the Passion." *PMLA* 106 (October 1991): 1083–93.

Stuard, Susan Mosher, "Fashion's Captives: Medieval Women in French Historiography." In *Women in Medieval History and Historiography,* ed. Susan Mosher Stuard. Philadelphia: University of Pennsylvania Press, 1987.

Suleiman, Susan Rubin, ed. *The Female Body in Western Culture: Contemporary Perspectives*. Cambridge: Harvard University Press, 1986.

Tavard, George. *Woman in Christian Tradition*. Notre Dame: University of Indiana Press, 1973.

Thompson, Edward P. "'Rough Music' Le charivari anglais." *Annales E.S.C.* 27 (1972): 285–312.

Todd, Mabel E. *The Thinking Body*. New York: Dance Horizons, 1937.

Travis, Peter W. "The Social Body of the Dramatic Christ in Medieval England." In *Early Drama to 1600*, ed. Albert H. Tricomi. *Acta*, vol. 13. Binghamton: SUNY Center for Medieval and Early Renaissance Studies, 1987 [for 1985].

Vickers, Nancy. "Diana Described: Scattered Woman and Scattered Rhyme." *Critical Inquiry* 8 (Winter 1981): 265–79.

Walsh, Martin W. "Divine Cuckold/Holy Fool: The Comic Image of Joseph in the English 'Troubles' Plays." In *Proceedings of the 1985 Harlaxton Symposium*, ed. W. M. Ormrod. Woodbridge, Suffolk: Boydell Press, 1986.

Warner, Marina. *Alone of All Her Sex: The Myth and Cult of the Virgin Mary*. New York: Knopf, 1976.

Warner, Marina, and Hilda Graef. *Mary: A History of Doctrine and Devotion*, 2 vols. London: Sheed and Ward, 1963–65.

Waugh, Patricia. *Feminine Fictions: Revisiting the Postmodern*. New York: Routledge, 1989.

Weedon, Chris. *Feminist Criticism and Poststructuralist Theory*. Oxford: Basil Blackwell, 1987.

White, Sarah Melhado. "Sexual Language and Human Conflict in Old French Fabliaux." *Comparative Studies in Society and History* 24, no. 1 (1982): 185–210.

Whitford, Margaret. "Rereading Irigaray." In *Between Feminism and Psychoanalysis*, ed. Teresa Brennan. London: Routledge, 1989.

Williams, Linda. "When the Woman Looks," In *Re-Vision: Essays in Feminist Film Criticism*, ed. Mary Ann Doane, Patricia Mellencamp, and Linda Williams. Los Angeles: American Film Institute, 1984.

Wilson, Katharina M., and Elizabeth M. Makowski. *Wykked Wyves and the Woes of Marriage: Misogamous Literature from Juvenal to Chaucer*. Albany: State University of New York Press, 1990.

Women and Language in Literature and Society. Ed. Sally McConnell-Ginet, Ruth Borker, and Nelly Furman. New York: Praeger, 1979.

Wood, Charles T. "The Doctors' Dilemma: Sin, Salvation, and the Menstrual Cycle in Medieval Thought." *Speculum* 56 (1981): 710–27.

———. "Queens, Queans, and Kingship: An Inquiry into Theories of Royal Legitimacy in Late Medieval England and France." In *Order and Innovation in the Middle Ages*, ed. William C. Jordan, Bruce McNab, and Teofilo F. Ruiz. Princeton, N.J.: Princeton University Press, 1976.

Contributors

MARGARET BROSE, Associate Professor of Italian and Contemporary Literature at the University of California, Santa Cruz, has published extensively on Romanticism, poetics, and modern Italian literature. She is currently working on a book, *The Rhetorical Structures of the Romantic Lyric*, and a series of essays, *Italy's Body: Figurality and the Female in Italian Verse*.

E. JANE BURNS is Professor of French at the University of North Carolina at Chapel Hill and author of *Arthurian Fictions: Rereading the Vulgate Cycle* (Ohio State University Press, 1985). A co-founder and editor of the *Medieval Feminist Newsletter*, she has edited, with Roberta L. Krueger, *Courtly Ideology and Woman's Place in Medieval French Literature (Romance Notes, 1985)*. Her book *Bodytalk: When Women Speak in Old French Literature*, is forthcoming (University of Pennsylvania Press, 1993).

THERESA COLETTI teaches in the English Department at the University of Maryland College Park. She is the author of numerous articles on medieval and contemporary literature and of *Naming the Rose: Eco, Medieval Signs, and Modern Theory* (Cornell, 1988).

WENDY HARDING (formerly Clein) is currently Assistant Professor of English at the University of Connecticut. She is author of *Concepts of Chivalry in Sir Gawain and the Green Knight* (Pilgrim Books, 1987) and of articles on medieval and contemporary theory. Current projects include a study of representations of motherhood in medieval literature and a book, with coauthor Jacky Martin, on Toni Morrison's novels.

LINDA LOMPERIS is Assistant Professor of Literature at Cowel College, University of California, Santa Cruz. She has published articles on medieval literature and contemporary feminist theory and serves on the advisory board of the *Medieval Feminist Newsletter*. She is currently completing a book on questions of women, politics, and authorial power in the writings of Chaucer.

GAYLE MARGHERITA is Assistant Professor of English at Indiana University in Bloomington. She is currently completing a book on sexuality and epistemology in Middle English literature and criticism.

PEGGY MCCRACKEN is Visiting Assistant Professor of French at the University of Illinois at Chicago and is working on a study of adulterous queens in Old French romances.

ELIZABETH ROBERTSON is an Associate Professor of English at the University of Colorado at Boulder. Her specialities are medieval literature and women writers. She is coeditor of *The Medieval Feminist Newsletter*. She is the author of *Early English Devotional Prose and the Female Audience* (Tennessee, 1990) and coeditor, with David Benson, of *Chaucer's Religious Tales* (Boydell and Brewer, 1990). She is now working on a book on rape and religion in Chaucer.

HELEN SOLTERER is Assistant Professor of French at Duke University. Her research, which has appeared most recently in *Signs* (Spring 1991), focuses on the problem of female figuration and its cultural ramifications. She is currently completing *The Master and Minerva*, a book on women's response literature in the French Middle Ages.

SARAH STANBURY teaches in the English Department at College of the Holy Cross and is the author of *Seeing the* Gawain-*Poet: Description and the Act of Perception* (University of Pennsylvania Press, 1991). Her articles on the female gaze in medieval literature have recently appeared in *PMLA*, *Studies in the Age of Chaucer*, and *Literature and Psychology*.

Index

University of Pennsylvania Press
NEW CULTURAL STUDIES
Joan DeJean, Carroll Smith-Rosenberg, and Peter Stallybrass, Editors

Jonathan Arac and Harriet Ritvo, editors. *Macropolitics of Nineteenth-Century Literature: Nationalism, Exoticism, Imperialism.* 1991.

John Barrell. *The Birth of Pandora and the Division of Knowledge.* 1992.

Bruce Thomas Boehrer. *Monarchy and Incest in Renaissance England: Literature, Culture, Kinship and Kingship.* 1992.

Julia V. Douthwaite. *Exotic Women: Literary Heroines and Cultural Strategies in Ancien Régime France.* 1992.

Barbara J. Eckstein. *The Language of Fiction in a World of Pain: Reading Politics as Paradox.* 1990.

Katherine Gravdal. *Ravishing Maidens: Writing Rape in Medieval French Literature and Law.* 1991.

Linda Lomperis and Sarah Stanbury, editors. *Feminist Approaches to the Body in Medieval Literature.* 1993.

Karma Lochrie. *Margery Kempe and Translations of the Flesh.* 1991.

Alex Owen. *The Darkened Room: Women, Power and Spiritualism in Late Victorian England.* 1990.

This book has been set in Linotron Galliard. Galliard was designed for Mergenthaler in 1978 by Matthew Carter. Galliard retains many of the features of a sixteenth-century typeface cut by Robert Granjon but has some modifications that give it a more contemporary look.

Printed on acid-free paper.